CONTENT ANALYSIS

The SAGE CommText Series

Editor:
F. GERALD KLINE
Director, School of Journalism and Mass Communication
University of Minnesota

Associate Editor:
SUSAN H. EVANS
Department of Communication, University of Michigan

This new series of communication textbooks is designed to provide a modular approach to teaching in this rapidly changing area. The explosion of concepts, methodologies, levels of analysis, and philosophical perspectives has put heavy demands on teaching undergraduates and graduates alike; it is our intent to choose the most solidly argued of these to make them available for students and teachers. The addition of new titles in the COMMTEXT series as well as the presentation of new and diverse authors will be a continuing effort on our part to reflect change in this scholarly area.

—F.G.K. and S.H.E.

Available in this series:

1. TELEVISION IN AMERICA
   George Comstock
2. COMMUNICATION HISTORY
   John D. Stevens and Hazel Dicken Garcia
3. PRIME-TIME TELEVISION: Content and Control
   Muriel G. Cantor
4. MOVIES AS MASS COMMUNICATION
   Garth Jowett and James M. Linton
5. CONTENT ANALYSIS: An Introduction to Its Methodology
   Klaus Krippendorff

additional titles in preparation

Klaus Krippendorff

CONTENT ANALYSIS
An Introduction to Its Methodology

Volume 5. The Sage COMMTEXT Series

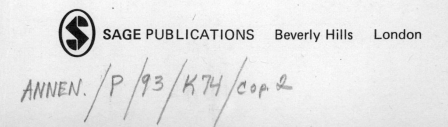

SAGE PUBLICATIONS   Beverly Hills   London

Copyright © 1980 by Sage Publications, Inc.

For information address:

SAGE Publications, Inc.
275 South Beverly Drive
Beverly Hills, California 90212

SAGE Publications Ltd
28 Banner Street
London EC1Y 8QE, England

Printed in the United States of America

Library of Congress Cataloging in Publication Data

Krippendorff, Klaus.
　Content analysis.

　(The Sage commtext series ; 5)
　Bibliography: p.
　Includes index.
　1. Content analysis (Communication) I. Title.
II. Series: Sage commtext ; 5.
P93.K74　　001.51　　80-19166
ISBN 0-8039-1497-0
ISBN 0-8039-1498-9 (pbk.)

SECOND PRINTING, 1981

CONTENTS

PREFACE

Potentially, content analysis is one of the most important research techniques in the social sciences, it seeks to understand data not as a collection of physical events but as symbolic phenomena and to approach their analysis unobtrusively. Methods in the natural sciences do not need to be concerned with meanings, references, consequences, and intentions. Methods in social research that derive from these "hard" disciplines manage to ignore these phenomena for convenience. Yet, nobody doubts the significance of symbols in society.

Currently, content analysis is somewhat at a crossroad. Its history is rooted in the journalistic fascination with numbers, supposedly making a quantitative statement more convincing than a qualitative one. Content analysis could continue the counting game which may lead to excitement but not to insights. Content analysis could also pursue more seriously than it has in the past what is involved in the claim to analyze something that is recognizably symbolic as a symbolic phenomenon, tracing its social role, effects, and meaning. The use of computers in natural language processing has taught us with painful clarity that this requires much more imagination and theoretical work than was previously anticipated. It also requires an appropriate logic, a methodology that is suitable to this end.

The book is addressed to a fairly wide audience of practicing social scientists, communication researchers, and students. It develops a new perspective. It can serve as a text in various social science curricula. It can be a practical guide in research contexts involving symbolic phenomena. And it also includes material that might help the critical user to evaluate content analysis findings.

I owe thanks to numerous students at Philadelphia's Annenberg School of Communication in interaction with whom the conceptual organization of the book arose, to several content analysis research projects whose conceptual and methodological problems showed repetition and pattern worthy of more general solutions, and to the Netherlands Institute for Advanced Study for providing the place to complete the work.

University of Pennsylvania   Klaus Krippendorff

7

FOREWORD

The term *content analysis* is about 50 years old. Webster's Dictionary of the English Language has listed it only since 1961. But its intellectual roots go far back in history, to the beginning of man's conscious use of symbols and language. Replacing magic, that consciousness has not only been shaped by several ancient disciplines, philosophy, rhetoric, art, cryptography but also furthered religious inquisitions and political censorship by ruling establishments. Today the concern for symbolic phenomena is institutionalized in literature, mass media criticism, education, in such academic disciplines as anthropology, linguistics, social psychology, sociology of knowledge, and in many practical pursuits, psychotherapy, advertising, politics, and so on. Virtually the whole spectrum of the humanities and the social sciences, including efforts to improve the political and social conditions of life, is concerned with symbols, meanings, messages, their functions, and effects.

However ancient these roots might be, their existence, if not persistence, should not distract from the fact that modern pursuits are significantly different in aim and in method. We see three marks of distinction.

First, *the pursuit of content analysis is fundamentally empirical in orientation*, exploratory, concerned with real phenomena, and predictive in intent. While many current terms related to language are indeed Greek in origin, for example, "sign," "significance," "symbol," and "logic," the Greek's interest in language was largely prescriptive and classificatory. Aristotelian logic was intended to lead to clear expressions and much of rhetoric was geared to a typology of proper argumentation. Only recently have the barriers of normative thinking been broken. For example, research on intelligent behavior has indicated that the human brain does not generally conform to Aristotelian categories. Slowly, a non-Aristotelian psycho-logic seems to be taking its place.

Analogous changes toward an open-minded empirical orientation distinguishes content analysis from classical epistemologies. Although speculations, generalizations, and theoretical constructions are needed indeed, they must ultimately prove their worth when applied to real data. With this empirical orientation, content analysis has joined other research methods in contributing to knowledge, specializing, however, in symbolic events to which other methods are generally insensitive.

Second, *content analysis transcends conventional notions of content* as an object of concern and is intricately linked to more recent conceptions of symbolic phenomena. This may be seen in the context of a changed awareness about human communication, the existence of new media, and the roles they play in the transmission of information in society. We probably are in the midst of the last of four revolutions concerning concepts of communication.

- The idea of *messages*—the awareness of the symbolic-representational nature of human exchanges—stems from a fertile combination of intercultural trade and science which surfaced in ancient Greece.

- The idea of *channels*—the awareness of the constraint that the choice of a medium imposes on human expression—stems from the increased use of communications technology, starting with printing and continuing with electronic media.

- The idea of *communication*—the awareness of the interpersonal dependencies, social relations, structure, and stratification surreptitiously created by the exchange of information—stems from the rapid social changes including the breakdown of traditional social institutions and human relationships in the beginning of this century.

- The idea of *systems*—the awareness of global and dynamic interdependencies—stems from the widespread use of complex communications technology; mass media; multichannel transmission networks and computers; the consequent dispersion of organizational forms; and the intermeshing of industry, government, the mass media, and other instititions.

It follows that an empirical concern with symbolic events can no longer study messages in isolation, it can no longer reduce communication to a psychological process or take the linguistic interpretations of a message as the basis of insights. The changed fabric of society calls for a *structural* definition of content, one that can take note of channels and constraints on information flows, communication processes and their functions and effects in society, and systems involving advanced technology and modern social institutions. We recognize this by defining content analysis no longer by its traditional domain of application (the meaning of messages) but by the process involved in analyzing data as symbolic entities (as opposed to in and for themselves). Perhaps the term *content analysis* no longer fits this larger context in which messages and symbolic data are and must be understood.

Third, *content analysis is developing a methodology of its own* that enables the researcher to plan, to communicate, and to critically evaluate a research design independently of its results. The need for such a methodology is clearly indicated by the larger perspective for content analysis, the increasing inability of a single individual to experience what complex symbolic events represent or foster, and the heavy reliance on organized research which requires coordination quality checks and the use of reliable techniques.

Since it concerns this book, methodology must not be confused with its subject matter. The purpose of methodology is to describe and to examine the logic of composition of research methods and techniques, to reveal their powers and limitations, to generalize successes and failures, to find domains of appropriate application, and to predict possible contributions to knowledge. The development of a methodology is always a major step in the natural history of a scientific pursuit. For example, it took thousands of years of retelling stories before von Ranke, about a hundred years ago, gave the "document" the methodological status it now has in the study of history. Content analysis was also first practiced before it could be codified. Although one can argue that all content analyses are different and that each discipline using the technique tackles somewhat different problems, we maintain that all content analyses share a logic of composition, a form of reasoning and certain criteria of validity. It is in these common procedures that we find the subject matter of content analysis methodology.

We disagree with the contention that "content analysis is nothing other than what everyone is doing when reading a newspaper, except on a larger scale." Content analysis may have started out that way and its methodology does not prohibit such orientations, but this characterization refers to an earlier, journalistic stage of content analysis. As newspaper readers we are perfectly justified in applying our idiosyncratic world view and in exerting our preferences. But as researchers we do our best to avoid biases, distrust a single individual's interpretation, make explicit what we are doing, share our findings so that others may examine or replicate them, and, above all, we are aware of the qualitative difference between a methodology that provides us with a platform from which we can talk about data and scientific procedure and what these phenomena mean to us individually.

This book introduces the reader to ways of analyzing data as symbolic communications. Its content can be grouped into three main concerns. The theoretical part begins with a brief history of content analysis, develops a definition distinguishing content analysis from other methods, and exemplifies its domain of practical application. The methodological-practical part begins with the logic of content analysis designs and then shifts to the procedures involved: unitizing, sampling, recording, the construction of data languages, analytical constructs, computational techniques, and the use of computers. The critical part concerns the two principal quality criteria for content analyses: reliability and validity. The book concludes with a practical guide summarizing the preceding from this special perspective.

The scholar who has never done a content analysis may want to begin by familiarizing himself with the conceptual foundations but should then start with a small project of his own, perhaps following the steps outlined in the Chapter 14. Attempting to describe and to justify what he is doing when interpreting his data symbolically, he will soon realize what this procedurally involves and how much substantive knowledge about the surrounding conditions of his data he requires before he can design a larger project. Such substantive knowledge is specific to a discipline or about the particular object of analysis and has to be acquired elsewhere. The researcher who has already performed content analysis may acquire a larger perspective and new tools for analysis, gain further insights into its methodology, and perhaps become more certain about whether his findings are defendable in the light of the framework developed here. The critical user of content analysis results obtained elsewhere will find the evaluative techniques and criteria most helpful because they may enable him to estimate how much he can rely on these results, thus gaining a critical attitude.

The book will have achieved its purpose if it has improved the social significance of some of the increasing number of content analyses done in the humanities and in the social sciences and if it has stimulated further developments of methods of inquiring into the symbolic reality.

1

HISTORY

Empirical inquiries into communications content date back to studies in theology in the late 1600s—when the Church was worried about the spread of nonreligious matters through newspapers. It has since mushroomed into numerous areas. This chapter surveys the historical growth of content analysis methodology. References are made to large-scale studies of the press, to sociological and linguistic inquiries, especially into newer media and for different purposes—ranging from concerns with political symbols and propaganda to myths, folktales, and riddles.

Probably the first well-documented case of quantitative analysis of printed material occurred in eighteenth-century Sweden. Dovring (1954-1955) described the incident involving a collection of 90 hymns of unknown authorship, entitled *Songs of Zion*. The collection passed the state censorship but was soon afterward blamed for undermining the orthodox clergy of the Swedish state church, being popular and contagious, and aiding a dissenting group. Outstanding in this case was the fact that good scholars participated in this controversy which crystallized around the question of whether the songs were in fact the carriers of dangerous ideas. One side started counting religious symbols in these songs, the other side counted the same symbols in the established song book and found no difference. The symbols were then counted in the contexts in which they appeared, compared with the results of a German study of the outlawed Moravian Brethren until it became clear what the difference was and how this could be explained. For these scholars the controversy stimulated a methodological debate on the level of which the issues were finally resolved.

Loebl (1903) published in German an elaborate classification scheme for analyzing the "inner structure of content" according to the social functions newspapers perform. The book was well-known in journalistic circles but did not stimulate empirical investigations.

At the first meeting of the German Sociological Society in 1910, Max Weber (1911) proposed a large-scale content analysis of the press but for a variety of reasons it did not get off the ground. During that time Markov (1913) worked on a theory of chains of symbols and published a statistical analysis of a sample of Pushkin's novel in verse, *Eugene Onegin*. Most of these inquiries were discovered only recently or influenced the content analysis literature indirectly. For example, Markov's work entered the content analysis literature via Shannon's (Shannon and Weaver, 1949) information theory and Osgood's (1959) subsequent contingency analysis.

QUANTITATIVE NEWSPAPER ANALYSIS

The turn of the century brought a visible increase in the mass production of newsprint in the United States, a concern to assess mass markets, and interest in public opinion. Journalism schools emerged, leading the demand for ethical standards and for empirical inquiries into the phenomenon of the newspaper. These demands plus a somewhat simplistic notion of scientific objectivity were met by what was then called *quantitative newspaper analysis*.

Probably the first analysis of this kind, published in 1893, asked the rhetorical question, "Do Newspapers Now Give the News?" (Speed, 1893). The author showed how religious, scientific, and literary matters had dropped out of leading New York newspapers between 1881 and 1893 in favor of gossip, sports, and scandals. A similar study attempted to reveal the overwhelming space devoted to "demoralizing," "unwholesome," and "trivial" matters as opposed to "worthwhile" news items (Mathews, 1910). By simply measuring the column inches a newspaper devoted to particular subject matters, journalists attempted to reveal "the truth about newspapers" (Street, 1909), believed they had found a way of showing the profit motive as the cause of "cheap yellow journalism" (Wilcox, 1900), became convinced that they had established "the influence of newspaper presentations on the growth of crime and other antisocial activity" (Fenton, 1910), or concluded that a "quarter-century survey of the press content shows demand for facts" (White, 1924).

The dominant methodological problem seemed to have been the support of journalistic arguments by scientific facts. To be irrefutable these facts had to be "quantitative." And the respect for numbers is old indeed. In a footnote, Berelson and Lazarsfeld (1948: 9) cite from a source of nearly 200 years ago:

> Perhaps the spirit of the battle over ratification is best reflected in the creed ironically attributed to each of the contending parties by its opponents. The recipe for an Anti-Federalist essay which indicates in a very concise way the class-bias that actuated the opponents of the Constitution, ran in this manner: "wellborn, nine times—Aristocracy, eighteen times—Liberty of the Press, thirteen times repeated—Liberty of Conscience, once—Negro Slavery, once mentioned—Trial by Jury, seven times—Great men, six times repeated—Mr. Wilson, forty times . . .—put them together and dish them up at pleasure" [From the *New Hampshire Spy*, Nov. 30, 1787].

Quantitative newspaper analysis bore many valuable ideas, however. In 1912 Tenney called for a large-scale and continuous survey of press content to establish a system of bookkeeping of the "social weather" comparable in accuracy to the statistics of the U.S. Weather Bureau. He demonstrated it on a few New York newspapers for different ethnic groups, but practical applications were not feasible. This approach to content analysis culminated in the sociologist Willey's (1926) study of *The Country Newspaper*. In this model study, Willey traced the emergence of Connecticut country weeklies, reported their circulation figures, changes in subject matter, and the social role they acquired in competition with large city dailies.

When other mass media became prominent, this approach—measuring volumes of print in subject matter categories—became extended initially to radio (Albig, 1938) and later to movies and television. Content analysis of this kind continues today and is applied to a wide variety of content such as textbooks, comic strips, speeches, and advertising.

EARLY CONTENT ANALYSIS

A second phase in the intellectual growth of content analysis is due to at least three factors. First, the new and more powerful electronic media of communication could no longer be treated as an extension of the newspapers. Second, the period following the economic crisis brought numerous social and political problems to which the new mass media were thought to be causal. Third, the emergence of empirical methods of inquiry in the social sciences.

For example, sociology started to make extensive use of survey research and polling. The experiences gained in analyzing public opinion gave rise to the first serious consideration of methodological problems of content analysis by Woodward (1934) entitled "Quantitative Newspaper Analysis as a Technique of Opinion Research." From writings about public opinion, interest in social "stereotypes" (Lippman, 1922) entered the analysis of communication in various forms. Questions such as how Negroes were presented in the Philadelphia press (Simpson, 1934), how the United States described her wars in her history textbooks as compared to those published by her former enemies (Walworth, 1938), or how nationalism was expressed in American, British, and other European children's books (Martin, 1936) now assumed importance.

One of the most important concepts that emerged in psychology during this time was that of "attitude." This added to content analysis such evaluative dimensions as "pro-con," or "favorable-unfavorable," and with further advances in attitude theory development. It opened the door to systematically assess biases, appealing to such standards as "objectivity," "fairness," and "balance." Among the explicit standards, Janis and Fadner's (1965) "Coefficient of Imbalance" deserves mention. Psychological experiments in rumor transmission led Allport and Fadner to study newspaper content from an entirely new perspective. Their "Five Tentative Laws of the Psychology of Newspapers" (1940) attempted to account for the changes that information undergoes as it travels through an institution and finally appears on the printed page.

The interest in political symbols added another feature to the analysis of public messages. McDiarmid (1937), for example, analyzed 30 U.S. presidential inaugural addresses in terms of symbols of national identity, of historical reference, of reference to fundamental concepts of government, and of fact and expectations. Above all, Lasswell (1938), viewing public communications within his psychoanalytical theory of politics, classified symbols in such categories as "self" and "others," forms of "indulgence," and "deprivation." His symbol analysis led to a "world attention survey" (1941) in which trends in the frequencies of national symbols were compared in prestige papers of several countries.

Several disciplines studied their own trends in scholarship as reflected in the topics of representative journals. This was probably first done in

Russia regarding physics (Rainoff, 1929) but most thoroughly in the field of sociology (Becker, 1930, 1932; Shanas, 1945) and later in journalism (Tannenbaum and Greenberg, 1961).

What distinguishes early content analysis from quantitative newspaper analysis is (1) that many eminent social scientists entered the development, bringing with them rich theoretical frameworks; (2) that rather detailed concepts were defined and recognized in data: attitudes, stereotypes, styles, symbols, values, propaganda devices; (3) that better statistical tools were brought to bear on the analysis, especially from survey research and psychological experiments; and (4) that content analysis data became part of larger research efforts (Lazarsfeld et al., 1948). The first concise presentation of these efforts appeared in a volume *Content Analysis in Communication Research* originally by Berelson and Lazarsfeld (1948) and later by Berelson (1952).

PROPAGANDA ANALYSIS

Content analysis received a major impetus for its probably first large-scale practical application during World War II. Before the war, content analysis largely aided and became virtually defined by the use of mass communications as data for testing scientific hypotheses and for criticizing journalistic practice. In the same spirit, propaganda analysis started out as an instrument for identifying individuals as "unethical" sources of influence. According to the Institute for Propaganda Analysis (1937) propagandists reveal themselves by their use of such tricks as "name calling," using "glittering generalities," "plain folks" identifications, "card stacking," "band wagon" devices, and so on. These were easily identified in religious or political speeches.

In the 1940s, with attention in the United States devoted to the war effort, the identification of the propagandist was no longer a problem. Neither was it sufficient to establish the mass media of communication as powerful agents of molding public opinion; military and political intelligence was needed. In this climate there emerged two outstanding centers devoted to propaganda analysis. Harold D. Lasswell and his associates worked with the Experimental Division for the Study of Wartime Communications at the Library of Congress, and Hans Speier who had organized a research project on totalitarian communication at the New School for Social Research assembled a research team at the Foreign Broadcast Intelligence Service of the American Federal Communications Commission (FCC). The work of the Library of Congress group (Lasswell et al., 1965) was devoted to basic issues of sampling, measurement problems, reliability and validity of content categories, and, in a sense, continued the tradition of early quantitative analysis of mass communications. The FCC group relied primarily on domestic enemy broadcasts to understand and predict events within Nazi Germany and its allies and to estimate the effects of military actions on war mood. Pressures of day-to-day reporting left the analysts little time to formalize their methods. After the war, George (1959a) worked through the volumes of reports left behind to ascertain the methods that evolved in the process and to validate the inferences that were made against documents that then became available. These efforts resulted in his *Propaganda Analysis* which made major contributions to conceptualizing aims and processes of content analysis. The assumption that the propagandist is rational, in the sense of following his own propaganda theory in the choice of his assertions, reoriented the analyst's focus from a neutral concept of "commonly shared content" to the conditions that explain a communication and the interests they might be expected to serve. "Preparatory propaganda" became a particularly useful key to understand the meanings of those broadcasts. In order to assure support for planned political actions, the population affected by them had to be prepared to accept such actions. The FCC analysts successfully predicted several major military and political campaigns, assessed Nazi-elite perceptions of their situation, political changes within the governing group, and shifts in relations between axis countries. Among the more outstanding predictions actually made by British analysts was the date of deployment of the German V-weapon against Great Britain. Monitoring Goebbels's speeches, the analyst inferred interferences with the production of these weapons and extrapolated the launching date which was accurate within a few weeks.

Among the lessons learned from this application was:

(1) that content is not an absolute or objective quality of communications. Sender and receiver may radically differ in the way particular broadcasts are interpreted. In addition, their ordering in time, and the particular situation of the receiver, is crucial for what particular communications mean. In other words, that aspect of content which is shared by all communicators is relatively insignificant to the understanding of the political process involved.

(2) that the analyst, looking "beyond the surface" of propaganda messages, makes predictions or inferences about phenomena without enjoying direct access to them. Content is not identifiable in the same way as one might identify finger prints. Quantitative newspaper analysts had made inferences, but failed to relate them to the situation from which their data stemmed and mistakenly denied their own contribution to the understanding of the messages that were analyzed.

(3) that in order to interpret or to make sense of propaganda messages, elaborate models of the system in which such communications took place were needed. The analyst constructed such models more or less explicitly. While earlier content analysis had viewed mass communications as isolated units, propaganda analysis responded to their systemic nature.

(4) that quantitative indicators are extremely insensitive and shallow in providing political insights. Even if large amounts of data are available as required for statistical analyses, they do not lead to the "most obvious" conclusions that political experts are easily able to draw upon and to agree upon by observing qualitative changes more in depth.

With the conviction that content analysis should not be inferior in exploring human intellect, numerous writers (e.g., Kracauer, 1947, 1952-1953; George, 1959) challenged the simplistic reliance of content analysis on counting qualitative data. Smythe (1954) called it an "immaturity of science" in which objectivity is confused with quantification. However, the proponents of the quantitative approach largely ignored the criticism. In his 1949 essay on "Why Be Quantitative," Lasswell (1965a) continued to present the quantification of symbols as the sole basis of scientific insights.

CONTENT ANALYSIS GENERALIZED

After World War II, and perhaps as the result of the first integrated picture of content analysis provided by Berelson and Lazarsfeld (1948) and Berelson (1952), content analysis spread to numerous disciplines. Although mass communications no longer remained its exclusive empirical domain, such applications were, and still are, predominant. In fact, some of the largest research projects concerned the public media. Lasswell (1941), for example, realized his idea of a "world attention survey" in a study of political symbols in French, German, British, Russian, and U.S. elite press editorials and key policy speeches. He wanted to test the hypothesis that a "world revolution" has been in steady progress (Lasswell et al., 1952). Gerbner's (1969) proposal for "cultural indicators" was exemplified by analyzing, now for the 10th consecutive year, one week of fictional television programming per year, mainly to establish violence profiles for different networks, to trace trends, to see how various groups, women, children, and the aged were portrayed on U.S. television (Gerbner et al., 1979).

In psychology, content analysis found three primary applications. The first is the analysis of verbal records to discover motivational, psychological, or personality characteristics. This application had been a tradition since Allport's (1942) treatise on the use of personal documents; Baldwin's (1942) application of *Personal Structure Analysis* to cognitive structure; and White's (1947) value studies. A second application was the use of qualitative data gathered in the form of answers to open-ended questions, verbal responses to tests, and the construction of Thematic Aptitude Test stories. Here content analysis acquired the status of a supplementary technique which allowed the researcher to utilize data that could only be gathered without imposing too much structure on the subject and to cross-validate findings obtained by different techniques. The third application concerned processes of communication in which content is an integral part. For example, Bales's (1950) *Interaction Process Analysis* of small group behavior used verbal exchanges as data through which group processes could be examined. Anthropologists started using content analysis techniques for the analysis of myths, folktales, and riddles with componential analysis of kinship terminology being one of many examples of discipline specific contributions to content analysis. Historians had always looked for more systematic ways to analyze large bodies of available historical documents and came to appreciate content analysis as a suitable technique. Educational material, long the focus of attention by social scientists, became recognized as a rich source of data both to make inferences about processes of reading (Flesh 1948, 1951) and to understand larger political, attitudinal, and value trends to be found in its textbooks. And the problem of identifying the authors of unsigned documents, long of interest to literary scholars, was successfully approached by the newly available techniques and so on. This proliferation brought a loss of focus. Everything seemed to be content analyzable and every analysis of symbolic phenomena became a content analysis.

In 1955, responding to the increasing interest, the Social Science Research Council's Committee on Linguistics and Psychology sponsored a conference on content analysis. The participants came from such disciplines as psychology, political sciences, literature, history, anthropology, and linguistics. Their contributions appeared in a volume edited by Pool (1959) *Trends in Content Analysis.* Despite obvious divergence in interest and approach, Pool observed a considerable and often surprising convergence on two points. There was a sophisticated concern with problems of inference from verbal material to its antecedent conditions as well as a focus on counting internal contingencies between symbols instead of the simple frequences of symbols (Pool, 1959: 2).

COMPUTER TEXT ANALYSIS

The late 1950s witnessed a considerable interest in mechanical translation, mechanical abstracting, and information retrieval systems. Computer languages specially suited for literal data processing were developed and even journals devoted to computer applications in psychology, the humanities, and the social sciences appeared. The often large volumes of written documents to be analyzed and the repetitiveness of the task made the computer a natural ally of content analysts.

After software developments made the computer more and more amenable to literal (as opposed to numerical) data processing, computer programs for word counts became available. They provided the basis, among others, of a new discipline later called "computational stylistics" (Sedelow and Sedelow, 1966) and revolutionized tedious literary work, the establishment of concordances, for example. Probably the first computer-aided content analysis was reported by Sebeok and Zeps (1958) who made use of information retrieval routines to analyze some 4000 Cheremis folktales. A Rand Corporation paper on "Automatic Content Analysis" by Hays (1960) explored the possibility of designing a computer system for analyzing political documents. Unaware of both developments, Stone and Bales, who were engaged in a study of themes in face-to-face interacting groups, designed and programmed the initial version of the General Inquirer system. A later version of this system and numerous applications ranging from political science to advertising, and from psychotherapy to literary analysis, was presented by Stone et al. (1966). Since that time the system has been improved, elaborated and expanded to other-than-English language domains.

Computer uses in content analysis were also stimulated by developments in other fields. Psychology became interested in simulating human cognition (Abelson (1963). Newell and Simon (1963) developed a computer approach to (human) problem solving. Linguistics developed numerous approaches to syntactical analysis and semantic interpretation of linguistic expressions. Artificial intelligence focused on the design of machines that understand natural language.

In 1967, the Annenberg School of Communications sponsored a major conference on content analysis. Researchers from numerous disciplines had a chance to present their own computational techniques, to compare the power of different approaches, and to project future needs. The conference also provided a platform for contrasting divergent approaches to content analysis. Discussions focused on difficulties of recording non-verbal (visual, vocal, and musical) communications, the need for standardized categories, the problem of drawing inferences, and, particularly, the role of theories and analytical constructs, all of which pose essentially methodological not computational problems. Barcus (1959), who had collected much of the content analysis literature, presented a survey of the use of content analysis in research and teaching in the United States. These contributions are summarized in a volume edited by Gerbner et al. (1969). Its publication coincided with Holsti's (1969) survey of the field.

Summarizing, one could say that content analysis has evolved into a scientific method that promises to yield inferences from essentially verbal, symbolic, or communicative data. Over and above its continuing involvement with substantive psychological, sociological, and political issues, the last 80 years have witnessed an exponentially increasing concern for using the technique and for establishing suitable validity criteria. We take this to indicate increasing maturity.

2

CONCEPTUAL FOUNDATIONS

Content analysis has its own approach to analyzing data. This stems largely from how the object of analysis, content, is regarded. This chapter develops the conceptual foundations of content analysis, presents a definition of content analysis; develops a framework for prescriptive, analytical, and methodological purposes; and contrasts content analysis with other social science techniques.

DEFINITION

We define:

Content analysis is a research technique for making replicable and valid inferences from data to their context.

As a research technique, content analysis involves specialized procedures for processing scientific data. Like all research techniques, its purpose is to provide knowledge, new insights, a representation of "facts," and a practical guide to action. It is a tool.

Any instrument of science is expected to be reliable. More specifically, when other researchers, at different points in time and perhaps under different circumstances, apply the same technique to the same data, the results must be the same. This is the requirement of a content analysis to be *replicable.*

In another definition by Berelson, content analysis is defined as "a research technique for the objective, systematic and quantitative description of the manifest content of communication" (1952: 18). The requirement of the technique to be "objective" and "systematic" is of course subsumed under the requirement of replicability in our definition. For a process to be replicable, the rules that govern it must be explicit and applicable equally to all units of analysis. However, several of Berelson's definitional requirements are excluded from our definition, largely because they are either unclear or too restrictive. For example, Berelson chose the attribute "manifest" merely to assure that the coding of data in content analysis be intersubjectively verifiable and reliable. His definition has led many scholars to believe that latent contents are excluded from the analysis. The requirement to be "quantitative" has been similarly restrictive. Although quantification is important in many scientific endeavors, qualitative methods have proven successful particularly in extracting intelligence from propaganda, in psychotherapy, and oddly enough in computer analysis of linguistic data where qualitative considerations turned out to be fundamental for the development of suitable algorithms.

The chief objection to Berelson's definition is that it does not spell out what "content" is or what the object of a content analysis should be. For some researchers, "content analysis" seems to denote nothing more than counting qualities (words, attributes, colors). For others the use of the term suggests a method for "extracting" content from the data as if it was objectively "contained" in them. Neither goes to the heart of the problem of content analysis.

Our definition attempts to be explicit regarding the object of content analysis. But since this might not be immediately clear, we proceed in small steps. Intuitively, content analysis could be characterized as a method of inquiry into *symbolic meaning* of messages. Most content analysts probably have such a notion in mind and the characterization would appear to be reasonable were it not for at least two misleading connotations which a good definition should avoid.

First, *messages do not have a single meaning* that needs to be "unwrapped." Data can always be looked at from numerous perspectives, especially when they are symbolic in nature. In any single written message, one can count letters, words, or sentences. One can categorize phrases, describe the logical structure of expressions, ascertain associations, connotations, denotations, elocutionary forces, and one can also offer psychiatric, sociological, or political interpretations. All of these may be simultaneously valid. In short, a message may convey a multitude of contents even to a single receiver. Under these circumstances, the claim to have analyzed THE content of communication reflects an untenable position.

Second, *meanings need not be shared.* Although consensus or intersubjective agreement as to what a message means would simplify a content analysis tremendously, it exists either only regarding the most obvious or "manifest" aspects of communications, or only for a few people that happen to share the same cultural and sociopolitical perspective. Generally neither condition is interesting. Thus, sharing can hardly serve as a presupposition for content analysis. In psychiatrist-patient interactions, a sophisticated expert talks with a layman about the layman's problems. Their perspectives cannot be presumed to be the same. Even experts in anthropological artifacts, art, nonverbal communication, and politics often disagree with their native-participant informers on how the symbols they use are to be interpreted. Public speakers tend to use ambiguous expressions in a calculated way and thereby demonstrate an asymmetrical awareness of the fact that messages may convey different things to different people. Thus, meanings are always relative to a communicator.

The most distinctive feature of messages is that they inform someone vicariously, providing the receiver with knowledge about events that take place at a distant location, about objects that may have existed in the past, or about ideas in other people's minds. *Messages and symbolic communications generally are about phenomena other than those directly observed.* The vicarious nature of symbolic communications is what forces a receiver to make specific inferences from sensory data to portions of his empirical environment. This empirical environment is what we refer to as the *context of the data.* We also note that it is always a specific *someone* who makes inferences from data to their context; and it is therefore that person who distinguishes whether his experiences are vicarious or direct, whether something is symbolic or nonsymbolic, or whether his datum is a message about something else or is an event that displays its own structure and existence. The content analyst, too, is a receiver of data. He is likely to differ radically from ordinary communicators who may assign meanings routinely, unconsciously, and without empirical justification. Although content analysis may concern itself with *making the kind of inferences that are made by some receiver when attempting to understand symbolic communications,* the technique has been generalized and is probably more successful when applied to nonlinguistic forms of communication where patterns in data are interpreted as *indices and symptoms* of which untrained communicators may no longer be aware.

Making specific inferences, which is the key to distinguishing between symbolic and nonsymbolic data processing and designates the domain of content analysis, is not entirely absent from other definitions. For example, Holsti and Stone argue for a definition that deviates from Berelson's in at least two important ways. First, it recognizes the inferential character of coding textual units into conceptual categories. Second, it makes these inferences a central concern: "Content analysis is a research technique for making inferences by systematically and objectively identifying specified characteristics within a text" (Stone et al., 1966: 5). Thus, although their definition recognizes the inferential nature of identifying the forms of ideas, values, and attitudes to which content analysis attends, it does not make explicit the importance of relating the classification, categorization, and frequency counts of these forms to other phenomena. This is necessary if the results of a content analysis are to be empirically meaningful. As early as 1943, Janis (1965) pointed to the need for validating the results of content analysis of mass communications by relating them to audience perceptions or to behavioral effects. We, too, demand content analysis to be predictive of something that is observable in principle, to aid decision making, or to help conceptualize that portion of reality that gave rise to the analyzed text. To this end we suggest that any content analysis must be performed relative to and justified in terms of *the context of the data.*

Moreover, we believe that all theories of meaning, all theories of symbolic phenomena, including theories of message content, are alike in concerning themselves with the relationship between data and their context. In its most elementary sense, data are physical stimuli or sign-vehicles such as the black and white marks on paper. However, most concerns with meaning start with higher levels of abstraction such as written documents, films, verbal dialogues, and paintings to name just a few. The context is their environment. Usually the analyst can choose the environment and its conceptualization. A linguist may limit his focus of attention to the linguistic environment of words and expressions. A sociologist may recognize the meaning of an act by placing it in the social context of the situation in which it occurs. A communication researcher may interpret the meaning of a message in relation to a sender's intentions, to a receiver's cognitive or behavioral effects, to the institutions within which it is exchanged, or to the culture within which it plays a role.

ELABORATIONS

Without further discussion of the wording, some examples might best illustrate how the definition applies to practical situations. Consider the situation of the wartime analyst of enemy broadcasts who may want to gauge popular support of elite policies. In peacetime such problems could be solved directly by public opinion surveys or on-site inspections. During a war, such information tends to be inaccessible and the analyst is forced to obtain it by indirect means. Here, the analyst tends neither to be interested in what the propagandist intends to say nor to be bothered if his inferences are not shared by ordinary listeners. In fact, he probably has good reasons to discard overt meanings as lies anyway. What he cannot ignore is that the "enemy broadcasts" are part of a real but inaccessible political process involving a civilian population, its governing elite, the military, and the socio-political-economic conditions of the country. By the analyst's choice, the actors in this process constitute the context of the broadcasts. The phenomena of interest, namely, popular support of elite policies, is located in this context. In order to make valid inference about popular support from domestic broadcasts, the analyst must have some knowledge about the relationships between the principal components of the political process.

Historians, too, are never mere collectors of documents. Their fascination pertains to the symbolic reconstruction of past events to which available texts may lead. Historians would surely love to interview Caesar, Nietzsche, or African slaves entering colonial America, if this were possible. But because letters, books, artifacts, and records kept by others do not anticipate the historian's questions, answers have to be found by indirect methods. When historians make an effort to infer events from documents (Dibble, 1963), they are, by definition, involved in content analysis. It is not surprising, therefore, that historians have always demanded that documents be placed in their appropriate historical context. Once this context is delineated, gaps in relevant detail are filled by drawing inferences from numerous bits of information. Historical methods help create a web of relationships that may ultimately answer the questions originally posed. The process of decreasing uncertainty in an unobservable domain is an inferential one and in fact the same that content analysis follows.

Psychology has a long tradition of developing theories and constructing empirical tests whose generality is established by repeated experiments.

The analysis of personal documents by psychologists (Allport, 1942) fits the description of content analysis clearly: The aim and context of such analyses tends to deal with such topics as a writer's cognition, attitudes, personality, or psychopathology which could have been measured by more direct techniques if the writer were available. In the course of analyzing personal documents, a variety of inferential techniques have emerged (e.g., type-token ratios, the discomfort relief quotient, graphology, the readability yardstick, thematic apperception tests) that are intended to link the syntax and expressions in written documents to characteristics of the writer. In psychology, content analysis is an honored practice although it may not always be labelled as such.

Mass communication is, of course, the traditional domain of content analysis. Communication researchers tend to be interested in communicator characteristics, audience effects, public attention, sociopolitical climates, processes of mediation of values, prejudices, cultural distinctions, institutional constraints, and so on. Although the context of mass communication is clearly implied when a content analyst is concerned with audience perceptions, for example, it is less clear when researchers claim to "merely describe" what the communications are about. It would seem that all inferences are then omitted and that descriptive aims would not satisfy our definition of content analysis. This is not the case.

Consider so-called purely descriptive accounts of political bias, of racial prejudice, or of violence on television. Although such accounts might be presented as "factual," they are meaningful only in the context of the social problems that render them significant. Rarely would someone undertake to systematically describe something without some implications in mind. How an analyst conceptualizes and describes biases, prejudices, and violence is never entirely arbitrary. The descriptive language may be that of the client of the content analysis, perhaps correspond to the perceptions of a specific audience, accommodate the interests of a network-producer, or reflect cultural stereotypes or literary conventions. Whatever the case, *any description entails inferences*, even when it is of a primitive sort. A quantification of television violence, for example, would hardly be justifiable without a demonstration of some correlation with other phenomena (aggressive behavior or crime), without an effort to show some correspondence with the perceptions by particular audience members, or without providing some hard support for policy formation. A content analysis, even with descriptive aims, must not be immune to validity considerations and has to be specific regarding the context to which the findings pertain.

FRAMEWORK

The definition of content analysis delineates the object of inquiry and places the researcher into a particular position vis-à-vis his reality. Based on previous work (Krippendorff, 1969a: 7-13) the following offers a conceptual framework within which his role can be represented. The framework is simple and general, employing only a few basic concepts:

- the *data* as communicated to the analyst
- the *context* of the data
- how the *analyst's knowledge* partititions his reality
- the *target* of a content analysis
- *inference* as the basic intellectual task
- *validity* as ultimate criteria of success.

The framework is intended to serve three purposes: prescriptive, analytical, and methodological. It is prescriptive in the sense that it should guide the *conceptualization and the design* of practical content analyses for any given circumstance; analytical in the sense that it should facilitate *the critical examination* of content analysis results obtained by others; and methodological in the sense that it should direct the *growth and systematic improvement of methods* for content analysis.

In any content analysis *it must be clear which data are analyzed,* how they are defined, and from which population they are drawn. Data are made available to the content analyst, their context is not. Data exhibit their own syntax and structure, are described in terms of units, categories, and variables, or coded into a multidimensional scheme. Data are the primitives for a content analysis and constitute the surface which a content analyst will want to penetrate. *The communication of data to the analyst is one way.* He is unable to manipulate reality. He has no corrective feedback with the source that, for reasons of its own, provides him with information. He is thus forced to study a portion of his universe unobtrusively. For example, the wartime propaganda analyst cannot possibly interact with members of the enemy elite he is interested in, and the mass media content analyst cannot influence or recreate the situation in which news items and entertainments were produced, disseminated, received, and turned into a variety of audience behaviors.

In any content analysis, *the context relative to which data are analyzed must be made explicit.* While data are made available, their context is constructed by the content analyst to include all surrounding conditions, antecedent, coexisting, or consequent. The need for delineating the context of a content analysis is particularly important because there are no logical limits as to the kind of context an analyst might want to consider. Any research effort must define the boundaries beyond which its analysis does not extend. In content analysis, disciplinary conventions and practical problems often dictate the choice of these boundaries. Psychologists tend not to be interested much beyond the individual, a writer, a politician, a historical personality, or psychiatric patient. Communication researchers tend to see messages in the context of their role in interactions between sender and receiver. The analyst of enemy broadcasts may have certain aspects of the enemy country in mind in the context of which elite propaganda behavior makes sense. Although the boundaries of a context are arbitrary, there is some advantage in defining them in such a way that there is some structural unity, some natural way of dividing the universe into what is relevant and what is not.

For any content analysis, the analyst's interest and knowledge determine the construction of the context within which inferences are realized.

It is therefore important that a content analyst has knowledge about the origin of the data and that he reveals the assumptions he makes about how the data and their environment interact. He must be able to distinguish between two kinds of knowledge. First, something whose nature is variable or unstable, about which the analyst is therefore uncertain as to which state, form or value it has. Second, that there are certain relationships between variables that are unchanging, stable, or fixed. As with all knowledge, this distinction will change in time. Indeed, content analysis uses available data and knowledge of stable configurations to remove uncertainties about the unstable pattern in the context of its data.

In any content analysis, the aim or *target of the inferences must be clearly stated*. The target is what the analyst will want to know about. Since content analysis provides vicarious knowledge, information about something not directly observed, this target is located in the variable portion of the context of available data. Although there is ample room for exploratory studies during which the researcher makes up his mind as to what his focus of attention will be, he has to come up with a clear direction. Only if the target of a content analysis is unambiguously stated can he judge whether the content analysis is completed and specify the kind of evidence eventually needed to validate the results.

The claim to have analyzed a representative sample of the *New York Times* may be specific about the data but vacuous regarding context and target. In fact, the analysis may have completely ignored the symbolic qualities of this medium. A title like "A Content Analysis of Chinese Wall Posters" is similarly uncertain, whereas "Prediction of Elite Decisions from Chinese Wall Posters" or "What the Chinese Public Learns from Wall Posters about Political Decision Making" at least refers to some context and indicates an aim.

In any content analysis, the task is *to make inferences* from data to certain aspects of their context and to justify these inferences in terms of the knowledge about the stable factors in the system of interest. It is by this process that data become recognized as symbolic or are rendered informative about something of interest to the analyst.

To accomplish or justify these inferences, a content analyst must have available, or construct an operational theory of, the relatively stable data-context relationships including the contributing or mediating factors. A theory of these relationships that is formulated so that the data appear as its independent variables and the target appears in its dependent variables is called an *analytical construct*. Thus, an analytical construct provides rules of inference. An analytical construct serves as the logical bridge between available data and the uncertain target in their context. It is not enough to know that data-context relationships are stable, one has to know their specific form as well. In attempting to predict the outcome of a political decision from mass media coverage, it is not enough to know that the mass media play an important role in the political process. One will have to know which elements, assertions, or arguments influence the process in one or in the other direction. What is needed is knowledge of the nature of this relation.

In any content analysis, *the kind of evidence needed to validate its results* must be specified in advance or sufficiently clear so as to make validation conceivable. Although it is the *raison d'être* of content analysis that direct evidence about the phenomena of interest is missing and must be inferred, at least the criteria for an ex post facto validation of results must be clear so as to allow others to gather suitable evidence and see whether the inferences were indeed accurate. Ex post facto validation is not merely a matter of curiosity. Just as one can learn only when success and failure become distinguishable, so can the methodology of content analysis advance only with systematic efforts at validating its results. Much too often content analyses are either regarded as unique instances with no repetition ever attempted or are conceptualized so poorly that it is impossible to pin down the researcher as to what a suitable validity test would be. Such content analyses are empirically vacuous and contribute little to the methodology of content analysis.

A good example of an ex post facto validation is found in George's (1959a) effort to examine documents captured after World War II to see how successful the wartime FCC propaganda analysts had been and to evaluate the different techniques used. Janis (1965) proposed an indirect method of validating inferred audience perceptions by correlating content analysis results with audience behavior (e.g., voting, consumption, or aggression).

The framework may be summarized in Figure 1, which suggests that data become dissociated from their source or from their surrounding conditions and are communicated one way to the analyst. The analyst places these data in a context that he constructs based on his knowledge of the surrounding conditions of the data including what he wishes to know about the target of the content analysis. Knowledge about the stable dependencies within the system of interest are formulated as analytical constructs which allow him to make inferences that are sensitive to the context of the data. Content analysis results must represent some feature of reality and the nature of this representation must be verifiable in principle.

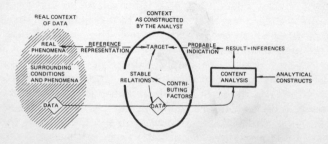

FIGURE 1:   The Framework for Content Analysis

DISTINCTIONS

Every research technique has its own empirical domain. It can be misused and applied where other methods may be more efficient. In order that content analysis be used at its highest potential, we contrast its empirical domain with that of other techniques of social research. Figure 2 summarizes these distinctions using the three most important dimensions of contrast. It shows content analysis at one extreme with other methods scattered throughout. We will state these contrasts in the form of propositions.

(1) *Content analysis is an unobtrusive technique.* Since Heisenberg we know that acts of measurement which interfere with the behavior of the phenomena being assessed create increasingly contaminated observations the deeper the observer probes. For the social sciences, Webb et al. (1966) have enumerated several ways in which subjects react to being the source of scientific information and thus introduce errors into the data being analyzed. Some of these are:

- the awareness of being observed or tested
- the subject's assumed or assigned role as interviewee or respondent
- influences of the measurement process on the subject
- stereotypes and preferences in casting responses
- experimenter-interviewer interaction effects on the subject.

Techniques that are especially susceptible to these errors are experiments, interviews, questionnaires, and projective tests. These are all conducted by an investigator who assumes control in varying degrees over the stimulus conditions to which subjects are asked to react.

In contrast, content analysis, information retrieval, modelling, the use of statistical records, and to a limited extent ethno-methodology share in being nonreactive or an unobtrusive research technique.

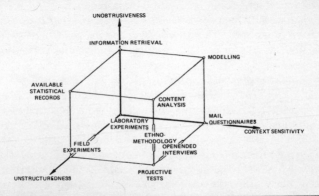

FIGURE 2:   Empirical Domains of Content Analysis and Contrasting Techniques

There are two reasons why a researcher may want to avoid reactive situations. *He may feel that undue constraints on the situation which gives rise to the data may jeopardize their validity.* For this reason, ethnomethodologists prefer to record data from natural settings, psychiatrists avoid questions that might distract the patient's attention from what he has in mind and economists take to investigating models of an economy rather than the system it represents. And *he may want to conceal his interest in the data so as to avoid the source's instrumental use of them.* Instrumental assertions are difficult to analyze. Had Goebbels known how, by which methods, and for which purpose his broadcasts were analyzed during World War II, he would have found ways of deceiving the analyst.

(2) *Content analysis accepts unstructured material.* There is of course considerable virtue in structuring a situation so that data come in analyzable forms. Mail questionnaires and interview schedules leave the respondent predefined choices whose meanings are easily coded. Subjects in experiments are virtually taught a data language that is not their own such as pushing buttons, indicating scale points by numbers, identifying shapes or forms, or administering electric shocks to other subjects. Also, modelling by computer and retrieving information from a data bank is prestructured by the formal requirement of manipulation and storage. Although survey research, psychological experiments, and computer applications owe their success to the ease of analyzing prestructured data, the researcher may not have that choice. *He may become interested in the material after it had been generated by a source* which employs a language, a logic, and categories that are neither needed for nor compatible with the requirements of the analysis. Historians, mass media content analysts, and psychologists using biographical data find themselves unable to obtain information in the desired form and have to take whatever is made available for reasons that have nothing to do with the analysis. Additionally, *he may not be able to anticipate all categories of analysis and forms of expression before the material has been obtained and examined.* For example, interpersonal communications tend to be so complex and a priorily uncertain in content that videotapes of them may have to be examined repeatedly, sometimes frame by frame, before the analyst understands what actually happened. Finally, *he may feel that undue constraints on the form of the subject's responses impede the validity of the data.* This is especially the case for content analyses of indigenous conceptualizations and expressions.

(3) *Content analysis is context sensitive and thereby able to process symbolic forms.* In analyzing responses obtained under various experimental conditions, data become dissociated from the symbolic meanings these responses may have had for the subjects involved and are analyzed as a collection of data regardless of their symbolic qualities. Thus, while experiments do not preclude the use of language, verbal responses tend not to be treated as symbolic phenomena except for the theoretical meanings attributed to them by the investigator. This constraint is also common to information retrieval procedures which employ syntactical matching and

search criteria that leave the symbolic interpretation of the data to the system's user.

Although it is admittedly easier to reduce the symbolic qualities of data to labels for categories, variables, and data points which have no consequence for the process of analysis and are meaningful only for the researcher who interprets his findings in these terms, there are two reasons for a researcher to prefer just the opposite. *An analyst may wish to analyze verbal data as symbolic phenomena* and in the process of transformation maintain the reference to what they represent, are associated with, cause, control, constitute, or reproduce within the original context. Thus, the political analyst following a case study approach to an international treaty or a President's speech simply cannot ignore the semantical and situational features. and the political consequences of such events. The direction of the analyst's interpretation is homomorphic to the symbolic process in reality. Or *he may wish to analyze data relative to a context that is neither shared with nor conceptualized in a manner similar to that of the individual communicators or subjects involved.* Valid theories, analytical constructs, or past experiences with a context may render the data "unconventional symbolic entities" which lead the analyst to inferences that the subjects may be unaware of, unable to agree to, or validate. This situation is epitomized in the use of projective tests: Here subjects respond to ambiguous and suggestive stimuli and do not know how they thereby inform the analyst about their personality, psychopathology, or aptitude. These data's symbolic qualities are recognized only by the researcher.

(4) *Content analysis can cope with large volumes of data.* Much of ethnomethodology, case studies in psychiatry, history, and political science focuses on small and unique bodies of text, attempting to infer contextual correlates in some depth. Although such a focus may be rewarding and is certainly not excluded from content analysis, especially at the preliminary stage, it tends to circumvent the use of quality controls for the statistical significance and reliability of findings. The data generated by content analyses can quickly exceed what a single analyst can do. Consider the following numbers of units of analysis:

481 Personal conversations (Landis and Bartt, 1924)
427 School textbooks (Pierce, 1930)
4022 Advertising slogans (Shuman, 1937, cited by Baelson, 1952)
8039 Newspaper editorials (Foster, 1938)
800 News of foreign-language radio programs (Arnheim and Bayne, 1941)
19553 Editorials (Pool, 1952)
15000 Characters in 1000 hours of television fiction (Gerbner et al., 1979).

As a consequence, *the content analyst may be faced with large volumes of linguistic data that can no longer be analyzed by a single person.* A large number of collaborators may have to be employed, processing may have to be spaced over large periods of time and aided by machines, requiring a research organization, quality controls, and a well-defined methodology.

3

USES AND KINDS OF INFERENCE

Distinguishing the forms of inference which analysts may employ allows one to encompass the tasks necessary for content analysis. The logical mechanisms employed to relate data to their context are examined here in terms of systems, standards, indices, linguistic representations, communications, and institutional processes.

Content analysis has an important place in the methodology of investigative tools. It is capable, first, of accepting relatively unstructured symbolic communications as data and, second, of analyzing unobserved phenomena through the medium of data connected with the phenomena, regardless of whether language is involved. Since most social processes are transacted through symbols, the widest use of content analysis is found in the social sciences and humanities. Several writers have identified and classified types and applications of content analysis.

Janis (1965) offers the following classification:

(1) *Pragmatical Content Analysis*—procedures which classify signs according to their probable causes or effects (e.g., counting the number of times that something is said which is likely to have the effect of producing favorable attitudes toward Germany in a given audience).

(2) *Semantical Content Analysis*—procedures which classify signs according to their meanings (e.g., counting the number of times that Germany is referred to, irrespective of the particular words that may be used to make the reference).

   (a) *designations analysis*—provides the frequency with which certain objects (persons, things, groups or concepts) are referred to, that is, roughly speaking subject-matter analysis (e.g., references to German foreign policy).

   (b) *attribution analysis*—provides the frequency with which certain characterizations are referred to (e.g., references to dishonesty).

   (c) *assertions analysis*—provides the frequency with which certain objects are characterized in a particular way, that is, roughly speaking, thematic analysis (e.g., references to German foreign policy as dishonest).

(3) *Sign-vehicle analysis*—procedures which classify content according to the psychophysical properties of the signs (e.g., counting the number of times the word *Germany* appears).

Berelson (1952) lists 17 uses:

- to describe trends in communication content
- to trace the development of scholarship
- to disclose international differences in communication content
- to compare media or "levels" of communication
- to audit communication content against objectives

- to construct and apply communication standards
- to aid in technical research operations (to code open-ended questions in survey interviews)
- to expose propaganda techniques
- to measure the "readability" of communication materials
- to discover stylistic features
- to identify the intentions and other characteristics of the communicators
- to determine the psychological state of persons or groups
- to detect the existence of propaganda (primarily for legal purposes)
- to secure political and military intelligence
- to reflect attitudes, interests, and values ("cultural patterns") of population groups
- to reveal the focus of attention
- to describe attitudinal and behavioral responses to communications.

Stone and Dunphy (Stone et al., 1966) describe applications of content analysis in such empirical domains as:

- psychiatry
- psychology
- history
- anthropology
- education
- philology and literary analysis
- linguistics,

with journalism and mass communication seen as the historical origin of the technique.

Holsti (1969), like Janis, places data in the context of communication between some sender and some receiver and surveys content analyses in terms of three principal purposes:

- to describe characteristics of communication—asking *what, how,* and *to whom* something is said
- to make inferences as to the antecedents of communication—asking *why* something is said
- to make inferences as to the effects of communication—asking *with what effects* something is said.

The following deviates from the above and will distinguish uses of the techniques in terms of the forms of inferences content analyses may make. These are:

- *systems*
- *standards*
- *indices and symptoms*
- *linguistic representations*
- *communications*
- *institutional processes.*

Our distinctions are motivated by differences in the mechanisms content analysts use to relate data to their context. They imply differences in the kind of contextual knowledge sought, in the analytical constructs needed, and in the way findings may be validated. The adequacy of either form is of course an empirical question.

The aim of this section is to define these forms of inferences and to illustrate how they have been used. A survey of the field is not intended.

SYSTEMS

A system is a conceptual device to describe a portion of reality. Minimally, it comprises:

- *components* whose states are variable
- *relations* that are manifest in constraints on the cooccurrence of states across components
- *transformations* according to which some relations imply other relations in time or in space.

Systems lead to extrapolations of existing data to yet unknown states of affairs and offer in this sense autonomous explanations. The solar system can be described in these terms with the configuration of planets following a definite temporal sequence. For someone who knows the system, data on one configuration imply all succeeding configurations. Kinship terminology also constitute a system in this sense. The relations between individuals are defined by the likes of descendency, marriage, adoption, and age difference, and a code prescribes how related individuals address each other. The system allows extrapolations to any new individual entering a relation. Systems of biological, symbolic, or social entities can become quite complicated, but retain the basic idea of a temporal or spatial linkage of relations between the many components. The inferences of interest to content analysis stem from transformations that are invariant to a symbol system and extendable beyond the time and space of available data.

The idea of a systems approach goes back to Tenney (1912), who asked "why should not society study its own methods of producing its various varieties of thinking by establishing (a) . . . careful system of bookkeeping? . . . What is needed . . . is the continuous analysis of a large number of journals. . . . The records in themselves would constitute a series of observations of the 'social weather,' comparable in accuracy to the 'statistics of the United States Weather Bureau." He had found some systematic interactions between subject matters within newspapers, suspected changes in such relations over time, and explored especially ethnic characteristics of these publications. He equated this dynamic of press coverage in an entire country with that country's thinking process but lacked data and presumably adequate methods for describing them systematically.

Recently Rapoport (1969) prepared the ground for a systems theory of "verbal corpuses," posing questions like what it means to describe a large body of symbolic data as behaving, changing, and evolving, and what the suitable components, relationships, and laws of interaction within such corpuses might be. Although he is aware that man's semantic environment both mirrors and constitutes much of human existence and that it is continuously enriched and may become polluted by individual acts and institutional policies, he suggests that the large-scale study of verbal outputs might be more fruitful when studied without reference to the symbol user, that is (at least for some time), as autonomous systems.

Trends

The prototype of a systems approach in content analysis is the extrapolation of trends. Speed (1893) compared several New York dailies published in 1881 with those published 12 years later and observed changes in subject matter categories. Although observations at only two points in time hardly lend themselves to solid predictions, Speed's discussion clearly showed such intentions when lamenting the decline of literary matters and the increase in gossip, sports, and fiction. Lasswell (1941) proposed a study and presented preliminary findings on trends in the frequencies with which references to various countries occur in different national presses. Loeventhal (1944) studied the changing definition of heros in popular magazines observing a still-ongoing drift away from working professionals and businessmen to entertainers. Other trend studies concern values in inspirational literature, advertising, political slogans, and frequency of publications in particular scientific disciplines. One of the more extensive content analyses using this perspective is Namenwirth's (1973) study of value changes in U.S. political party platforms, ranging over a 120-year period. He discovered two independent cycles in these data explaining global value changes as an autonomous system.

Pattern

Another systems notion in content analysis is the predictive use of patterns. In folklore, the structural analysis of riddles, proverbs, folktales, and narratives aims quite specifically at identifying patterns that have a high degree of predictability within a genre regardless of particular contents (Armstrong, 1959). Such an analysis begins by identifying the principal constituent elements within a genre and aims at the logic that relates these elements. Thus, Sebeok and Orzack (1953), analyzing Cheremis charms, found that a "purely factual statement" about the world is followed by a "motif of an extremely improbable eventuality." Labov's (1972) analysis of narratives follows a similar tradition. The analysis of genealogies within a body of literature through patterns of citation is another example. Scientific publications tend to cite other publications and thereby tie themselves into a web of literature. Garfield (1979) uses this fact in his citation index. In communication research, the charting of "who says (what) to whom" yields different patterns—communication networks that resemble sociograms. And the study of co-occurrences of words within a sentence, paragraph, or within a whole document leads also to patterns of co-occurrences from which inferences about a body of literature may be drawn.

Combining *trends* with *patterns* has led to many interesting content analyses. Bales's (1950) *Interaction Process Analysis* yielded patterns of communication, evaluation, control, decision making, tension reduction, and reintegration, all of which were defined on 12 basic categories of verbal exchanges within small groups. Holsti et al. (1965) analyzed the succession of public assertions made during the 1962 Cuban Missile Crisis by major decision makers in the United States and the Soviet Union into perceptions and expressions and they described each in terms of the values of the evaluative, strength, and potency dimensions of Osgood's attitude theory. They thereby gained data for a dynamic interdependency model which proved to be moderately predictive of the emotional responses each group of decision makers made to the other.

Differences

All systems approaches are concerned with extrapolating differences into new situations. Indeed a large body of literature in content analysis assesses the differences in messages generated by two communicators, by one source in two different situations, differences in audiences addressed, and differences between input and output. Differences in news coverage of political campaigns have been correlated with editorial endorsements (Klein and Maccoby, 1954). Differences in coverage of civil rights issues have been explained in terms of various newspaper characteristics including geographical location, ownership, and political orientation (Broom and Reece, 1955). Differences between newspapers that either face competition or have a monopoly have been studied (Nixon and Jones, 1956). How different ideological and class orientations turn up in the stream of messages was demonstrated in the reporting of an apolitical crime by the French press (Gerbner, 1964). Messages from one source may also vary when different audiences are addressed. This was shown by comparing John Foster Dulles's political speeches before groups of different make-up (Cohen, 1957; Holsti, 1962). Fiction written for upper, middle and lower class readers differs (Albrecht, 1956) and so does advertisement in magazines with black or white readership (Berkman, 1963). Differences between input and output are exemplified by studies relating sources of information available to a newspaper to what appears finally in print (Allport, 1940), analyses of what happens to a book when it is adapted into a movie (Asheim, 1950) or comparisons of scientific findings with their popularized versions.

A good example of combining *differences* between media and *trends* is the Hoover Institution's study of Revolution and the Development of International Relations (RADIR). It identified such key symbols for "democracy," "equality," "rights," and "freedom" in 19,553 editorials that appeared in American, British, French, German, and Russian prestige papers during 1890-1949. The analysis of these data led Pool (1951) to observe-predict that proletarian doctrines replace liberal traditions, that an increasing threat of war is correlated with growth in militarism and nationalism, and that hostilities toward other nations are related to insecurity. Although these symbols refer to aspects of a political reality, they were categorized, counted, and analyzed by an analyst without regard to what these symbols represent. Pool's observation that symbols of democracy appear less frequently when a representative form of government is accepted than where it is in dispute would suggest though that this symbol system is not entirely autonomous. Gerbner et al.'s (1979) study of

television violence has now accumulated enough data on fictional programming to make extrapolations of interest to policy makers. His term
message systems analysis (Gerbner, 1969) intends to do this concerning
four general interests:

(1) the frequencies with which a system's components occur, or "what is"
(2) the order of priorities assigned to the components, or "what is important"
(3) the affective qualities associated with the components, or "what is right"
(4) the proximal or logical associations between the components or "what is
    related to what."

Unfortunately, most practical uses of systems notions in content analysis have been marred by their still-archaic forms. The study of trends has
often been concerned with only one variable, or has taken only one
variable at a time such as frequencies, volume, growth, definition, or
values. Patterns have often been conceptualized in binary relation such as
succession, contrast, proximity, cause, or communication. And differences
have rarely been explained in terms of interactions that may enhance or
diminish them in time. One problem is the sheer volume of data required
to find characteristics that are sufficiently invariant to warrant systemic
inferences. As this problem is beginning to be handled with the use of
electronic information-processing capabilities, another problem comes into
the foreground. How can we develop suitable systems conceptions that
lend themselves to the computation of symbolic data as systems in their
own right?

STANDARDS

Common to processes of identification, evaluation, and auditing is the
existence of a standard with which an object is compared so as to establish
what kind or how good it is. Although it might appear that these processes
do not involve inference, the fact is that identities do not reveal themselves
in a vacuum. Evaluations are meaningless without a purpose and audits
remain inconsequential unless the criteria in use have institutional support.
The outcome of such processes depends on the interaction between an
object's characteristics and a standard, varies with different standards, and
thus involves inferences though of a simple sort.

Evaluations

The evaluation of press performance has been a major preoccupation
since the emergence of quantitative newspaper analysis. The concern with
changes from quality to quantity of news reporting (Speed, 1883) or with
increases of trivial, demoralizing, and unwholesome subject matter at the
expense of worthwhile information (Matthews, 1910) assumes evaluative
standards, albeit implicitly. Although one may share the concern that
prompted those studies, it is difficult to agree on a sufficiently acceptable
scale that places newspapers between good and bad. Many of the evaluative studies have limited themselves to measuring biases toward one or the
other side of a controversy. For example, Ash (1948) attempted to
determine whether the public was given a fair opportunity to learn both
sides of the controversial Taft-Hartley Labor Act.

Most evaluative studies suffer from the lack of defensible criteria. Janis and Fadner (1965) published a "coefficient of imbalance" that measures the degree to which favorable statements outnumber unfavorable ones. Formally, the coefficient is impeccable; but whether, or under which circumstances, journalists should be impartial remains an unsettled issue. In the last days of Nixon's presidency, it was hard not to take sides. Merrill (1962) used a battery of evaluative criteria on journalistic presentations (attribution bias, adjective bias, adverbial bias, contextual bias, photographic bias, and outright opinion) but the catalogue is far from complete. Berelson and Salter (1946) used the racial composition of the U.S. population as a standard against which they evaluated the population of fictional characters in magazines, an idea that led to many other evaluative studies (Berkman, 1963). But whether the population of fictional characters in magazines, on stage, or in television should be statistically representative of such audience characteristics as ethnicity, sex, age, and especially the kinds of activities they engage in is also not clear. The Council on Inter-racial Books for Children (1977) proposed and demonstrated a method for evaluating history texts in the United States by comparing them with known "historical facts." Again, some selectivity in the presentation of history is probably unavoidable. What is worrisome and should provide the decision point for all evaluative efforts is systematic excesses, not adherence to a fixed standard.

Identifications

While evaluations assess the degree to which something conforms or deviates from a standard, identifications have a more *either/or* quality. Dibble (1963), who considered the kind of inferences of interest to historians, exemplified his category of "documents as direct indicators" somewhat like this: Suppose a historian wants to know whether the British ambassador to Berlin communicated with the foreign ministry the day before World War I began. The letter in the file of the foreign ministry then provides direct evidence of its having been sent. His inference involves identifying the letter by certain required characteristics. Identifications of this kind include authentications of a piece of art, verifications of a will, or certifications of a signature. Even on the micro-level, identifications are important ingredients of computer content analysis. For example, the General Inquirer (Stone et al., 1966) categorizes the words in a text into classes of semantically similar words. Since the computer program does not recognize similarities in meaning, this idea is built into a "dictionary" which reduces the task of classification to one of "identification of specified characteristics." Much of content analysis involves a categorization of sign vehicles by identifying the meanings they convey to a specified audience or receiver (Janis, 1965).

Audits

Audits, too, involve judgments on data relative to a standard with the additional provision that the standard is *prescribed or legitimized* by an institution. For example, when the FCC requires that each television station maintain a certain proportion of commercial, local live, sustaining, and public issue programming, it implies a form of measurement and criteria. Decisions on obscenity, plagiarism, discriminatory communication practice, and even on whether fictional programming could stimulate a crime might be based on evidence obtainable through a content analysis provided that the law is specific enough as to the nature of admissible evidence. Unfortunately, most legal issues pertaining to communication content are not formulated in a language that is easily operationalizable. Nevertheless, the results of content analyses have been accepted in court at least since Lasswell's (1949b) comparative analysis of publications of suspected foreign agents (see his *Content Analysis*, 1948).

INDICES AND SYMPTOMS

An index is a variable whose significance in an investigation depends on the extent to which it can be regarded as a *correlate of other phenomena*. Pierce required an index to be causally connected with the event it signifies—as smoke indicates fire—or based on physical necessity rather than arbitrary convention (symbol) or similarity (icon). In medicine, indices are called symptoms. Many diseases and biological disorders turn out to have visible side effects that are not consciously controllable by the patient. A significant part of a physician's diagnosis involves interpreting visible changes of the human body as symptoms about an illness. "An index . . . does not depend on the physical entities or events from which it is derived" (Rapoport, 1969).

Likewise, many content analyses use measurable entities as indices of not so directly measurable phenomena. Typically, linguistic (or para-linguistic) data are measured in such a way that they achieve the status of an index of nonlinguistic phenomena: the speech disturbance ratio as a measure of a patient's anxiety during a psychiatric interview (Mahl, 1959); the frequency of a certain class of words as an index of the motive to achieve (McClelland, 1958); typographical and space measures as indices of public attention to a particular subject matter (e.g., Budd, 1964); television violence index (Gerbner et al., 1979); indices of citizen dissatisfaction computed from letters of complaint (Krendel, 1970); Flesh's (1948, 1951) readability yardstick; Broder's (1940) adjective-verb ratio as an index of schizophrenia (Mann, 1944); and improbable co-occurrences of nouns as indicators of associations in the speaker and receiver (Osgood, 1959).

In mass communication research, three indices have had a long history of use:

- The *frequency* with which a symbol, idea, or subject matter occurs in a stream of messages tends to be interpreted as a measure of *importance, attention,* or *emphasis.*

- The balance in numbers of *favorable and unfavorable* attributes of a symbol, idea, or subject matter tends to be interpreted as a measure of the *direction or bias.*

- The kind of qualifications made and associations expressed toward a symbol, idea, or subject matter tends to be interpreted as a measure of the *intensity or strength* of a belief, conviction, or motivation.

The use of such easily computable quantities as indices is not without problems. Chomsky (1959), taking Skinner to task for suggesting that promptness of response, repetition, voice volume, and the like are natural indices of the intensity of motivation, compares two hypothetical women, each receiving a luxurious bouquet. The first woman, instantly after seeing the flowers, shouts "Beautiful! Beautiful! Beautiful! Beautiful!" at the top of her lungs, thus giving evidence, according to Skinner's criteria, of a strong motivation to produce the response. The second woman, upon opening the box, says nothing for 10 seconds, then whispers, barely audibly, "Beautiful." Presumably she exhibits a "weak motivation to respond" (Rapoport, 1969).

Frequency indices of attention are equally problematic. It is one thing to use frequencies or repetitions to gain certainty about a hypothesis, and quite a different matter to use it as an indicator of a phenomenon that is to correlate with it. The former pertains to scientific procedure, the latter to an empirical property. In his famous "Why Be Quantitative" in content analysis, Lasswell (1965a) confuses this distinction. Frequency measures are likely to be successful indicators when the underlying phenomena is likewise frequency related. For example, the number and kind of letters of complaint to city hall (Krendel, 1970) are likely to be indicative of the same kind of dissatisfaction that would manifest itself in mayoral elections. In a critical moment, Berelson (1952) wondered what a Martian might infer when finding high frequencies of love and sex in the mass communications that survive from our time—a promiscuous society or a repressive one? Pool (1952b) observed that symbols of democracy occur less frequently where democratic procedures are accepted than where they are in dispute. Although most learning theories suggest that repetition strengthens beliefs, repetitions are also known to lead to semantic satiation, such as the loss of meaning.

The difficulties involved in establishing an index may be demonstrated in the use of the *discomfort-relief quotient*. Based on learning theoretical considerations, Dolland and Mowrer (1947) derived it as an index of anxiety of the speaker. The quotient is computed as the proportion of the number of discomfort or drive words and the sum of the number of discomfort or drive words plus the number of comfort or relief words. Despite theoretical arguments in its favor, tests of the indicative power of this quotient have led to mixed results. Significant correlations with palmar sweating have been reported but correlations with other measures of anxiety seem to be demonstrable only in very restricted circumstances. Murray et al. (1954) compared the discomfort-relief quotient with several other motivational and conflict measures during therapy and found the quotient not to be sensitive to changes in therapeutic progress. What the quotient might indicate is therefore far from clear.

Somewhat more successful is the use of indices for readability. Clearly, the use of foreign expressions, long and compound words, and complex grammar and punctuation makes reading difficult. Flesh (1948) aggregated the proportion of pairs—such as foreign to native words and long to short words—into a single figure, his readability yardstick, which correlated with reading ease as reported by readers. Subsequent studies have taken many more measures into account, factored out human interest, comprehension, and reading speed, and thus came to measures that correlate better than the original "yardstick." One might suspect that the reason for this success, however moderate it may be, lies in an additive notion of reading ease: Each difficulty that a reader encounters presumably adds to the overall judgment of the difficulty in ways similar to the way in which difficult words are counted. This may not hold true for other magnitudes.

Indices have also been successful in settling disputes about authorship. Yule (1944), an insurance statistician, reconsidered whether Thomas à Kempis, Jean Gerson, or one of several others wrote *The Imitation of Christ.* He correlated frequencies of nouns in works known to have been written by each prospective author, thereby developing discriminating indices to their identity and applied these indices to the disputed work. The inference was in favor of à Kempis. Mosteller and Wallace (1964) found function words rather than nouns more distinctive in deciding on the disputed authorship of 12 *Federalist Papers.* The evidence favored Madison.

Again, the establishment of indices is not a matter of verbal definition. Counting frequencies and calling it a measure of attention does not make it an index of attention. And even if empirical data are used in developing an index, there remains the problem of generalization. For example, Morton and Levinson (1966) analyzed Greek texts of known authorship and extracted seven discriminators of style which, according to the authors, taps the unique elements of any person's writing: sentence length, frequency of the definite article, third-person pronouns, the aggregate of all forms of "to be," and the frequency of the words *and, but,* and *in.* After an analysis of the 14 Epistles attributed to Paul, Morton (1963) concluded that they were written by six different authors and that Paul himself had written only four. Ellison (1965) applied these constructs to texts of known authors; this led to the inference that *Ulysses* was written by five different authors none of whom wrote *Portrait of the Artist as a Young Man.* Even Morton's own article was found to be written in several distinct styles. This casts serious doubt on the utility of Morton's stylistic indices of an author's identity.

LINGUISTIC REPRESENTATIONS

A discourse involves language in a systematic exposition and argument including a methodical discussion of the facts and principles involved and conclusions reached. A discourse is concerned with a limited portion of reality or with some of its experiential features. It may stem from one person or a group of people in interaction. It may define its own subject matter, remain open to the inclusion of new facts, and accept modifications of facts previously held true or claimed by others. To analyze a body of text as a discourse involves relationships between two or more sentences provided that these relationships bear on the knowledge about the reality this body represents.

Hays (1969) exemplifies some typical streams of linguistic data that social scientists may be interested in as follows:

- *A sequence of editorials.* The staff of a newspaper, experiencing an epoch, produces a series of essays, recapitulating some of the day's events, placing them with respect to historical trends, theory, and dogma. It expresses opinions about the true nature of situations that are necessarily not fully comprehended, and opinions about the responses called for.

- *International exchanges of an official character.* This kind of correspondence might well be compared with a sequence of newspaper editorials, except that there are two or more parties involved, each pursuing a policy of its own.
- *Personal documents.* These may be letters, diaries, or written materials of other kinds. Except for the particularity of content, these materials could be compared with newspaper editorials or governmental notes.
- *Interview transcripts.* Usually there are two parties. One of the parties is naive, and the other is sophisticated. The purpose of the interview may be, for example, therapeutic or diagnostic.
- *Social interaction.* Two or more persons participate, discussing a fixed task or whatever topics they deem suitable.

Even if one ignores the sequential aspect of these examples—journalistic accounts of an event, testimony by a witness in court, reports on the findings of an investigation, scholarly treatises, and political documents— all share the use of language for representing a portion of reality, ideally excluding the feelings, interests, and subjective perspectives of the source. The intuitive notion of "content," too, seems to point to a linguistic representation of facts and experiences. Surprisingly, content analysts have felt more comfortable with the use of indices that, although computed from linguistic data, do not rely on, and in fact ignore, the power of language. Although there may be good reasons for content analyses to process data in ways different from those who generate them, it is a fundamental fact of human communication that language is used to convey knowledge and to understand the knowledge conveyed by others. Therefore, one task of content analysis is to achieve this kind of understanding of linguistic data and to draw inferences on the basis of this understanding.

The most rudimentary form of understanding what language may convey involves classifying words or linguistic expressions by the references (denotations, connotations) they make. Consider the many ways a U.S. President may be referred to in the press: by his official title, by his names, by his ordinal number, by his years in office, by his residency (the White House), or by his major political accomplishments. A considerable linguistic and political knowledge is required to isolate such references from their contexts and to put them into one category for the occupant of this office. Although differences among referentially synonymous expressions might be indicative of attitudes or personal relationships, to name just two, when focusing on what a discourse is about, one might be justified in ignoring these. In quantifying "the amount of attention paid to television violence," two components must be distinguished. The first is the quantitative *index* for the magnitude of attention and, second, the qualitative distinction between *references* to portrayals of violence and nonviolence. It is the latter use that is of interest here, and it is not tied to quantification.

Obviously, a mere collection of references does not do justice to the knowledge a language may convey. One use of linguistic representations in content analysis is the development of cognitive *maps*. Gerbner and Marvanji (1977) develop the maps of the world as seen from U.S., Eastern

European, Western European, Soviet, and some third world newspapers, using the volume of foreign news as a criteria of size. Lynch (1965), though coming from a different tradition, maps all verbal statements about moving within a city into a map of that city as seen by residents. Allport (1965), analyzing personal *Letters from Jenny*, shows what the world of the writer of these letters looks like and what kind of psychological inferences might be drawn from it. Marginal examples of discursive representations may be found in simulations of cognitive processes (Abelson, 1968) and its application to political campaigns (Pool et al., 1964).

Perhaps it is because human analysts are so efficient in interpreting linguistic assertions referentially that detailed techniques for drawing inferences from discursive representations are not so well formalized. Let us see the kind of inferences that could be drawn from such representations. Allen (1963), proposing some kind of logical content analysis, shows which options are left open to the signatories of an arms limitation agreement. This leads him to infer the directions into which the parties to this agreement can or may intend to move, and where further conflicts among them could arise. Emphasizing constraints rather than options, Newell and Simon's (1956) Logic Theory Machine shows how a sequence of logical implications (a proof) from available evidence (premises, axioms) may be used to make decisions within a problem area (the validity of a theorem). Obviously political documents, newspaper accounts, research findings, and the like are of interest primarily because of the *implications* that can be drawn from them regarding problems of interest to the user.

The best model for a content analysis using discursive representations is found in *question-answering machines*. These are governed by computer programs, accept natural language data (with some constraints), and can answer specific questions by ascertaining what available data implicitly "say" about that question. This type of machine has little to do with information retrieval devices which reply to a query by retrieving an explicitly stored idea according to some index. It should also not be confused with abstracting devices which extract key words or the most representative sentence from a given text. The principal feature of such a content analysis is the reliance on a map of the discourse territory. It does include the analyst's target into which linguistic data are entered and whose implications can be explored.

Considering how recent developments in computational linguistics have aided content analysis, Hays (1969) proposes such a model, calling it a "conversationalist." A content analysis of this kind would have to consider what the contributors to a discourse can be presumed to know. It would accept a stream of linguistic data, the discourse, a dialogue, a treaty, and the like, and it would answer the analyst's questions regarding implications, intentions, disagreements, or options.

COMMUNICATIONS

Communications are messages that are exchanged between interlocutors. The composition and content of these messages are to some extent intended by the originator and may have a variety of consequences. Most important, communications are exchanged in the context of existing relationships among the communicators and modify the relationships in the process. On the lowest level, communications may serve to explain causes and effects that are symbolically mediated. Communications may also serve to explain the dynamics of behavior, individual or collective consequences of exchanging information, psychopathologies, the emergence of conflict and consensus, and the transformation of material culture. Although this conception of communications seems obvious, content analyses that employ it in their procedures are rare indeed. Exchanges between purposeful beings clearly go beyond mere linguistic representations. While the hope to study the interaction through messages certainly predates content analysis, suitable conceptions for drawing inferences are of relatively recent origin.

Attempting to infer anxiety from recorded speech, Mahl (1959) considered how intentions affect word choices. Although his problem was eventually solved by developing suitable indices that are not consciously controllable, his discussion of the instrumental use of language reveals a form of meaning that is rooted in the essential circularity of communication effects: An assertion is instrumental to the extent that it stimulates a desired feedback to the communicator regardless of semantical contents. The interpretation of linguistic data as communications allows the analyst to draw inferences about circular causal pattern.

INSTITUTIONAL PROCESSES

Besides being indicative, conveying content, or having instrumental or unintentional consequences, messages may also serve functions within social organizations and societal institutions. Communication has been likened to the glue that holds social organizations together. Indeed, families, bureaucracies, and societies are unthinkable without regular and standard forms of ongoing processes of communication. Within organizations, messages may serve many purposes, only the more obvious one is the provision of information from the outside. Messages are a living organization's symbolic backbone and content analyses may aim at inferring the institutional structures and processes constituted by the data at hand.

Lasswell (1960), for example, distinguishes between three principal societal functions of communication about which an institutional approach to content analysis may want to make inferences:

(1) the surveillance of the environment
(2) the correlation of the parts of society in responding to the environment
(3) the transmission of the social heritage from one generation to the next (culture),

to which Wright (1964) adds:

(4) entertainment.

Any society seems to have institutions that specialize in such activity. Some of them are journalism, politics, education, literature, and the arts.

Mass communication may serve such purposes simultaneously, more or less adequately, and thereby affect institutional arrangements in society. Although these distinctions arose in sociological theory and in political analysis, they are also applicable in analyzing smaller social organizational phenomena and particular institutions.

Without going into the details of very many, not always thoroughly designed content analyses employing some institutional framework or another, let me propose four primary propositions for content analyses in institutional contexts.

Communications tend to be governed by institutional rules prescribing conditions under which they are disseminated and used within an organization. A bank check delivered to a teller must conform in design and in writing to what a bank recognizes as a valid check. When all conditions are met, the teller is obligated to enact a financial transaction, and knowing the institutional role of a check, an auditor can infer how much money has been transferred. Knowing the institutional role of *Pravda* to be the official organ of the Soviet government, an unsigned article on national matters can be inferred to represent the view of a high governmental official or the party and may thus be interpreted as due process, a transaction within the government with possible policy implications. The knowledge that allows such inferences to be made represents the stable aspects of the institutional web of which *Pravda* is a part. Institutional approaches in mass communications research have focused on legal, economic, sociopolitical, and technical-structural conditions that shape media contents and may in turn be inferred from available communications.

Legal in the sense that communicators must be licensed, maintain membership in professional associations, pay dues or be otherwise entitled to participate in the process of communication. Within social organizations the right to use a particular channel of communication is regulated and whatever data one obtains in such contexts, they reveal what an institution deems permissible. This includes which legal constraints are no longer obeyed and which constraints are implicitly accepted.

Economic in the sense that the costs of production, transmission, and consumption must be paid by someone. In the United States, television programs are paid for by advertising and whatever. is aired serves the interests of its sponsor. The effects of ownership, monopolies, industrial connections have been frequent targets of inferences from content analyses. Most communications can be assessed in terms of institutional costs and benefits.

Sociopolitical in the sense that communications can rarely be confined to particular institutional channels and may then become subject to constraints that range from formal codes of ethics to informal value judgments by potentially powerful interest groups. The Watergate scandal exemplifies the disregard for powerful sociopolitical conditions of political acts. Newspapers, television stations, even industries that expect to have some longevity cannot afford to displease a powerful minority or governing elite of a country. Communications in institutional contexts, particularly public communications, thus reflect the dominant power configurations of senders and potential receivers.

Technical-structural in the sense that communications must be producible and communicable by existing means. The film and television industry employs techniques of mass production that are vastly different from those employed in newspapers or in a small circus. What is found on the screen, read in the newspaper, or seen in a circus is constrained by their respective technical means of production and the social forms of organization of these media. Content analysis can infer some of these conditions from the messages one is able to gather.

Communications, created and disseminated under the operating rules of an institution, *tend to reinforce the rules under which they are created* and disseminated. Within institutional contexts, the activity of saying something is often more important than what is being said. Ceremonial speeches may come to mind. Their primary purpose is to move a ritual performance from one stage to the next and demonstrate an institution's success in completing the sequence.

The *properties of the medium* for recording and disseminating information *have a profound effect on the nature of the institutions that their communications can sustain.* Comparing oral with written communications, Innis (1951) suggests that writing has the effect of freezing traditions, proving to be more permanent and reliable and is thus able to support empires that extend control over larger geographical areas than word-of-mouth communications could. Radio and television with their virtually instantaneous transmission over vast distances tend to support the development of geographically widely dispersed organizations. But they are also far less capable of retaining access to past histories. Media of communications, or certain of its properties, are thus seen as the principal agent of social change and of the development of social structures. In the process of mediation, control is conferred to particular institutional forms. Content analyses of these media in institutional contexts can lead to inferences regarding competition of communication modes for dominance, which social changes are speeded up or retarded, or how power is distributed in a society.

Communications transmitted through institutional channels *tend to assume the syntax and form such channels can transmit most efficiently.* Content analyses have shed light on the systematic changes in content when a book is made into a film (Asheim, 1950); what happens to news and shows with controversial content, the gate-keeping mechanisms (White, 1964); how news is made as opposed to reported (Gieber, 1964); the social role of the magazine cover girl as a function of channels of distribution (Gerbner, 1958); and also how expectations about an institution can shape the forms of petitions by users (Katz et al., 1967). Most mass communication studies employing this perspective support the contention that the need for repetition (mass production) tends to preserve and strengthen social stereotypes, prejudices, and ideologies rather than correct them (Adorno, 1960). There are proposals, however, to anticipate major social changes from content analyses of avant-garde literature. These focus on communications that may undermine or escape institutional controls (Bell, 1964).

4

THE LOGIC OF CONTENT ANALYSIS DESIGNS

The sequential nature of content analysis designs is laid out below: data making, data reduction, inference, and analysis lead the content analyst to processes of direct validation, testing for correspondence with other methods and testing hypotheses.

SCIENTIFIC INFORMATION PROCESSING

Probably the most distinctive commitment any content analyst must make concerns the way he processes information. Scientific findings are never accepted at their face value, whether they are aimed at better understanding a phenomenon or at improving some conditions of life. The researcher is held accountable for the process leading to these findings: He must describe the conditions under which data are obtained, justify the analytical steps taken, and see to it that the process is not biased in the sense that it favors one kind of finding rather than another. Explicitness about the process is required so that others may evaluate his work, replicate the process, or qualify the findings.

The procedural network of analytical steps through which scientific information is processed is called the research design. It accounts for the way data were obtained, what was done to them in the course of an analysis, and provides others with instructions as to what to do in order to replicate the results. *Any research report must contain a description of the research design.*

For content analysis, more so than for other techniques, the research design as a whole must be appropriate to the context from which the data stem or relative to which data are analyzed. For example, when attempting to infer the psychopathology of a mental patient from his answers to questions, it would not seem to make sense to cut these answers into words, scramble them up, and draw a random sample for analysis. Such a procedure would be justifiable only if the information wanted was contained in the occurrence of isolated words. Most probably, the question-answer pair may have to be taken as a unit whose internal organization is deemed significant. Or, attempting to create a sociological profile of a newspaper, it would not be appropriate to apply intelligence test type items to its content. Categories have to be justified in terms of what is known about the data's context. Content analysis research designs have to be *context sensitive.* There must be some explicit or implicit correspondence between the analytical procedure and relevant properties of the context.

Research designs in content analysis tend to be *sequential* in nature. One step is followed by another and decisions on one procedure are not made (or reconsidered) depending on the outcome of a subsequent procedure. It follows that any error that may have entered a research design without detection is carried over to the end. In sequential processing of information, errors are thus cumulative or multiplicative. If one component of a research design is defective, by destroying relevant information, for example, a subsequent component cannot compensate for this loss or recreate what was destroyed. If observers do not record their observations reliably, subsequent analysis, however carefully it may be executed, will yield results which cannot be trusted.

TYPES OF DESIGNS

Looking at content analysis research designs holistically, we can distinguish three types. The typology depends largely on how the results of a content analysis are embedded in larger research efforts.

Designs to estimate some phenomena in the context of data are most basic. They conform directly to the definition of content analysis and are used when *content analysis is the sole method* being used. One could further distinguish whether some parameter is estimated or whether hypotheses between several estimated parameters are tested. However. the way these research designs relate to reality, specifically that the empirical findings are interpreted as being indicative of the context, renders them essentially the same. Graphically the two situations are presented in Figures 3 and 4.

Examples of single-parameter estimates include inferences regarding the level of anxiety of a psychiatric patient during an interview, assessment of a speaker's attitudes, ideological positions or values, attempts to gauge the war mood of a population by elite broadcasts directed toward this population, or estimates of the amount of public attention devoted to a social issue. Examples of within-content hypotheses include correlations between (1) personality attributes of television characters which are indicative of stereotypes and formulae and (2) studies of the domination and displacement of different subject matters over time.

One could also differentiate between cases where the content analyst has reasons to believe that the research design corresponds to, models, or replicates the relationship between data and their context and, therefore, where he accepts the results of the process as representative of contextual phenomena. Or, where his past successes with the method lead him to be confident about what his results represent regardless of the structural correspondence between his research design and contextual relations involving the data. These two alternatives are not mutually exclusive. Content analysts tend to reject totally implausible results or a research procedure that includes processes that are obviously alien to what they know about the source of the data. Often the content analyst knows a small part of the target and a small part of the relations.

Crucial for this design is that the content analyst utilizes all the knowledge he has about the system of interest in interpreting *one* set of

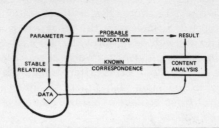

FIGURE 3: Content Analysis Design for Estimation

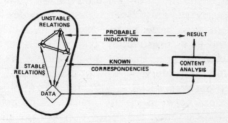

FIGURE 4: Content Analysis Design for Inferring Relations

unstructured or symbolic data. He does not rely on other methods to validate his results and he cannot simultaneously consider different sets of data in relation to which additional insights might be obtained.

A second type are *designs to test the substitutability* of one method by a content analysis. Here, two or more methods are applied to the same data or to different data obtained from the same situation to test whether the two methods yield comparable results or, when more than two methods are involved, which one is better. Figure 5 depicts this design graphically.

Examples range from comparisons of the discomfort-relief quotient as applied to interview data and judgement by a panel of psychiatrists on the level of anxiety of the speaker (Dollard and Mowrer, 1947), to attempts to establish correlations between several methods of measuring public attention. Usually, one of the methods is considered more valid than the content analysis but the latter is in some respect more advantageous whether in terms of cost, speed, or unobtrusiveness. Perfect correspondence may not say much about the validity of either method but may indicate functional equivalence and hence mutual substitutability (see the later section on validity). Much of content analysis research is motivated by the search for techniques to infer from symbolic data what would be either too costly, no longer possible, or too obtrusive by the use of other techniques.

Often a whole battery of different methods, including content analysis, is applied to data from the same situation. Without a priori knowledge as to which one is "best" or more valid, high correlations among their results are then interpreted as indicating that they assess the same underlying phenomena. This research design provides the basis for what has become known as *multiple operationalism* (Webb et al., 1966). It demands that research results be consistent across different methods all of which purport to be sensitive to the same phenomena. It thereby aims at preventing findings that may be an artifact of a single method and possibly unrelated to other research results.

Designs to test hypotheses, shown in Figure 6, compare the results of a content analysis with data obtained independently and about phenomena not inferred by the technique. Very often, content analyses are only a part of larger research efforts. There may be several kinds of data available, only some of which are unstructured or concern symbolic communications that must be content analyzed. This research design provides insights into the relations that might exist between the phenomena a content analysis is concerned with and their surrounding conditions. For example, one may content analyze television programs for the presence of a certain characteristic and match this with interview data of program preferences to ascertain a relationship between social stratification and the characteristic in question. Correlations between stated intentions and actual behavior of the speaker may reveal whether the content serves mere strategic purposes. Correlations between message content as inferred from a content analysis with a variety of behavioral indices also yields insights about antecedent conditions and effects. So the number of children in magazine fiction was correlated with birthrates (Middleton, 1960), the volume of news coverage on selected subject measures such as consumer prices, unemployment, and ecology was analyzed relative to public opinion fluctuations and actual figures (Zucker, 1978). And correlations between the frequency of widely circulated suicide stories and airplane accident fatalities revealed a causal or "triggering" relationship (Phillips, 1978).

COMPONENTS OF CONTENT ANALYSIS

Looking now at content analysis research design in detail, one can distinguish several different components or steps in the process:

- data making
    unitization
    sampling
    recording
- data reduction
- inference
- analysis,

to which comes:

- direct validation
- testing for correspondence with other methods
- testing hypotheses regarding other data.

Figure 7 gives a graphical account of how these components might be assembled into a content analysis research design.

In subsequent sections these components will be described in some detail, like a tool-kit, including its problems and practical solutions, so that a content analyst may tailor components to his needs. The remainder of this section will make a few more general comments on these components.

Data Making

A datum is a unit of information that is recorded in a durable medium, distinguishable from other data, analyzable by explicit techniques, and relevant to a particular problem. So defined, data are not absolute facts. They are cast into a particular form for some particular purpose and much effort in content analysis is devoted to bringing unstructured and vicarious information of often momentary existence into an analyzable form.

Data must be information bearing in the sense that they provide the link between information sources and indigenous symbolic forms on the one side and theories, models, and knowledge concerning their context on the other. Data must be representative of real phenomena.

The need to record data in a durable medium follows from the requirement of replicability. Only somewhat durable records are reanalyzable. The sound of the human voice vanishes soon after it is made and cannot be considered data. To be content analyzed, human speech must be written down or at least tape recorded.

The need for data to be analyzable by explicit techniques relates data to the analytical capability of a researcher. A few years ago the written word could not be considered data. It required human interpreters to make sense of them. With the advent of linguistic data processors, words, sentences, paragraphs, chapters, and whole books are acceptable as data. A consistent trend in the history of science is to make more and more phenomena subject to measurement and analysis.

Data in content analysis typically stem from complex symbolic forms in an indigenous language. Cartoons, private notes, literature, theater, television drama, advertisements, film, political speeches, historical documents, small group interactions, interviews, or sound events have their own syntax and semantics and are rarely analyzable in their original manifestation. Within such unstructured forms:

- The phenomena of interest must be distinguished and segmented into separate units of analysis posing problems of *unitizing*.
- These units may appear in unmanageably large numbers posing the problem of *sampling* a smaller portion from all possible units.
- Each unit must be coded and described in analyzable forms, leading to problems of *recording*.

Unitizing, sampling, and recording are somewhat interlinked. Sampling one proportion from one kind of unit and another proportion from another kind of unit, for example, requires the ability to distinguish between the two kinds which is an important part of the recording process. Unitizing

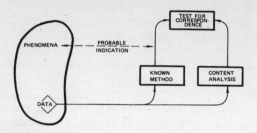

FIGURE 5:   Content Analysis Design To Compare Different Methods

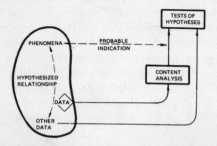

FIGURE 6:   Content Analysis Design To Test Hypotheses

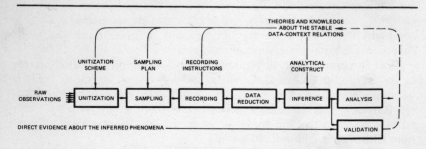

FIGURE 7:   Procedures in Content Analysis

can also be done during the recording phase of a content analysis. An example would be when phases of a group process are distinguished because the differences in behavior are larger across than within these phases. When the whole population of data are analyzed, sampling is not needed.

Data Reduction

Data reduction will not be elaborated in this section because it either presents no problem or can be treated under analysis. Although it may occur everywhere in the research design, it is principally geared to ease computational efforts, tailoring the form of available data into one required by the analytical technique. Data reduction may be statistical, algebraic, or simply a question of omitting what turns out to be irrelevant detail.

Inference

Inference is, of course, the *raison d'être* for any content analysis and will be described in some detail. It "consumes" all the knowledge a content analyst may have about the way data are related to their context and this knowledge will be strengthened with inferential successes. The arrow indicating the result of validation efforts characterizes this.

Analysis

Analysis concerns the more conventional processes of identification and representation of patterns that are noteworthy, statistically significant, or otherwise accounting for or descriptive of the content analysis results. By definition, we do not require an analysis to be context sensitive as all preceding procedures are required to be.

According to the above, a research design must be replicable, and what must hold for the whole is required to hold for each detail. When a component is standardized, such as contingency analysis by computer programs that cannot be subject to random fluctuations, replicability is virtually assured. But where analytical procedures involve individuals, errors and uncertainties invariably creep in. The assessment of these errors is discussed under reliability. But the primary condition for the replicability of a research design is that each component is explicitly described. (Figure 7 summarizes the procedures involved in a content analysis.)

5

UNITIZING

This chapter explicates the units in content analysis, their purposes, and the processes needed for defining them—be they sampling units, recording units, or context units—in a manner that is efficient and reliable.

The first task of any empirical research is to decide what is to be observed, recorded, and thereafter considered a datum. There are good reasons for using the plural of "datum," for empirical research requires a multitude of information bearing units: "data." Unitizing involves defining these units, separating them along their boundaries, and identifying them for subsequent analysis.

TYPES OF UNITS OF ANALYSIS

Unitizing the world of observations and messages poses many epistemological questions that cannot be addressed here, except to say that units are not absolute. They emerge in interaction between reality and its observer. They are a function of empirical facts, research purposes, and demands made by available techniques. In content analysis three kinds of units deserve distinction: *sampling units*, *recording units*, and *context units*. Their analytical purpose and use will be elaborated below after which five different ways of defining such units are discussed.

Sampling Units

Sampling units are those parts of observed reality or of the stream of source language expressions that are regarded independent of each other. Here "independent" is synonymous with unrelated, unbonded, unordered, or free so that the inclusion or exclusion of any one sampling unit as a datum in an analysis has neither logical nor empirical implications for choices among other units. A statistical definition of such units would stress "that there is very little freedom for variation within it but much freedom at its boundaries" (Pool, 1959: 203). However, the choice of sampling units is rarely statistically motivated.

A political speech may serve as an example. While an ordinary listener may well respond to it holistically by liking or disliking the speaker, a political analyst may see the speech as addressing several separate political issues. He may thus partition the speech and, ignoring the connections between these parts, probe into the structural details of some or of all of these parts to reveal attitudes or patterns of reasoning. A linguist, on the other hand, is likely to break the speech into sentences. Since there are no grammatical rules that would make one sentence construction dependent on another, he sees no need for considering units larger than a sentence. For him, the collection of sentences contains all relevant information to explore the linguistic performance of the speaker. On the other hand, a computer program for word counts that ignores the syntactical position of the words would unitize the text in ways useless to the linguist. Similarly would the political analyst find little of interest in a linguist's collection of sentences for his insights stem from the semantical and rhetorical organization of the speech which the linguist's way of unitizing ignores.

Obviously, sampling units are of concern to sampling: A sample is drawn unit by unit from a population of sampling units. Sampling units are also important for the use of inferential statistics. Objects that are to be counted must be independent or else frequencies will be meaningless. Survey researchers who use inferential statistics extensively take great pains to insure that their interviewers do not interact. Experimenters make sure that the events they manipulate to test statistical hypotheses are independent.

Interdependencies among sampling units, if they exist, are not only lost in sampling but also confound the findings. Suppose, during a study of television violence, one notices in one program that one violent incident triggers a long chain of violent encounters which constitutes the theme of the drama while in another program many violent encounters are separately provoked and not precipitated by others, the theme being something else. How could meaningful sampling units for violence by defined and enumerated? Should the chain of violent encounters be regarded as one sampling unit or separated into many? Should each carry the same weight? Perhaps violent encounters might not constitute meaningful sampling units. Unless one finds units that are independent as far as the phenomenon of interest is concerned, breaking a highly organized message into separate sampling units invariably distorts the information contained in the resulting data.

Recording Units

Recording units are separately described and can therefore be regarded as the separately analyzable parts of a sampling unit. While sampling units tend to have physically identifiable boundaries, the distinctions among recording units are achieved as a result of a descriptive effort. Holsti (1969: 116) defines a recording unit as "the specific segment of content that is characterized by placing it in a given category." Dependencies that might exist within sampling units are retained in the individual description of its recording unit.

Suppose fictional television programs are sampled with the aim of studying the population of characters on television. Programs have a definite beginning and a definite end and thus constitute natural sampling units among which decisions regarding inclusion or exclusion in a sample can easily be made without looking into the content of these programs.

The characters within these programs are far from independent of each other. They interact, they are defined with regard for each other and they assume specific roles in a highly organized script. Because of these interdependencies, it would be impossible to cut a program into individually meaningful segments, one for each character. But it is possible to describe each character individually, including in the description the position he assumes within the network of interpersonal relations, the order of his appearance, and the interactions he is involved in. In the process of such description, individual characters become recording units which can be analyzed individually and collectively although not always meaningfully.

Another reason for choosing recording units that differ from sampling units is that sampling units are often too large, too rich, or too complex to serve as a unit for description. For example, a film that makes creative use of documentary materials is difficult to categorize as presenting either fact or fiction. It contains both. However, by describing smaller units, scenes, editing shots or individual frames, for example, one is likely to yield unambiguously codable recording units.

It is possible, though often difficult, to describe recording units in such a way that the whole sampling unit of which they are a part can be reconstructed. It requires that relevant information about the organization of the sampling unit be retained in the collection of recording units. The analyst then has the option of analyzing different levels of units.

A common practice in content analysis is to define larger units structurally. In such definitions a certain structure between smaller units must be identifiable in order for the larger unit to be admitted for analysis. A good example is the action-actor-target framework. Each may be characterized individually and hence be analyzed separately but all three must co-occur in a recording unit if it is the goal to analyze co-occurrences across units.

Context Units

Context units set limits to the contextual information that may enter the description of a recording unit. They delineate that portion of the symbolic material that needs to be examined in order to characterize a recording unit. By defining a larger context unit for each recording unit, the researcher recognizes and makes explicit the fact that symbols codetermine their interpretation and that they derive their meanings in part from the immediate environment in which they occur. Context units neither need to be independent nor separately describable. They may overlap and contain many recording units.

How much the characterization of a recording unit and ultimately the research results depend on the size of the context unit was demonstrated by Geller et al. (1942) who had subjects judge the way such symbols as "democracy" were evaluated using as context units a sentence, a paragraph, three sentences, and the entire article. While the four methods were generally in agreement as to the direction of the bias (favorable, neutral, unfavorable), they differed in extent. As the size of the context increased, the number of neutral evaluations decreased significantly. Evidently, the context of a symbol does contain a great deal of evaluative information.

The use of larger context units is marred, however, by problems of reliability and efficiency. To describe the treatment of characters in the context of a novel requires reading the entire book first and then assigning each character to the appropriate categories. Not only is this process time consuming but also often unreliable because individuals may approach a novel differently and the whole novel has to be kept in mind when making the judgment. Going through a document sentence by sentence, or through other data by scenes, by encounters, or by editing shots might be more efficient and more reliable but less meaningful.

Other texts on content analysis (e.g., Holsti, 1969) also mention *units of enumeration*. Their importance was tied to the early definitional requirement of content analysis to be quantitative (Berelson, 1952), which simply meant that data be accounted for numerically, in terms of frequencies of occurrence, in terms of space (column inches of news print) or time (minutes of broadcast), or in terms of typographical characteristics (headline boldness or picture sizes). However, the conceptual status of these units is confusing. In content analysis, quantities may have at least three different origins. First, quantities may result from counting repetitive occurrences. This associates *a magnitude with a class of identical recording units* and merely reduces the analytical effort. Second, measures like the size of a photograph or the column inches of an article become *descriptive of one recording unit*. Third, measures like the number of issues of a newspaper printed or the Nielson ratings of a television program are associated with a whole sampling unit and *shared by all recording units* in that sampling unit. In older content analyses the coder had to quantify everything and the distinction between these three quantities therefore became blurred. Quantities of the first kind come up in the process of analyzing data. In obtaining correlation coefficients and distance measures, for example, frequencies and magnitudes of classes of units are merely computational. The coder need not bother about them at all. Quantities of the second kind are of concern to coders in that they must be measured on each recording unit. Square inches, centimeters, or number of lines require no specialized concept, however. They have the status of a numerical category just like the values on a semantic differential or intensity scale. Quantities of the third kind tend to be supplied by other sources and are rarely obtained from judgments by coder. Thus, while it is important to know what is quantified in content analysis, units of enumeration deserve no specialized attention here.

Units are thus distinguished by the function they serve in content analysis. Sampling units are of concern to sampling and provide the basis for statistical considerations. Recording units collectively carry the information within sampling units and provide the basis for the analysis. And context units are of concern to the process of describing the recording units.

WAYS OF DEFINING UNITS

Despite their functional differences, most content analyses use one or more of five different ways of delineating and identifying these units:

- physical units

- syntactical units
- referential units
- propositional units (and kernels)
- thematic units.

These are now described.

Physical Units

Some units seem so obvious that they hardly deserve attention: books, financial reports, issues of a newspaper, letters, poems, or posters. These units are physically delineated. They seem obvious because the boundary of the message they contain coincides with the boundary of the medium.

Even when events are continuous or the stream of source language expressions exhibits few natural boundaries, physical distinctions may nevertheless be imposed on them. Physical units partition a medium by time, length, size, or volume rather than by the information carried. Osgood (1959) sampled pages of Goebbel's diary. Ekman and Friesen (1968) used frames of film as the smallest recording unit. Dale (1937) analyzed newsreel foot by foot and Albig (1938) provided his observers with a clock and requested that they summarize each minute of broadcasting. Time units are common in studies of interpersonal behavior (Weik, 1968). Imposing a rectangular grid over a photograph and describing each square has the same effect.

Syntactical Units

Syntactical units and items are "natural" relative to the grammar of a communications medium. They do not require judgments on meaning.

Words are the smallest and as far as reliability is concerned the safest recording unit of written documents. Lasswell's world attention survey (Lasswell, 1941; Lasswell et al., 1952), many literary detection efforts (Yule, 1944; Mosteller and Wallace, 1964), the analysis of style (Miles, 1951; Herdan, 1960), psychodiagnostic inferences (Dollard and Mowrer, 1947), and research on readability (Flesh, 1948, 1951; Taylor, 1953) all rely on words or symbols.

Syntactical units in the nonverbal media are the television shows (as listed in the *TV Guide*), the acts in theatrical performances, encounters in drama, news items in broadcast, or editing shots in film. To recognize syntactical units requires familiarity with the medium. Syntactical units are more natural than physical units because they utilize distinctions made by the source.

Referential Units

Units may be defined by particular objects, events, persons, acts, countries, or ideas to which an expression refers. So the 37th President of the United States may be referred to by "he" (the context being unambiguous as to who he is), as ',the first president to visit China," as "Richard M. Nixon," as "Tricky Dick," or as "the occupant of the White House between 1969 and 1974." Each denotes the same person though in different ways and it is unimportant whether the reference is made in one word or many, directly or indirectly.

Referential units are indispensable when it is the task to ascertain how an existing phenomenon is portrayed. Much of early work in symbol analysis (Pool, 1959) defined symbols (usually single words) by their denotata and explored values, attributes, and qualifications associated with them. In attempts to infer the attitudes, preferences, and beliefs of authors referential designations of the attitude objects of interest are required just as is the case in all efforts to develop profiles of particular classes of individuals (heros, teachers, Spanish-Americans).

Propositional Units (and Kernels)

The exclusive use of referential units implies a data language that merely recognizes objects and their attributes. It does not approach the complexities of natural language. One way of delineating somewhat more complex units is by requiring them to possess a certain structure. For example, Osgood et al. (1956) proposed to study all propositions that can be phrased into one of two forms:

Attitude Object/Verbal Connector/Common Meaning Term

and

Attitude Object$_1$/Verbal Connector/Attitude Object$_2$.

According to which the sentence: "He was fighting a losing battle against the powerful establishment." would yield:

The student leader/was fighting a battle/against the establishment.

The establishment/is/powerful.

The student leader/is/unsuccessful.

This form of kernelizing a complex sentence into propositional units is the basis for evaluation assertion analysis.

Holsti (in North et al., 1963: 137) instructed coders to edit and rephrase political documents in terms of an action framework containing the following units:

- the perceiver and incorporated modifiers
- the perceiver other than author of the document and incorporated modifiers
- the perceived and incorporated modifiers
- the action and incorporated modifiers
- the object acted upon (other than an actor-target) and incorporated modifier
- the auxiliary verb modifier
- the target and incorporated modifiers.

Each such propositional unit thus had up to seven components and could have originated in one or more sentences. Similarly, Gerbner (1964) extracted propositions from news reporting to analyze ideological biases which would not be apparent in single words or in reference to a particular object.

Thematic Units

These are identified by their correspondence to a particular structural definition of the content of narratives, explanations, or interpretations. They are distinguished from each other on conceptual grounds and are contrasted with the remaining portion of irrelevant material by their possessing the desired structural properties.

Thematic units require a deep understanding of the source language with all of its shades and nuances of meaning and content. While it is often easy for ordinary readers to recognize themes, it is generally difficult to identify them reliably. Although the purpose of the research is important in judging which kind of units are most meaningful, for many content analyses thematic units are probably the most preferable. But because of the long chains of cognitive operations involved in the identification of thematic units, even carefully trained observers can be easily led astray. Thematic units are therefore often avoided in content analysis or at best used to circumscribe the fuzzy universe from which a sample or propositional units are drawn.

A good example of the use of thematic units is provided by Katz et al. (1967) who analyzed written letters in order to shed light on the use of administrative services in Israel. His thematic units were defined as requests to authorities for favors or exemptions that include as constituent elements descriptions of the writer's personal qualifications and the reasons why the request should be granted.

Thematic units are common in the analysis of folklore. Unitizing folkloristic items goes back to Thompson (1932), whose list and description of motifs fill six large volumes and aim at an exhaustive recording scheme. Armstrong (1959) reviewed some of the problems with using thematic units in folkloristics. Treating history as a kind of folklore, the Council for Interracial Books for Children (1977) published a list of sexist and racial themes to identify recurring stereotypes, distortions, and omissions in U.S. history texts.

EFFICIENCY AND RELIABILITY

The five units just discussed differ mainly in the kind of cognitive operations required for their identification. Generally, unitizing is the more efficient and reliable the simpler and more "natural" the cognitive operations are. But simple units may not be productive analytically. The researcher will thus have to optimize productivity without too much loss in efficiency and reliability.

Physical units require essentially a mechanical device. Cognitive operations are minimal and therefore efficient and reliable. However, unless the boundaries of physical units coincide with those of the content to be described, they can cause unreliabilities in recording and may not yield interesting findings. Although there are virtues in delineating sampling units by the physical characteristics of the medium, recording units are rarely defined in these terms.

Syntactical units require familiarity with the grammar of the source language, the medium, or form of the material to be unitized. The identification of these units tends to be efficient and reliable but not always productive in subsequent analysis. Context units are often defined in these terms.

Referential units require familiarity with the semantics of the source language, with the symbols, and with the referential meaning of elements. The identification of referential units is still quite efficient but not always reliable, the principal difficulty being that references are not always clear unless one restricts the units to words or short denotative phrases. Referential units are preferred for defining sampling units and recording units.

Propositional units require considerable familiarity with the syntax, semantics, and logic of the source language, with linguistic transformations such as rephrasing, completion, decontextualization, and kernellization. Because the identification of these units often calls for rewriting a whole document according to some format, the process can become quite inefficient and may be only moderately reliable.

Regarding unitization, the general recommendation is to aim for the empirically most meaningful and productive units that are efficiently and reliably identifiable and that satisfy the requirements of available techniques. This often involves considerable compromises. Sometimes it simply means letting unreliable information go by unitizing propositions instead of themes or by unitizing references instead of propositions.

6

SAMPLING

As in most endeavors, the social analyst must use some form of sampling plan to make the task executable. This chapter lays out the various sampling strategies available with specific concern for the needs of content analysis.

Communication has always penetrated all spheres of life. But the mass production of print, the availability of sound- and video-recording equipment, copying machines, and electronic computers have vastly increased the availability of symbolic material. As soon as a content analyst poses a problem for which newspapers, film, governmental records, and the like may contain answers, he becomes flooded with information produced by these institutions. And when a researcher decides "to simply tape" the group experiments he conducts, the man-hour requirements for a content analysis of these tapes can easily be between 10 and 100 times the time covered by the tape. The universe of available raw data tends to overwhelm even well-equipped research operations.

Faced with such volumes, the content analyst has to make two kinds of decisions. First, he has to employ all knowledge he can possibly obtain to distinguish relevant and irrelevant material. Information leading to the intended inferences may be unequally distributed over different media, publications, documents, time periods, or geographical areas. Second, if, after exhausting all available knowledge, the volume of relevant material is still too large, he has to employ random methods to select a sample that is large enough to contain sufficient information and small enough for analysis.

Suppose inferences concerning how the incumbent president and the challenger to this office differ regarding their sensitivity to audience beliefs and attitudes. The researcher must first identify the sources of relevant information. Taped speeches by both candidates may be only a starting point. These must be supplemented by evidence about audience characteristics to which either candidate may have had access, such as public opinion surveys or newspaper accounts of what the group of people that are addressed do expect, how they voted in the past, or what their concerns are. There may be good reasons for sampling among newspapers, circulars, and announcements according to the media preferences of these audience members for they, like the candidates, may learn about each other through their own media. These decisions begin to delineate the *population of raw data* that are relevant to the intended inferences.

Once this population of relevant material is delineated, decisions of the second kind, *sampling*, may be required. The practical need for sampling is to reduce a large volume of potential data to a manageable size. The methodological justification of sampling concerns whether the process yields a sample from which generalizations can safely be made. However, in content analysis one tends to sample from one population in order to make generalizations about another population. Here sampling concerns two potentially very different populations.

There is the population of possible observations, or the universe of possible data that could be obtained if resources are unlimited. In the example, any written accounts of political expectations, voting preferences, publicly voiced concerns, and the campaign speeches that followed these expressions would constitute this population. But there is also the context to which inferences are directed, which concerns how the speaker adjusts his expressions, promises, and reflection of values to audience characteristices known to him. This is the universe of possible inferences. Drawing a sample that is representative of possible data is different from drawing a sample that is representative of what is to be inferred. A content analyst must decide what sampling is to accomplish.

TYPES OF SAMPLING SCHEMES

Sampling processes are guided by a *sampling plan*. It specifies in sufficient detail how a researcher proceeds to obtain a sample of units that are collectively representative of the population of interest. To obtain a representative sample, the sampling plan assures that, within the constraints imposed by available knowledge about the phenomena, each unit has the same chance of being represented in the collection of sampling units. It assures that there is no bias in the inclusion of units in a sample.

Random Sample

Assuming no a priori knowledge about the phenomena, a sampling plan for drawing a simple *random sample* involves listing all relevant units (issues of newspapers, documents, speeches, or sentences) about which generalizations are intended. To determine which unit is then to be included in the sample, the plan may call for the use of dice, a roulette wheel, a random number table, or of any other device that assigns equal probabilities to each unit. Content analysis uses this or any of the following four kinds of procedures.

Stratified Samples

Stratified sampling recognizes several distinct subpopulations within a population, called strata. Each sampling unit belongs to one stratum only. Random sampling is carried out in each stratum separately so that the resulting sample reflects a priori distinctions known to exist within the population.

Newspapers, for example, have been stratified by geographic area of distribution, by frequency of publication, size of readership, or audience composition such as readers of prestige papers versus the boulevard press.

Another example is to compose a typical week of television programming by stratifying a whole year's programming into weekdays and time slots and then randomly selecting for each time slot 1 out of the 52 possibilities.

Systematic Sampling

Systematic sampling involves selecting every k^{th} unit of a list into the sample after determining the starting point of the sequence at random.

In content analysis, systematic sampling is favored when data stem from regularly appearing publications, sequences of interpersonal interaction, the stringlike order of writing, film, and music. The chief problem with systematic sampling is that the interval of length k is constant and will create biased samples if it coincides with natural rhythms like seasonal variations and other cyclic regularities. For this reason it is advisable not to select every seventh issue of a daily, but, say, every fifth. A study of marriage announcements in the New York *Times* Sunday edition exemplifies this bias. It concluded that during 1932 and 1942 there were no announcements of marriages in Jewish synagogues (Hatch and Hatch, 1947). Later it was found that the systematic sampling of all June issues during this period coincided with a period during which tradition prohibits Jewish marriages (Cahnman, 1948).

Cluster Sampling

Cluster sampling uses groups of elements as sampling units. Groups exhibit natural designations and boundaries. The selection of one group brings all of its elements into the sample and, because groups contain unknown numbers of elements, the probability that a unit will be included in a sample depends on the group sizes.

When a researcher wants to study how minorities are portrayed on television, it is impossible to enumerate or to know the population of television characters in advance of the study. However, he can begin with the list of programs. In fact, almost all mass-media material is "packaged" or comes in natural "chunks" (see syntactical units): Regular publications, daily news, advertisement slots, books, reports, patients' medical records, and fairy tales are easily identifiable although the content and composition may vary considerably. But, by selecting television programs for convenience, unequal numbers of characters will be brought into the sample. This would also be the case when newspapers are selected by issues within which a variable number of news items are identified, counted, or compared. In fact, whenever sampling units and recording units are not equivalent, clustering may be involved surreptitiously.

Clustering is a practical response to the inability to individually list the elements in the population as opposed to listing the groups in which they occur. The results of clustering are almost always subject to greater sampling errors. The variance within a sample tends to be exaggerated. Clustering is preferable to individual selection of elements if the saving in effort per element due to the clustering is greater than the increase in variance per element.

Varying Probability Sampling

Varying probability sampling assigns probabilities of inclusion in a sample to each unit according to some a priori criterion. Subsampling with probabilities according to size is the most common procedure yielding what are often called *proportional samples.* The criteria for assigning probabilities must be explicit (unlike in clustering) and justified in terms of the overall research design.

Varying probability sampling is important to content analysis because of its commitment to making inferences about phenomena not included in the sample (neither directly observed nor sampled). For a hypothetical example, suppose a content analyst wants to infer opinions within the USSR population about the United States and is limited to the use of available newspapers only. In designing such a study, one would have to consider the fact that newspaper accounts are systematically biased samples of opinions held in the population. First of all, population groups have unequal access to the media and, second, some opinions are more likely to be printed than others. A sample that is drawn to be representative of all available newspapers would build this bias right into the data and yield invalid inferences about individual opinions. In drawing a sample of newspapers from which inferences about a population of individuals could be made, the effects of this self-sampling process need to be undone. This can be accomplished by assigning to each expressed opinion a probability that is inversely related to the probability with which that opinion is expected to find its way into print. The pronouncements by official spokesmen might thus appear less frequent in the sample than assertions by ordinary individuals appearing in print.

An interesting application of this procedure in the analysis of newspaper content is reported by Maccoby et al. (1950) who were interested not in newspapers as an institution but in the information to which readers are exposed. The researchers listed all dailies within each of nine census districts (strata), added their circulation figures, and assigned probabilities to each newspaper according to its share in total circulation. While issues of newspapers were the sampling units, readership determined the probabilities assigned to them.

Varying probabilities represent the statistical knowledge a researcher has about the context of the data, that is, about the way the phenomena of interest are probabilistically indicated in the data actually obtained. Such knowledge being often uncertain or hypothetical, varying probability samples are difficult to justify and should be drawn only with extreme caution.

Multistage Sampling

Frequently samples are drawn using one or more sampling procedures in succession. This is called multistage sampling and may be considered a modification of clustering. For example, newspapers may be sampled after stratification by geographical area and readership level, issues within newspapers may be drawn systematically, and articles within issues may be selected with probabilities assigned proportional to their length. Multistage sampling does not need to use different procedures; to get an idea of the literature on a subject, one may start with a set of recent articles on that subject, draw a random sample from the literature cited in these articles, and draw a second random sample from references found in the cited literature until the inclusion of new elements does not change the proportional composition of the sample.

Although there seems to be considerable freedom in devising any sampling plan whatever, its chief aim is to yield samples that are representative of the phenomena of interest. Its justification is generally more difficult in content analysis than in survey research, from which most of the techniques and terminology of sampling stem, because the phenomena of interest are only indirectly manifest in available material. In content analysis the data are not the object of analysis, but rather are the stepping stone to other phenomena.

SAMPLE SIZE

After settling the issue of how to draw a sample, the next question usually is how large it must be. There is no set answer. When all sampling units are exactly identical, a sample size of one is satisfactory. This is often assumed in engineering and consumer testing. When there are a few rare and significant incidents on the list of units, the sample will have to be large and will include the whole population when each sampling unit is unique. In practice, this uncertainty is not quite so threatening. While each additional unit in a sample adds to the costs of an analysis, there comes a point at which a further increase will not appreciably improve the generalizability of the findings. This is the point at which the sample size is most efficient. It is a cost-benefit question which depends largely on how the property to be generalized is distributed in the sample.

Stempel (1952) compared samples of 6, 12, 18, 24, and 48 issues of a newspaper with the issues of an entire year and found, using the average proportion of subject matter as a measure, that increasing the sample size beyond 12 did not produce significantly more accurate results. Unfortunately such recommendations are confined to studies using similar measures on newspapers with similar distributions of content.

A test for the appropriate size of a sample, which does not require an analysis of the whole population, is the so-called *split-half technique* where a sample is randomly divided into two parts of equal size. If either part supports the same statistical conclusions within the same level of confidence, the whole can be accepted as an adequately sized sample. This test may be repeated for several equal splits as it should hold for as many splits as is demanded by the confidence limit. If this test fails, the researcher may want to increase the sample size until the conditions are met.

7

RECORDING

In making data from observations or text, it is important to consider the characteristics of the coders, their training, the syntax and semantics of the data language being used, and the administration of data processing. Procedures of developing suitable instructions are explicated with examples in this chapter.

Recording is one of the basic methodological problems in the social sciences and in the humanities. The proposition, accepted in the natural sciences, that reality is not accessible as such except through the medium of a measuring instrument, applies here as well. One cannot analyze what is not suitably recorded and one cannot expect that source material comes cast in the formal terms of a data language. Recording is required whenever the phenomena of interest are either unstructured relative to the methods that are available or symbolic in the sense that they carry information about phenomena outside their physical manifestations. Indigenous symbolic forms are replete with fuzzy structures and omissions, full of ambiguities and context dependencies that physical measuring instruments can rarely register. Symbolic communications in the form of writing, sound records, and videotapes must largely be transcribed in formal terms before they can be used for data processing and inference.

In content analysis, recording has been such an important problem that older definitions virtually equate content analysis with the process of recording, for example:

> "Content Analysis" may be defined as referring to any technique (a) for the classification of the *sign-vehicles* (b) which relies solely upon the *judgements* (which theoretically may range from perceptual discrimination to sheer guesses) of an analyst or group of analysts as to which sign-vehicles fall into which categories, (c) provided that the analyst's judgements are regarded as the report of a scientific observer [Janis, 1965: 55].

Or, in another characterization one reads:

> In order to handle larger blocks of verbal material in a statistical way, it seems necessary to reduce the variety of alternatives that must be tabulated. This can be accomplished by putting a wide variety of different word patterns in a single category [Miller, 1951: 95].

Recording is a necessary consequence of the fact that content analysis accepts unstructured material but should not be confused with content analysis of which it is a part.

We argued above in more general terms that explicit instructions should contain *all* that is needed to replicate the data making process, using different individuals. Janis's call for explicit instructions refers primarily to the semantics of the data language—the rules for assigning sign-vehicles to categories. Explicit *recording instructions* should contain:

- the characteristics of the observers (coders, judges) employed in the recording process
- the training and preparation these observers undergo to prepare themselves to qualify for the task
- the syntax and semantics of the data language used including, when necessary, an outline of the cognitive procedures to be employed in placing messages into categories
- the administration of data sheets.

OBSERVERS

Observers, coders, and judges should, of course, be familiar with the nature of the material to be recorded but also capable of handling the categories and terms of the data language reliably. These dual qualifications are not easily met. If the problem is to record a local vernacular, for example, it is easy to find indigenous speakers but a lot more difficult to find one with appropriate training in scientific method. Content analysts therefore often approach the problem from the other end and use social-science-trained individuals, such as students, who have to become acquainted with the phenomena to be recorded. Although distortions are then probably less noticeable, a white, middle-class college student will still inevitably have a hard time appreciating the subleties of the local slang. Even when it comes to describing television shows, themes, and characters to which many more people are exposed, socioeconomic and linguistic backgrounds and educational differences among coders are often decisive in whether data can be recorded reliably.

Recording instructions should therefore include a characterization of the kind of individuals for which these instructions are written and with respect to which these instructions have been tested for reliability. One simply cannot assume that recording instructions are universally unambiguous and can be followed by everyone in exactly the same way. Generally, the practical problems of assessing replicability are less severe if instructions are written for observers:

- who can be found frequently in the population
- whose dual qualifications are easily identifiable.

TRAINING

Training of coders is a common preparatory task in content analysis. Not only do individuals have to be acquainted with the peculiarities of the recording task—rarely do procedures and definitions perfectly conform to intuition—but these coders are also often instrumental in shaping the process, especially during the preparatory phase of a content analysis. Researchers typically report months of training sessions during which categories are refined, processes are altered, and data sheets are revised until the individuals feel comfortable and can do their job reliably and efficiently. Sometimes the initial ideas are modified beyond recognition. A good example of how definitions of the data language emerge concurrently with the training of coders is described in a study of Soviet-American attitudes:

> The purpose of the study was to generate an accurate picture of Soviet and American foreign policy goals and strategies as far as they might be reflected in elite articulations regarding (A) the international environment, (B) the distribution of power, (C) the other's operational code, and (D) their own operational code.

> The procedure followed two main phases: designing and refining our coding procedure and applying it. The first phase followed six more or less distinct steps:

> 1. The questions that seemed most germane to the study at hand were compiled. These were, of course, based on a multiplicity of sources: the author's general knowledge of the subject, the parameters of his own social science conceptual schemes, and those dimensions of foreign policy suggested by the writings and research of others in the field.
> 2. Once a tentative set of essentially *a priori* dimensions was set up and arranged, these dimensions were discussed, criticized, and modified by the author, his assistants, some consultants, and several professional colleagues.
> 3. This set of dimensions was then applied by the coders to a sample of the material to be coded, resulting in the deletion of some dimensions, the rephrasing of others, and the addition of a few new dimensions.
> 4. The author then reappraised the dimensions and further tightened up the three categories under each dimension, in order to maximize mutual exclusiveness as well as exhaustiveness of the categories under each dimension.
> 5. The dimensions and their categories were then pretested by the coders themselves to ensure that:
>   a. The literature to be coded made frequent enough reference to the dimensions to be worth coding,
>   b. The dimensions themselves did not overlap one another (except in a few cases where some subtle shadings of attitude were being sought),
>   c. The dimensions themselves were clear and unambiguous enough to assure that independent coders would have a high agreement that a specific article should or should not be coded along that dimension,
>   d. The three category alternatives under each dimension were as mutually exclusive as possible, yet exhaustive of the possible ranges or relevant response.
> 6. When the pretests had demonstrated (by agreement between two or more independent coders) that the dimensions and categories were adequately refined and clarified, they were settled upon as final. (Singer, 1964: 11-12)

Such steps are typical:

- The research designer formulates his initial data requirements.
- He familiarizes himself with the way relevant information is expressed in the source material.
- He formulates written recording instructions.
- Working with the coders who are to apply them, instructions are jointly interpreted and modified until they meet suitable reliability requirements.

Calibration occurs in the last step and in the above example the problem lies in its implicitness. In the process, some kind of homeostatis is reached between what the research designer wants, what the observers see and are capable of learning, what the instructions imply, and how the source material can be interpreted without violating intuition. As a consequence, only those who participated in this mutual adjustment process will work consistently. Group specific interpretations change the written instructions which are then no longer solely representative of the recording process. Summarizing the use of content analysis in psychotherapy, Lorr and McNair observe the effects that such implicit adjustment processes have on replicability:

> Even though most investigators publish respectable indices of inter-rater agreement in categorizing the responses, these are open to serious questions. Usually the published inter-rater agreement is based on two people who have worked together intimately in the development of a coding scheme, and who have engaged in much discussion of definitions and disagreements. Inter-rater agreement for a new set of judges given a reasonable but a practical period of training with a system would represent a more realistic index of reliability. Trials with some existing systems for content analysis suggested that reliabilities obtained by a new set of judges, using only the formal coding rules, definitions, and examples, are much lower than usually reported. Often they do not meet minimum standards for scientific work [1966: 583].

Ideally, the individuals that take part in the development of suitable recording instructions should not be involved in recording the data. After recording instructions have been developed by whatever method, a final step must be added to the above list:

- Recording instructions are tested for reliability with a fresh set of independent observers.

Individuals should be able to work with the recording instructions as their sole guide. They should have only minimal, if any, access to sources of uncontrollable information (e.g., the history of the instructions) else these instructions are amended in unanticipated directions. And they should work with an absolute minimum of informal communication among themselves else surreptitious agreements on interpretations emerge. Any modification of the instructions that might be necessary must be incorporated into the written instructions.

If training is required, it should be standardized so as to be replicable elsewhere. We once devised a detailed self-teaching program for recording incidents of television violence: Individuals were merely briefed about the nature of the task and thereafter worked by themselves through a standard set of television shows. After each unit was identified and recorded on one data sheet, trainees found the obstensibly correct scores (established by a panel of experts) on another. The comparison provided immediate feedback on their own performance and enabled them to adapt to a standard interpretation of the instructions. The method allowed us not only to plot the increasing reliability but also to decide at the end of the period which individuals were suitable for the task. With such a self-teaching program in hand, the process can be easily replicated and yields similar results almost by necessity.

Probably the worst practice in content analysis is when the investigator develops his recording instructions and applies them all by himself or with the help of a few close colleagues and thus prevents independent reliability checks. The practice is often justified by the lack of resources. But test after test has shown such a process to be largely unreliable. One must wonder, indeed, what kind of contribution a study can make that only the author can replicate.

SEMANTICS OF DATA
(WAYS OF DEFINING THE MEANING OF CATEGORIES)

The *syntax and semantics* of a data language are essentially embodied in the rules governing the assignment of units into categories or the code. The checkmarks on a data sheet, the holes of a punch card, the cryptic annotations an analyst might write in the margins of the source text are information bearing to the extent that rules are followed reliably. But they are meaningful only to the extent that the properties that give rise to the data are recognizably represented in them. Data are symbolic entities.

Recording instructions must not only assure that data are reliably recorded but should also explicate their meaning. Only when the semantic relation between data points and source material is clear can findings based on these data lead to insights about real phenomena. When recording instructions or coding manuals are lost, data may exhibit their syntax, but because the researcher no longer has access to their semantics, inferences are uncertain. Often the semantics of the data are merely polluted by unreliable coding, by changes in instructions while coding is in progress, or by using specialized operational definitions which are later equated with the intuitive concept that may have given rise to these definitions. Noise, ambiguities, and counterintuitive perspectives in the semantics of a data language make subsequent interpretation of the findings difficult.

That "categories must be exhaustive and mutually exclusive" is an often stated requirement. It pertains to the semantics of a data language in that it fixes a relation between the phenomena to be described and the data representing them. "Exhaustive" refers to the ability of a data language to represent all recording units, without exception. No unit must be excluded because of the lack of descriptive terms available. "Mutually exclusive" refers to the ability of a data language to make clear distinctions among the phenomena to be recorded. No unit may fall between two categories or be represented by two distinct data points. This dual requirement demands that the semantics of a data language partition the universe of possible recording units into *distinct classes* and that the members of each class are represented by a *different datum* so that the distinctions made in the world are unambiguously represented in the data.

A nonexhaustive set of categories can be rendered exhaustive by the addition of another category that represents all units not representable in the initial set. Such categories are often labelled "not applicable," "other," or "none of the above." Because such a fail-safe category does not represent a clearly designated set of phenomena, except by exclusion of all others, it contributes little, if anything, to research findings and should therefore be avoided whenever possible.

This solution does not apply to categories that lack mutual exclusivity. To add a category "ambiguous" to the set that would catch all units for which the assignment to categories is unclear or multivalued, such as when two or more categories apply, prevents the assessment of reliability and, more important, biases research results in the direction of easily describable phenomena. There is no remedy for ambiguous recording instructions.

How categories are defined and how numerical values or data points are made representative of real phenomena, observations, and message characteristics is an art. Little is written about it. Nevertheless, a few *ways of delineating the semantics* of a data language may be distinguished:

- verbal designations
- extensional lists
- decision schemes
- magnitudes and scales
- simulation of hypothesis testing
- simulation of interviews
- constructs for closure and inferences.

Verbal Designating

Verbal designations are most frequent and apparently obvious. The sex of a dramatic character may be either *male, female* or *indeterminate.* This latter designation may be due to insufficient information, a child without a sex role, or some other perspective. But single-word designations of characteristics or properties including names for individuals, concepts, or classes of events are successful only when the differentiations fully conform to common linguistic meanings. This may not be the case for any scientific discipline invariably develops its own theoretical conceptions. The following set of categories exemplify distinctions that are no longer shared with untrained observers or, as it were, with psychiatric patients whose level of anxiety was to be assessed (Mahl, 1959). Longer definitions and examples are then apparently required.

(1) *"Ah."* Wherever the definite "ah" sound occurs, it is scored.
(2) *Sentence correction* (SC). A correction in the form or content of the expression while the word-word progression occurs. To be scored, these changes must be sensed by the listener as an interruption in the word-to-word sequence.
(3) *Sentence incompletion* (Inc). An expression is interrupted, clearly left incomplete, and the communication proceeds without correction.
(4) *Repetition* (R). The serial superfluous repetition of one or more words—usually of one or two words.
(5) *Stutter* (St).
(6) *Intruding incoherent sound* (IS). A sound which is absolutely incoherent as a word to the listener. It merely intrudes without itself altering the form of the expression and cannot be clearly conceived of as a stutter, omission, or a tongue-slip (though some may be such in reality).
(7) *Tongue-slip* (T-S). This category includes neologisms, the transpostion of words from their correct serial position, and the substitution of an unintended for an intended word.
(8) *Omission* (O). Parts of words, or rarely entire words, may be omitted. Contractions are exempted. Most omissions are terminal syllables of words.

Extensional Lists

An extensional list specifies the semantics of a data language by indicating for each term in the source material the category to which it belongs. Although a conceptual scheme may be underlying the construction of such a list, the coder is not required to know it. Extensional lists are a requirement for certain computer approaches to content analysis. For example, the General Inquirer involves a procedure called the dictionary for mapping a multitude of terms in the input text into a small set of tags.

Extensional lists are necessary where linguistic conventions and conceptual differentiations are absent and are advantageous where they are difficult to communicate to coders. An example of the latter is provided by O'Sullivan (1961), who attempted to quantify the strength of relationships reported to hold between variables in the theoretical writings on international relations. Prior commitments to factor analysis required that "strength of relation" be conceptualized as correlation. But in training coders it soon became apparent that verbal designations of the underlying idea did not lead to reliable differentiations, hence the use of a list:

.2 is less likely to; in certain situations induces; may lend some; may be due to; may be, to the extent that; can be used without; possible consequences seem to follow;

.3 has introduced additional; not merely a function of, but of the; is a factor of; will depend not only on—but upon; depends in part on; possibility of;

.4 leads; is likely to be; tends to produce; would tend to; will tend to induce; tends to; tends toward; tends to introduce;

.5 makes it improbable that; strongly affects; is most likely to result from; is most likely to occur; creates essentially; depends primarily on; depend primarily on; is a major source of; creates a problem of;

.6 will heighten; requires at least; will enhance; necessitates; will determine; produces; depends on; is inevitable; produces; depends; is the result of; will reflect; will impose; prevents; will override; weakens; strengthens; offers maximum; will be less; will add to;

.7 will; any—must first; are least—when; as—will be; puts a; has; is a; is less—when there has been; if it is—this is; there is; there has been, and is; is directly related to; will be enhanced in direct relation to; is inversely related to; will influence—in direct proportion to; is directly related to; there is a direct relationship between; stand in marked contrast to; to the extent that; the longer—the more; the greater; the greater—the greater—the more; the greater—the less—the greater; the greater—the greater—the greater; the greater—the more; the wider—the less; the more—the less; the more—the more; the more—the larger—the more; the more—the greater; the more—the less likely; more—than; the wider—the greater; the wider—the more; the higher—the greater; the longer—the less; the shorter—the greater must be; the fewer—the greater; becomes more—as the; is more likely to be—the more; the less—the fewer; the less—the less; will be more—the larger; the larger—the more;

Decision Schemes

Decision schemes regard each datum as the outcome of a predefined sequence of decisions. Its use has several important advantages. First, decision schemes can avoid problems arising from categories that are on different levels of generality or overlapping in meaning. Schutz (1958) exemplified the case by a study of comic strips which classified places of action in the following terms: United States, foreign, rural, urban, historical, and interstellar. A rearrangement of these categories as the outcome of several dichotomous decisions is diagramed in Figure 8 in which the terminal categories are the categories of the data language and the others merely intermediary concepts. Second, when recording units are multidimensional, decision schemes offer the opportunity of decomposing a complex judgment into several simple decisions and thereby achieve levels of reliability not obtainable otherwise. Third, decision schemes drastically

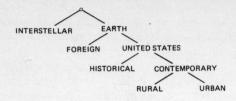

FIGURE 8: Decision Scheme for Recording

reduce the number of alternatives to be simultaneously considered at each step.

Magnitudes and Scales

Magnitudes and scales demand of the coder that the source material is conceptualized as a continuum, as ordered or as having a metric. The semantic differential scales proposed by Osgood et al. (1957) may serve as an example.

strong	:	:	:	:	:	:	:	:	weak
active	:	:	:	:	:	:	:	:	passive
good	:	:	:	:	:	:	:	:	bad

Each scale is conceptually anchored by polar opposite terms and, without spelling out the meanings of the intermediate scale points, the coder is asked to describe the attributes of each recording unit as how far away they are from the two polar extremes. Incidentally, these three scales correspond to what has been found to be three basic dimensions of human affective cognition: the potency, the activity, and the evaluative dimension (Suci, 1957; Osgood, 1962).

Not all concepts can be placed on a continuum between opposites. The law may regard the attributes "legal-illegal" as binary opposite attributes while the distinction "news-fiction" is not clearly unidimensional. Forcing a scale on something that does not lend itself to this conception causes unreliability. In fact, in many content analyses, semantic differential scales turn out to be unreliable mainly when information about the attribute to be recorded is absent or insufficient. For example, some television characters are highly developed within a drama while others appear only during a short scene. Bipolar personality scales are naturally more reliable for main characters than for minor ones. Judgments on the extent to which information on a characteristic is provided are clearly on a level different from judgments regarding what this characteristic is. A scale that avoids this difficulty was introduced by Zillman (1964) under the name of "semantic aspect scale." Its six scale points are interpreted "not present—very little—little—medium—much—very much." This unipolar scale is appropriate when attributes, qualities, or phenomena can appear more or less present, more or less significant, more or less intense, or more or less frequent and appeal to a ratio (absolute zero point) conception of the continuum.

Simulation of Hypothesis Testing

Most verbal expressions carry presuppositions and have logical implications over and above the attributes and references they make. For example, "he was reading the *New York Times*" presupposes that he had reasonable eyesight, sufficient lighting, knowledge of English, and is at least six years old. It also implies that he received some information on what this newspaper deemed "fit to print." Although it is probably impossible to prepare a complete list of such inferences, it is less difficult to cognitively link them with predefined statements or hypotheses. Generally, a hypothesis is a statement whose truth is rejected by counter example, by disproof, or by statistical evidence in favor of the contrary. As a recording strategy, the simulation of hypothesis testing demands of a coder that he cognitively-logically link each verbal recording unit with any one of several mutually exclusive hypotheses and ascertain to which it pertains and sometimes how strongly it supports or rejects either alternative.

A classical example for the simulation of hypothesis testing is found in Lasswell's (1965b) approach to the detection of foreign propaganda in domestic news sources during World War II. Lasswell extracted four basic propaganda aims from the public pronouncements by Nazi party and governmental officials and asked his coders to judge whether news items and commentary about events implicitly supported or rejected any one or more of these propaganda aims.

The simulation of hypothesis testing by cognitive-logical processes has uses beyond the mere establishment of bias. One can ascertain the degree to which the description of psychological phenomena conforms to one or the other theory of human behavior, how accidents are explained, which popular conceptions underlie discussions of illness and medical treatment, or the kind of communication theories a writer implicitly assumes when reporting research.

Simulation of Interviews

The simulation of interviews provides a means of obtaining survey-type data through the medium of the "respondent's" writing. The coder is asked to familiarize himself with the author's work, in the course of which he develops a mental construct of the author's personality, knowledge, and beliefs, and then, going through it a second time, he is asked to look for evidence that would indicate whether the author is likely to say yes or no, or any shade in between, to each of a set of prepared questions an interviewer would have liked to put to him if he could.

An example of such a simulated interview situation is given by Klausner (1968), who based his inferences on a stratified sample of 199 out of 666 child-rearing manuals published in the United States over a period of two centuries. The author's attitudes and conceptions were recorded in terms of 80 questions with predefined answers. One of these questions is as follows:

Terms of data language		Questionnaire items and answers of source language
Col. Number	Punch	Question:
32		How does the book legitimate the authority of the parent in the parent's eyes (basis on which he appeals to parent to attend the child)
		Answers:
	1	Not discussed
	2	Legitimation assumed, but no specific basis given
	3	The parent has superior knowledge to the child
	4	The parent is morally superior to the child (appeal to sense of personal responsibility)
	5	The parent is a moral representative of the community
	6	The parent influences the child morally; intellectually whether or not he wills it and so has the responsibility for the consequences of his own acts
	7	Parent influences the child psychologically whether or not he wills it
	8	Other
	0	NA (question not applicable and does not deal with question)

While the simulation of hypothesis testing relies primarily on the coder's logical and linguistic ability, the simulation of interviews relies on the coder's additional ability to assume the writer's role. Naturally, this adds unreliabilities, particularly when the volume of writing is large and less topical. The shorter the writing, the more topical it must be to avoid an excessive use of the category "no answer" or "other." The advantage of simulations of this kind is that interviewees do not react to the interviewer, embarrassing questions are admissible (Barton, 1958), and interviewees are "available," however indirectly, for an indefinite period of time.

Constructs for Closure and Inferences

One of the marks of experienced psychodiagnosticians is that they can study what a patient avoids saying rather than what he overtly expresses. Similarly, political analysts are inclined to "read between the lines" and cultural critics attempt to identify patterns in what is suspiciously absent. These efforts can be likened to "closing an incomplete figure." When left to unconstrained intuition, such closures can of course become highly subjective and projective. But it is also possible, at least occasionally, to specify in advance "the abstract organization of the figure" or the cognitive constructs that are to be employed to obtain such closures reliably.

An example is found in George's (1959a) account of the FCC's inferences from domestic enemy broadcasts during World War II. In the course of their work, the analysts developed elaborate constructs which were intended to explain why certain broadcasts came into being and what, therefore, the antecedent perceptions and conditions were. In this example the distinction between recording data and making inferences was not so clear. We will mention details of the approach in the section on analytical constructs. Here it suffices to say that the analysts developed and utilized highly specific constructs of the situation, including generalizations regarding the political behavior and propaganda behavior of the governing elite which allowed them to obtain a considerable amount of military intelligence.

The cognitive processes which such coders employ in coming to the desired conclusions are well-described by George:

> The analyst's reasoning takes the form of filling in, or assigning a value to, each of the major unstable variables which are not already known, and supporting this reconstruction both by generalizations and by logic-of-the-situation assessments. This type of inferential reasoning may be likened to an effort to reconstruct the missing pieces in a mosaic. Certain parts of the mosaic are given or readily assumed. Other pieces in the mosaic, however (including the conditions which the analyst particularly wants to clarify), are missing. In effect, therefore, the analyst rehearses in his mind the different possible versions of each particular missing variable which he wants to infer, trying to decide which version is the most plausible, given the known value of the content variable and the known or postulated values of other antecedent conditions [1959: 61].

This list of methods for operationalizing the semantics of a data language is by no means complete. Only major types are described here. They may serve as a spring board for new and better methods of recording.

While there are obvious differences between these methods regarding reliability and efficiency, it is impossible to state preferences. We know that short extensional lists are better than long ones, but the point at which coding by verbal designations becomes superior to extensional lists depends on so many circumstances that simple generalizations do not help the research designer. As a rule, recording is more reliable and more efficient the more familiar the concepts, the simpler the cognitive operations, the shorter the inferential chains, the fewer the categories, and the less training coders require.

DATA SHEETS

Data sheets contain information in its primary, and most explicit, form. When the phenomena to be recorded are ongoing without leaving physical traces, like group discussions and live television, data sheets may be the *only* records of these phenomena, and when the phenomena of interest are unstructured, as taped speeches or handwritten letters tend to be, data sheets contain *all* the information about these phenomena that a content analysis can possibly consider. Perhaps the term *data sheet* is not general enough because some primary data may be recorded directly on magnetic tape (Janda, 1969) or on film (Ekman and Friesen, 1968) but our most common form of record is on paper.

The design of primary records may employ considerable ingenuity. Because the demands made on them are so varied, it is impossible to suggest a standard or optimal form. A few recommendations can be made, however. The requirement that all recording units of the same kind must be described in terms of the same set of categories, coupled with available duplicating and printing technology, clearly favors the separation of data sheets by recording units, not by observers or variables. Thus, recording units of the same kind should be recorded on the same kind of data sheets which may be duplicated or printed. A content analysis requires as many separate records as there are recording units.

Data sheets contain several kinds of information: some obvious, others easily overlooked. Briefly, these are:

- administrative information
- information on data organization
- information on the phenomena to be recorded, the data.

Administrative Information

Administrative information guides the handling of the data in the office. The need for space for this kind of information cannot be underestimated. It often happens that data sheets get out of order, making it impossible to reconstruct the sequence. Much time is wasted when one finds a set of completed forms and can no longer ascertain with certainty to which part of the study it belongs, whether it has been verified, punched, or stored. Administrative information includes:

(a) An identification of the *content analysis project* for which data are recorded including the phase of development of the recording instrument, if it is being changed, and perhaps an identification of the general type of data and the kind of unit to which it is applied. This information may be printed on each sheet and serves to differentiate among projects or phenomena being analyzed.

(b) An identification of the *state of the data sheet:* completed, verified, filed (by number), duplicated, transferred to another sheet, punched, or whatever. However it is processed, the research administrator should be able to identify how it has been handled and what is still to be done with it before it is filed away.

(c) An identification of the *individuals involved* in data handling, specifically the observer who coded the original phenomena, but also those who checked and processed the data and may have to be consulted if errors are later encountered.

(d) Instructions as to *how data are to be punched* (column numbers for variables, numbers for categories) or otherwise prepared for computer processing.

In some studies, the amount of administrative information may appear to be disproportionately large, but it is necessary.

Information on Data Organization

Information on data organization is important when an analysis employs several kinds of recording units. To make use of one kind of data in the analysis of the other, information on data organization must be added either in the form of a master file outlining how the different kinds of data fit together or in the form of special entries indicating where the data belong relative to others.

For example, in a study of newspaper editorials, there may be one kind of data sheet for the newspaper in which the editorial appeared (containing circulation figures or frequency of publication, one kind of data sheet for the content of the editorial and another for the news items associated with the editorial. To merely repeat information on newspapers for each editorial contained in it is not only time consuming but also prevents a separate analysis with newspapers, rather than editorials, as the unit of enumeration. Here, arbitrary reference numbers to the newspaper in which an editorial occurred and to the news item that is referred to by the editorial maintains accessibility to the different kinds of data. Similarly, in a content analysis of interaction pattern among television characters, we recorded personality traits and other characteristics that are stable and idiosyncratic to the character on one kind of sheet and entered the communicative contacts into an interaction matrix containing reference numbers to the characters involved. This allowed us to compare characteristics across individuals.

Data

Information on the phenomenon to be recorded, the data, proper, are, of course, the raison d'être of the whole recording process. The first and most obvious requirement is that information must be easily entered by the observers, easily read by those who have to process it, but not too easily altered by wear and tear or by dishonest intentions. Optical scanning devices make special demands on the kind of pencils to be used, making it more difficult to verify the marks. When data are to be punched, data sheets are often organized so that the manual entries are easily translated into the 80-column format of a punch card. When the analysis proceeds manually, some abbreviated terms are probably best for understanding.

Besides the ease of entering and reading the data, the form of data sheets should minimize errors. One typical source of errors is the use of illegitimate entries. Consider the following three ways of recording the outcome of interpersonal interactions:

Enter appropriate number	Encircle one only	Check whichever applies
☐ 0 - favorable to neither	*favorable to* neither	☐ favorable to initiator
1 - favorable to recipient	recipient only	☐ favorable to recipient
2 - favorable to initiator	initiator only	
3 - favorable to both	both	

Their difference lies primarily in the kind of errors they invite. The left version can receive numbers larger than 3 that are nowhere defined, hence illegitimate, and relies more than the others on the idiosyncracies of handwriting. The middle version invites the use of double codes while the right version cannot bear illegitimate markers at all. Although it is not always possible to entirely prevent the occurrence of illegitimate entries, data sheets can minimize these errors.

Another primary source of errors is coupled with the question of how much of the data language's semantics needs to be repeated on the data sheets. Because recording instructions can be easily forgotten, one extreme is to repeat all definitions of categories. This assures high levels of consistency but is also both time consuming and costly. The other extreme, merely presenting the coder with a large grid into which he inserts numerical entries, invites a host of confusions of rows and columns and of what these numerical entries mean in each case. We found it useful (1) to include on data sheets some indication of what each variable and preferably each option means, (2) to use checkmarks and avoid numbers and letters when they do not have an intrinsic relation to the phenomena to be recorded, and (3) to utilize the special organization of the data sheet to convey some of the organizational features of the recording units. This applies specifically to the recording of iconical properties, spatial distributions, temporal sequences (before and after can become left and right), and conceptual distinctions between sender, message, and receiver.

8

DATA LANGUAGES

Categories and measurements mediate between the world of real phenomena and scientific facts, and thus condition analytical success. This chapter considers a system of categories and measurements as a data language. Its semantics tie a datum to observations and messages, and its syntax links it to scientific procedure.

The descriptive apparatus into which terms an analyst casts his data is called a *data language*. A data language mediates between the world of real phenomena and scientific facts and often is the bottleneck to scientific insights. It has syntax and semantics. *The semantics of a data language roots a datum in the real world while its syntax links it to scientific procedure.*

The problem of defining the operational meanings of the categories of an analysis is the principal focus in *recording*. The conflicting recommendation of deriving categories either from the source material or from relevant theories comes up in the emic-etic distinction. And the lack of ambiguity in the representation of real phenomena is considered in *reliability*. This section concerns the *syntax of data languages* of interest to content analysis. Generally:

- Data languages must be free of syntactical ambiguities and inconsistencies.
- Data languages must satisfy the formal demands made by an analytical technique to be applicable.
- Data languages must possess the descriptive capacity to provide enough information about the phenomena of interest to be conclusive.

The first of these three requirements calls for data languages to be formal or formalized. Only formal languages are computable in principle. Being context sensitive, ordinary human beings are well-equipped to cope with syntactical ambiguities. Explicit analytical techniques are not. For example, an ordinary reader with access to the context of the sentence "They are flying planes." has no difficulty deciding whether "they" refers to a group of pilots or to several objects seen in the sky. For computer processing this syntactical ambiguity will have to be removed either by specialized procedures or by such editorial additions as identifying "flying" as verb or as adjective. "Jim or Joe and Mary are coming" is similarly ambiguous and requires editorial additions to distinguish "(p or q) and r" from "p or (q and r)." As a rule, unless an analysis ignores the syntactical features altogether, as in word counts in which the position of these words is irrelevant, natural language expressions have to be coded and transcribed, or at least edited, to become syntactically unambiguous and computable. *The syntax of a data language must be definite.*

The second requirement takes account of the fact that each analytical technique makes its own specialized demands on the form of data. While this seems obvious, it is surprising to see how often researchers find they cannot meet the requirements of an analysis after the data have been collected. For example, readership data and an account of newspaper contents, each analyzed separately, do not help to explain reader's content preferences. The reason is that correlational and associational techniques require data to be recorded in pairs. Here, each reader would have to be paired with what he exposes himself to. Time series analysis requires that some object of analysis be observed at different points in time. Data on a sample of objects at one time and data on a sample of objects at another time do not meet this requirement. Another common error arises when the variables of a study do not have a metric that is powerful enough for the technique to apply. Variance analysis requires interval data. A rank ordering would disqualify the data for such an analysis. When data do not satisfy the requirements of a particular analytical technique, the results are generally uninterpretable (for an opposing view, see Tukey, 1980).

The third requirement derives from the target of content analysis, the intended inferences. Lasswell (1960) once characterized communication research as asking: "Who says what, in which channel, to whom and with what effect?" and then characterized content analysis as specializing in the question "says what," and audience research as concerning itself with "to whom." Making these distinctions, he failed to see that answering questions of "who," "what," "to whom," "which effects," separately will not yield insights about communication as a mediational social process. To study the latter requires a data language that is powerful enough to trace the flow of information as a multidimensional phenomenon (Krippendorff, 1970). Data languages may fail to provide enough information either by assuming a perspective from which the whole cannot be comprehended, as in Lasswell's separation of content analysis from the analysis of other facets of communication phenomena, by leaving out important variables, or by making too few distinctions. All of these have the effect of omitting important structural details. The informational requirements, whether for testing the validity of scientific hypotheses, for estimating the success of planned actions, or for removing uncertainties about a problem, can often be spelled out in advance. *A data language must provide at least as much information as demanded by the target of a content analysis.*

With these requirements in mind, we can define a data language in terms general enough to cover most content analysts' concern.

DEFINITION

A data language prescribes the form in which data are recorded and consists of:

- *variables* whose values represent the variability in recording units within a conceptual dimension

- *constants* with fixed operational meanings specifying relations between variables
- *a syntax* whose rules govern the construction of well-formed records (formulas, expressions) from variables and constants
- *a logic* that determines which records imply each other or are to be considered equivalent. It specifies logical (a priori) dependencies among variables.

In the algebraic formula

$$ax + b = c,$$

"a," "b," "c," and "x" are variables, each of which may assume a numerical value. "+" and the implicit multiplication sign are constants denoting well-defined algebraic operations. "=" is a logical sign designating the two parts of the formula as equivalent and mutually replaceable. Both parts of the formula are also well-formed. According to the rules of algebra, the string of symbols "abxc = +," for example, is not well-formed. In the process of recording, variables are replaced by particular values. Obviously not all combinations of values satisfy this formula, logic and syntax thus define a constraint on the range of permissible configurations of values.

A syntax rules out certain combinations of values within variables as illegitimate, *a logic equates certain combinations* of values within variables (makes some distinctions superfluous). Both reduce the variation a set of variables can record to the variations actually needed.

In content analysis, the syntax and logic of data languages are often very simple or absent and data are recorded in their most *basic form*. Each recording unit is described in terms of a fixed number of variables whose values are inserted in the cells of Figure 9. Here the constants merely assign an arbitrary position to each variable.

The syntax and logic of a data language is mentioned here mainly because exciting developments are taking place in other fields, notably in linguistics, which have to be considered in content analysis. For example, transformational grammars whose syntax includes rewrite rules that are aimed at characterizing natural language expressions cannot, or can only very awkwardly, be represented in a fixed number of variables format. Even less ambitious content analyses may include recursive forms. For example, a content analysis of native-foreigner attitudes in Africa (Piault, 1965) recorded answers to open-ended questions in terms of:

(a) an ordered set of variables concerning social characteristics of the interviewee
(b) the origin of the judgment, for example:
    X judges Y to be (   )
    X talks about Y judging X to be (   )
    X talks about Y talking about X. . . .
(c) relations between Xs and Ys, relative to the origin of the judgment
(d) themes, that is, three classes of arguments associated with each judgment
(e) a lexicon consisting of variables (675 terms) and constants (logical operators "and," "or," and such) that may be used to represent each argument lexically.

Here b includes a recursive definition of a well-formed record and e cannot be represented by a fixed number of variables. The analysis of Piault's data

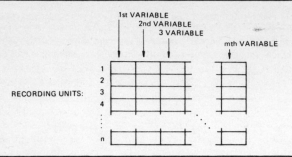

FIGURE 9:   Basic Form of m-Dimensional Data in Content Analysis

relied on information retrieval routines whose syntactical demands met those of this data language. Although syntactical rules and the logic of a data language are important, this is as far as we can go. The following concerns the use of variables and their ordering.

VARIABLES

A variable is a symbol which stands for any one of a set of two or more mutually exclusive values such as objects, states, categories, qualities, or elements). Webster (1967) defines a variable as something "able or apt to vary, changeable." Variation is what enables data to be *informative.* Indeed, unless there are males *and* females, the variable sex would have no descriptive significance; unless journalists have the option of leaning toward one *or* the other side of a controversy, the measure of "bias" would be meaningless. In a content analysis, each recording unit must be characterizable by one of several alternative values in each variable and the choice of such a value is exclusive of all others. This leads to another way of defining variables: *a variable partitions the set of all recording units into mutually exclusive classes.*

Because notions of variable and value are general, one finds them expressed in different words. Here are some correspondences:

variable	—	value
set	—	element
collection	—	member
dimension	—	point
scale	—	score
category set	—	category
space	—	location
gauge	—	measure
system	—	state
typology	—	type

When content analysts describe problems of category construction, when psychologists construct 7-point rating scales, when systems theorists define a system by the states it takes, the notion of "variable" is underlying all of these activities.

Variables may be *open-ended* or *bounded*. Age is an open-ended variable because its values have no logical upper limit. Marital status is a bounded variable because categories are limited in number and are known in advance. Although it is always recommended that variables are defined in terms of a single conceptual dimension, bounded variables do not need to conform to conventional distinctions as long as they yield distinct values or categories. Generally, the researcher has more conceptual freedom in defining bounded variables than open-ended ones.

A complete list of values provides an *explicit* definition of a variable. An *implicit* definition is exemplified by a coding scheme that calls for rephrasing a text into the form:

$$(\qquad) \text{ says } (\qquad) \text{ to } (\qquad).$$

For example, (Jim) says ("hi") to (Mary). Here original names and rephrased messages are entered as the values or categories of three variables that are implicitly defined by relational constants. They are also open-ended because these variables can accommodate any two communicators' names and any message that might be exchanged. In contrast, a polar opposite scale is also an implicitly defined variable but one that is bounded:

healthy |————————————————————————| unhealthy.

Whether and however many scale points may be identified in such a scale, they tend to be chosen by some intuitive function of the distances from either extreme. What ordering methods or schemes coders may have in mind is not so clear.

Variables may also be derived, that is, *defined on other* (primary) *variables*, abstract certain features from them, or take the form of indices that thereby discard some of the undesirable variation in the original. For example, one can record the 20 possible "communication networks" within five-person groups as one variable, as opposed to recording the presence or absence of the 10 possible "communication links" between pairs of members of this group. One can compute velocity rather than speed or combine several different measures into a single score. Gerbner et al.'s (1979) violence index and Budd's (1964) attention measure, for example, yield such derived or secondary measures by defining them on primary records or on combinations of values within certain variables.

Content analysts often publish their "conceptual scheme" or "system of categories" without being clear as to which variables are in fact employed in the study. Consider the following scheme (Herma et al., 1943) as reported in the literature:

Standards for rejecting Freud's dream theory

A. Depreciation through value judgment
   1. Ridicule and mockery
   2. Rejection on moral grounds
   3. Denial of validity
B. Denial of scientific character of theory
   1. Questioning analyst's sincerity
   2. Questioning verification of theory
   3. Questioning methodology
C. Exposure of social status of theory
   1. Disagreement among experts
   2. Fashionableness
   3. Lack of originality.

One interpretation is that there is but one variable consisting of nine values A1, A2, through C3, with the divisions into A, B, and C merely grouping these values into three less-detailed categories. A second interpretation is that there are three variables (A, B, and C) with 1, 2, and 3 serving as values, respectively. This would assume that each argument against Freud's dream theory has a valuational, a scientific, and a social dimension. The third interpretation is that there are nine variables whose values are "present" and "absent" with the breakdown into A, B, and C serving merely as a conceptual guide to the coder. A clue to deciphering just how the variables are defined lies in the variation that it can represent. A second clue lies in the enumeration of the data. Since each variable must partition the set of all recording units, without exception, the sum of the frequencies associated with the values of each variable must add up to the sample size. In this case, the first interpretation was in fact employed. Relative frequencies in the nine values add up to 100% and the grouping allows findings to be represented in terms of three values as well.

Nominal Scales

Nominal scales consist of a set of two or more values possessing neither order nor metric. Nominal scales are the most basic forms of variables, requiring nothing more than that its values are distinct. Data recorded in nominal categories are also called *qualitative* because *the difference between any two values of a nominal scale is the same* for all possible pairs of values.

Examples of nominal scales include lists of names for individuals, countries, cities, occupations, ethnic groups, kinds of words, types of expressions or arguments. Their alphabetical arrangement has nothing to do with the units named. Even if numerals are used to identify the values of a nominal scale, such as for football players or for lottery tickets, the numerical differences between these values has no meaning in a nominal scale. Another way of stating this property is that *the distinctions within a nominal scale are preserved under all permutations of its values.*

To distinguish between variables other than nominal scales, we employ the two concepts

- order
- metric

Order has to do with the arrangement of values, the network of relations between them. The difference between a hierarchical organization and a flat one is a difference in order of arrangement. Metric has to do with the kind of mathematical operations applicable on these ordering relations. Two incomes in dollars may be added, subtracted, or multiplied, whereas the attributes that distinguish between a shoemaker and a candlestick maker cannot. This difference is one of metric. All formal distinctions between variables boil down to answering questions regarding *which differences between recording units are represented by the values of a variable.* If such differences between recording units are significant to a study, the values of a variable must reflect them; and if the relations between the values of a variable possess the desired properties, analytical techniques must not distort them in the course of an analysis.

In this context only a few formal distinctions are made. Table 1 gives distinctions that are especially important to content analysis.

ORDER

Since each recording unit is described in terms of one and only one value of each variable, any relationship that might exist between two or more such units must be represented implicitly. Examples of such implicit representations are cognitive networks of concepts used by a writer (Baldwin, 1942), the semantical network of a text as stored in a computer (Klir and Valach, 1965), and the pattern of associations that might be utilized for answering questions, or the hierarchy of offices in an organization. Just

Table 1
Types of Variables by Order and Metric

metric \ order:	groupings	chains	loops	cubes	trees	partition lattices
absent	nominal scale	--	—	--	—	-
ordinal	classification	ordinal scale	cycle	multivariate crosstabs	typology	
interval	-	interval scale	π e.g time	space		
ratio	--	ratio scale	--	absolute vector space		

for simplicity, consider a road map of the Amtrak System of Passenger Rail connections. By specifying how cities, places, and intersections are linked with each other, directly or indirectly, including alternative routes, loops, or dead ends, the network orders the set of mutually exclusive points on a map. By taking only certain structures into account or tracing one feature at a time, the analysis of such networks often regards them as simpler than they are. In content analysis, data are often recorded in very simple and analytically tractable forms. For the convenience of the research designer, six common types of order are delineated below.

Groupings

Groupings within variables indicate that the values in one group have more in common than values in different groups. White's (1951) categories for the analysis of personal values are arranged in eight groups, each of which contains between one and six values. The following is another two-level classification:

A. *Physiological*
  1. Food
  2. Sex
  3. Rest
  4. Health
  5. Safety
  6. Comfort

B. *Social*
  1. Sex-love
  2. Family-love
  3. Friendship

C. *Egoistic*
  1. Independence
  2. Achievement
  3. Recognition
  4. Self-regard
  5. Dominance
  6. Aggression

D. *Fearful*
  1. Emotional security

E. *Playful*
  1. New experience
  2. Excitement
  3. Beauty
  4. Humor
  5. Creative self-expression

F. *Practical*
  1. Practicability
  2. Ownership
  3. Work

G. *Cognitive*
  1. Knowledge

H. *Miscellaneous*
  1. Happiness
  2. Value in general

The grouping suggests that the difference between food and sex is the same as the difference between food and rest and that both are smaller than the difference between food and achievement, for example.

Grouping may not always be motivated by the need to consider unequal distances between the values of a variable. One motivation already mentioned is to increase coding efficiency, especially when the number of categories is large. By regarding such a variable as a nominal scale, the ordering affect of the grouping is ignored.

Chains

Chains are completely ordered sets of values. A chain has two extreme values or ends, each of which has exactly one immediate neighbor. All

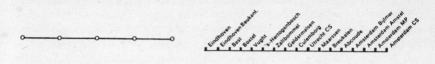

FIGURE 10:   Chains

other values have exactly two. Figure 10 gives two examples. Other examples include the (linear) passage of time, a waiting line, all measuring scales, and a path without loops. Chains are the most favored forms of variables in the behavioral sciences, the differences between ordinal scales, interval scales, and ratio scales being one of metric.

Loops

Loops are chains without ends. Each value of a loop has exactly two immediate neighbors. None is particularly outstanding. In fact, moving from any value in one direction brings one eventually back to the start which is arbitrary to begin with. Figure 11 shows this graphically. Examples of phenomena recorded by loops include cyclic or repetitive behavior, seasonal fluctuations, inconsistent preferences, and self-reference. Many cultures assume circular conceptions of time, biologists often describe biological phenomena in terms of life cycles, and cyberneticians tend to trace the effects of self-feeding loops in complex systems. Within a railroad network, a round trip that does not involve travelling the same track twice is a loop. An example of a two-dimensional loop is the system of coordinates for the earth's surface. Although traditional analytical techniques can rarely cope with loops and unwind them instead into a chain conception, loops have important properties which chains cannot represent.

FIGURE 11:   Loops

Cubes

Cubes involve multidimensional representations of data. Each value of a cube has as many immediate neighbors as there are dimensions, with the number of parallel paths between any two values depending on their dissimilarity or Euclidian distance (see Figure 12). Cubes often arise implicitly. Consider Lasswell and Kaplan's (1950) eight value categories:

Power
Rectitude
Respect
Affection
Wealthy
Well-being
Enlightenment
Skill

Superficially, these eight values resemble a nominal scale with no apparent order. But Lasswell and Kaplan allow any recording unit, person, symbol, or expression to score high on more than one value. This would violate, however, what would be required if these eight values were to be regarded as an unordered variable: Its values must be mutually exclusive. Hence it is not a nominal scale. In fact, these value categories are *attributes* and any instruction to "code as many as apply" defines a cube whose values are combinations (a selection from a fixed number) of attributes.

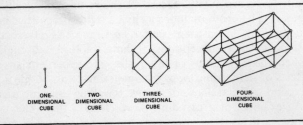

ONE-DIMENSIONAL CUBE   TWO-DIMENSIONAL CUBE   THREE-DIMENSIONAL CUBE   FOUR-DIMENSIONAL CUBE

FIGURE 12:   One- to Four-Dimensional Cubes

Trees

Trees or hierarchies have one designated end-value on the one side and several end-values on the other, and, depending on the side from which a tree is constructed, all other values occupy either branching points or merging points, respectively. The end values of the two sides are linked by chains that may share some members. A graphical example of a tree is seen in Figure 13. The *names* in the Linnean system of classification in biology constitute a tree. The system starts with the most general conception of

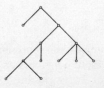

FIGURE 13

living things on top, differentiates somewhere in the middle between mammals and reptiles, and ends up with the most detailed differentiation among varieties or species and cultures in the biological world. Other examples include a family tree, decision, or branching processes that provide alternative paths at each state and so on.

Trees are of considerable importance in content analysis because they can represent different levels of abstraction which are common in natural language expressions. According to the Aristotelian theory of meaning, a definition names the genus to which the definiens (the word to be defined) belongs and distinguishes it from all other species of that genus. A reference to Europe implicitly refers to France, Italy, Germany, and so on. The relation between "Europe" and "France" is one of one-way implication (the former's extension includes that of the latter). A tree does represent such implications. The positions within hierarchical social organization form trees.

It is important not to confuse trees with groupings on the one side and with partition lattices on the other. Regarding the former confusion, the Linnean system clearly groups an otherwise unordered set of living beings. There is no abstract animal called "mammal," for example. "Mammal" is the *name* for a diverse class of biological organisms. Names may differ in generality, animals do not. The Linnean system indeed defines a *tree for names* but groups *the animals named.* Regarding the latter confusion, Europe may indeed be seen as partitioned into states, each of which into regions, districts, and so on. *While a tree can be regarded as one chain in a lattice of partitions*, the values of a tree represent the parts of these partitions, not the partitions themselves.

Partition Lattices

Partition lattices are variables that consist of partitions as its values. A partition is a set of mutually exclusive sets of elements. In a partition lattice, any two partitions have a meet (which represents the distinctions within either partition) and a join (which represents the distinction both partitions have in common), see Figure 14.

In everyday life, partition lattices are more common than one might expect even though they rarely enter the catalogue of descriptive devices

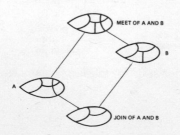

in the social sciences. Consider Lasswell's (1963) suggestion that politics concerns "who gets what, when, how." Accordingly, political science develops theories about and collects data on how resources are distributed among political actors. Presumably political interests are manifest in the partitions each has in mind, and the differences between the universal meet and the universal join of the partitions is what a political process aims to reduce. Taking Lasswell's contention seriously means that much of political theory requires data in the form of partition lattices. Partition lattices are also indispensable in research on coalition formation and similar processes which result in different partitions of the same whole into mutually exclusive parts.

METRIC

Within ordered variables, differences between values may have different properties called "metrics." A metric is defined by the kinds of mathematical operations applicable, neither distorting the differences represented in them nor introducing spurious quantities. For example, the algebraic operations of addition and multiplication may make sense when population figures are recorded, but not when the prominence of character traits are merely ranked. The literature distinguishes between ordinal, interval, and ratio metrics (Stevens, 1946) although not always by this name, with unordered variables or nominal scales being defined by the absence of any metric.

Ordinal Metrics

Ordinal metrics result from such comparisons of recording units as "larger than," "more than," "precedes," "causes," "is a condition of," "is a refinement of," "transmits to," "is contained in," "supervises," and many more. Ordinal scales (chains with an ordinal metric) are probably most common in the social sciences. Consider the coding of an index of the importance of a newspaper article as expressed in typographical terms:

(1) upper left quadrant of front page
(2) upper right or lower left quadrant and center of front page
(3) lower right quadrant of front page
(4) above center fold of an inside page
(5) below center fold of inside page.

How judgments regarding the relative prominence of an attribute might be recorded:

absent ————— barely ascertainable ————— present but not predominant ————— predominant

or how an identification scale for television characters is constructed:

(++) unqualified hero
(0+) a good guy/gal
(00) sometimes good and sometimes bad or undefined
(0−) a bad guy/gal
(−−) unqualified villian.

Even if some equal distances seem to be suggested by graphics such as this:

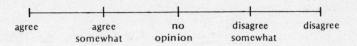

| agree | agree somewhat | no opinion | disagree somewhat | disagree |

without empirical evidence as to how far these values are apart all one can be sure of is their rank. An ordinal metric would render these three chains structurally equivalent:

agree	>	agree somewhat	>	no opinion	>	disagree somewhat	>	disagree
5	>	4	>	3	>	2	>	1
2570	>	569	>	568	>	12	>	.001.

Interval Metrics

Interval metrics can represent certain quantitative differences between recording units, specifically those that are expressible in terms of distances, similarities, or associations. Typical examples include distances travelled, time elapsed, balance in change (of money), movements of attitudes or beliefs in a suitable space, measures of differences in interpersonal attraction, agreement, amounts of political support, or amounts of communication. All of which imply some quantitative notion of "how different" two values are. An interval metric is the metric of a continuous space, one that may have many dimensions but neither beginning nor end. The finite representation of such a space is but an arbitrary section of this space cut out of the continuum by the choice of an analyst.

Interval scales provide the traditional backbone of empirical research in the social sciences. Variance analysis, correlational techniques, and factor analysis, for example, all require chains with interval metrics. In content analysis, interval scales are not as frequent.

Ratio Metrics

Ratio metrics possess an absolute zero point relative to which all values are expressed. Length, weight, speed, absolute temperature (in degrees Kelvin), income, column inches of newsprint, frequencies, but also quantities of disagreement, and of communication are examples of ratio scales whose zero point is absolute (unlike degrees Fahrenheit which can be negative). Another example is the polar scale which has two opposite reference points, as for judgments between good and bad, 0% and 100%, predominant and absent, relative to both of which values are quantified. Only because appropriate techniques of analysis are not readily available for this kind of scale are they often computed as interval scales. A ratio metric is the metric for a continuous space of any number of dimensions with one (or two) reference point(s) from which vectors are considered originating or destining (or both).

Mathematical Operations

As suggested above, metrics may be defined in terms of the kinds of mathematical operations that will not affect the differences between recording units that the values of a variable may represent. For example, if one simply adds "4" to all points of an interval scale ranging from "−3" to "+3," one obtains a scale whose values now range from "1" to "7," in which numerical differences remain the same. When the values of an interval scale are multiplied by a constant, the numerical differences change but their ordering still remains the same.

The four metrics are not merely different, their strength is also considered ranked. From the most powerful ratio metric an interval metric is derivable, from which an ordinal metric is derivable, from which an unordered variable is derivable. In this process the relational information in the original is stepwise degraded until only distinctions remain.

It is important to understand the properties of different metrics not only becuse they curtail the representation of real differences but also because some of the demands analytical techniques make are expressible in these terms. For example, all variance-based forms of analysis involve the computation of sums, average, and differences between values. For differences to be meaningful, at least an interval metric is required. For sums and averages to be meaningful, transitivity is required. This excludes loops and calls for chains. Variance-based forms of analysis thus require interval scales. Ratio metrics would contain more information than an interval technique can cope with while unordered variables and variables with ordinal metrics would contain too little for an interval technique to be applicable. Each analytical technique makes its own demands on the nature of a data language.

9

CONSTRUCTS FOR INFERENCE

Following the previous distinctions of systems, standards, indices, linguistic representations, communications, and institutional processes, this chapter provides illustrations of common usage in the operationalization of the interdependencies between data and context.

In previous sections, context sensitivity was considered the most important feature of content analysis. Context sensitivity is displayed (1) whenever the researcher feels that the processing of his data must not impair their symbolic qualities and (2) to assure that these qualities are retained, the analytical procedures used represents significant features of the context within which the data are considered. *An analytical construct operationalizes what the analyst knows about the interdependencies between data and context.*

In its most simple form, an analytical construct is a collection of if-then statements. Such statements should have some empirical base. In effect, the analytical construct of a content analysis can be likened to a *model of the stable interdependencies* in the context, the unstable characteristics being those toward which inferences may be directed. Like models, analytical constructs should correspond in function if not in structure to the characteristics they claim to represent. The extent of such correspondence is a measure of context sensitivity. Figure 15 depicts this notion graphically.

Analytical constructs may also be characterized as a *theory about a context* which is operationalized in such a way that its independent variables are capable of representing all possible data and its dependent variables represent what the content analyst wishes to infer, predict, or learn about the context of his data.

Since the context is not accessible when the data are content analyzed, the knowledge that goes into the development and justification of analytical constructs must be, or must have been, obtained through other sources. Where this knowledge comes from, how it is operationalized, and the form analytical constructs may take is the subject of this section.

SOURCES OF UNCERTAINTIES

Inferences never yield absolute certainties. A content analyst should therefore assess as well as he can the probabilities with which available

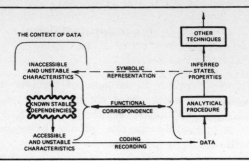

FIGURE 15:   Context Sensitivity of Analytical Procedures

data can be said to lead to the inferences he intends to draw. These probabilities stem from three principal sources:

- the relative frequencies of the observed contextual dependencies
- the confidence in the validity of the analytical construct
- the appropriateness of the construct in a situation.

While the numerical assessment of these probabilities is rare, it is nevertheless important to consider what influences these uncertainties.

The relative frequency of the observed contextual dependencies is the more obvious case in point. In a strictly deductive argument, probabilities have no place: From the premise "if A then B" and data in the form of "A," one infers "B" with certainty. But suppose past experiences are based on the following observations:

B followed A	8 times
B did not follow A	2 times
B did not follow when A was absent	10 times

If these observations are properly incorporated into an analytical construct (the premise), then, if A is observed, the probability of B is .8 and the probability of not B is .2. If A is absent, then the probability of B is zero and its converse is 1.0. In the social sciences most knowledge is probabilistic in this sense. Each rule has its exception.

The confidence in the validity of the construct is the inductive probability that the construct is not an accidental product of the circumstances under which past experiences were acquired. The clearest operationalization of this probability is found in the notion of *statistical significance*. In the above example, a sample size of 20 observations is very small indeed and inferences that might be drawn on this ground are highly tenuous. If the same relative frequencies were based on 200 observations or more, the confidence that the relative frequencies represent true probabilities would be enhanced, its upper limit being reached when the sample includes all possible cases or is infinite in size.

Since not all analytical constructs are derived from statistical findings, the confidence in their validity is often obtained by arguments in favor or against their purported truth. The number of different theories that lead to the same construct, the number of experts agreeing with its form and content, and the amount of research that went into gathering appropriate evidence all may be cited to establish the confidence in the validity of an analytical construct.

The appropriateness of the analytical construct in a situation recognizes that no two situations are exactly alike and that experiences, however definite and valid, obtained under one condition or at one point in time may not be or are only to a limited extent generalizable to other conditions or to different points in time. A good example in content analysis is the development of an analytical construct under laboratory conditions and its subsequent application on freely available data. The probability that the construct leads to valid inferences depends on how realistic the laboratory conditions actually were. Another example is that the situation in which a content analysis is attempted has surreptitiously changed from the situation in which experiences about the contextual dependencies had been acquired. This is a problem of propaganda analyses which tend to be executed by individuals whose experiences with the hostile country is restricted to prewar conditions. It is also a problem with analyzing historical documents with contemporary analytical constructs. The modes of expression and meanings may have changed. Granting that an analytical construct has been developed under conditions that are somewhat different from the situation of its application, the argument for the appropriateness of such a construct boils down to assessing the similarity between the data for content analysis and the data that went into the analytical construct.

SOURCES OF CERTAINTIES

Inferences that are correct to a degree better than chance require knowledge and, in examining the kind of arguments content analysts' engage when developing or justifying their analytical constructs, one finds basically four kinds:

- past successes
- contextual experiences
- established theories
- representative interpreters.

Let these arguments be considered one by one.

Past successes enhance the investigator's confidence in applying his analytical construct, provided only that the features such a construct represents are stable or unchanging in reality. Besides this assumption, pointing to past successes implies no knowledge and yields no particular insights into the nature of the contextual relationships a successful analysis accounts for.

The use of past success as evidential support for an analytical construct is exemplified in Stone and Hunt's (1963) computer analysis of real and simulated suicide notes. Real notes were collected from court records in Los Angeles. Simulated notes were written by a panel of individuals matching population characteristics (sex, age, race, occupation, and so on). Fifteen pairs of notes with known identity (real or simulated) were used to develop a discriminate function, or an analytical construct, that would enable the researcher to infer whether a note was fake or had to be taken seriously. Three variables were found to discriminate:

(1) references to concrete things, persons, and places
   (higher for real notes)
(2) use of the actual word *love* in the text
   (higher for real notes)
(3) total number of references to processes of thought and decision
   (higher for simulated notes).

By subtracting the score on the third measure from the sum of the first two, an index was developed that correctly discriminated 13 of the 15 pairs of notes.

Having been successful in 13 out of 15 cases, the analytical construct that had emerged was then applied to 18 more pairs of notes whose identity was not revealed to the researchers. It turned out that the procedure correctly inferred the identity of 17 out of 18 cases. The fact that these inferences were significantly better than human judgment, which had been obtained independently, lent further support to the validity of the construct.

In the example, the three distinguishing variables were extracted without any theory in mind. Also the idea of adding and subtracting scores seems to be an artifact of the procedure rather than motivated by knowledge about suicidal behavior. Nevertheless, the discriminate function worked convincingly and evidence for this fact should not be considered inferior. Ultimately, all content analyses must lead to inferences whose validity is significantly better than chance if not perfect.

Contextual experiences are obviously helpful in interpreting data. But such experiences are also more personal and perhaps less shared with others and therefore tend to carry the shadow of subjectivity. In content analysis as in all other scientific endeavors, inferences ought to be independent of the analyst, however, experts may not rest assured on their reputation alone. A content analyst who develops an analytical construct *de novo* must at least explicate the premises of his inferences. Explication makes possible the sharing of these experiences and their critical examination by others. Explication also facilitates the dialogue within the community of social scientists in the course of which alternative constructs may be explored and counter arguments may emerge.

A fascinating example of how a "hard" analytical construct developed from experiences with the context from which the data stem is provided by Leites et al. (1951). The analysts, all experts on the politics of the Soviet Union, were concerned with the distribution of power within the Kremlin and tried to make inferences about the succession in Soviet leadership, a process that remains largely hidden to outside observers. The researchers had at their disposal the public speeches made by politburo members on the occasion of Stalin's 70th birthday in 1949. All expressed the same adulation of Stalin with many nuances attributable to individual styles and therefore of no interest to political analysis.

The clue to a differentiation among members of the politburo, Leites et al. argued, lies in the modes of expressing nearness. For this, Soviet political use of language provides two distinct approaches. One set of "symbols of nearness and intimacy (father, solicitude, and so on) appears most frequently in the popular image of Stalin and (is) stressed for that audience which is far removed from him." The other set of symbols derives from the prevailing "depreciation of such nearness in political relationships. The ideal party member does not stress any gratification he may derive from intimacy for political ends. . . . Those closer to Stalin politically are permitted to speak of him in terms of lesser personal intimacy ('leader of the party,' etc.)," and are thus privileged to refrain from the crudest form of adulation. The authors conclude their argument by suggesting that the relative emphasis on the Bolshevik image or on the popular image of Stalin therefore "not only reflects the Bolshevik evaluation of the party as distinguished from and superior to the masses at large, but also indicates the relative distance of the speaker from Stalin" (1951: 338-339).

Leites et al. tabulated their findings, ranked the speakers, found Molotov, Malenkov, and Beria (in this order) to have the highest number of references to Stalin's Bolshevik image and inferred that they were probably closest to Stalin. The power struggle immediately after Stalin's death clearly confirmed the validity of the inferences made. A refinement of this construct is discussed elsewhere (Krippendorff, 1967: 118ff).

Established theories relating data to their context are the most unequivocal sources of certainty for content analysis. Sometimes theories take the form of fairly specific propositions that have been tested in a variety of contexts, for example, concerning the correlation between speech disturbances and the speaker's level of anxiety, between the frequency of reported crimes and public fear of the deterioration of law and order, or how members of television audiences group or classify advertisement appeals. Sometimes such propositions are derived from more general theories, for example regarding the expression of emotions, linguistic manifestations of psychopathologies, or how and according to which criteria the mass media and their audiences screen and present news. Unfortunately, a general theory of symbolic communication is not in sight and the content analyst has to search for pertinent theories wherever he can find them. Berelson and Steiner (1964) have developed an inventory of 1025 scientific findings in the social and behavioral sciences that might be consulted.

An example of the use of established theories for the construction of analytical constructs is Osgood et al.'s (1956) "evaluative assertion analysis." The technique is derived from a version of dissonance theory which assumes

(1) that concepts (attitude objects) are evaluated, liked or not, in degrees ranging from positive through neutral to negative

(2) that all linguistic assertions can be decomposed into pairs of concepts (attitude objects) which are to some degree associated or dissociated

and which postulates a psycho-logic according to which

(3) individuals perceive, believe, or express only concept pairs that are balanced, that is, assertions containing associations between similarly evaluated concepts or dissociations between dissimilarly evaluated concepts. Imbalanced concept pairs, that is, assertions containing dissociations between similarly and associations between dissimilarly evaluated concepts, are rejected or modified to achieve balance.

The authors go further and postulate a quantitative relationship between the degree of positive (or negative) evaluation of a concept, the degree of positive (or negative) evaluation of a second concept, and the degree of association (including dissociation) between them according to which the assertions are balanced (or imbalanced).

The analytical construct so derived leads the researcher to infer attitudes and implicit evaluations from explicitly evaluated concepts and associations between them. In evaluative assertion analysis one would define a statistic over the explicit and implicit attitudes occuring in a text and thus come to an overall picture of the attitudes of a writer.

Naturally, the use of an established theory has its drawbacks, too. In the course of deriving specific propositions and defining an analytical construct in operational terms, some content of the theory may get lost or become too distorted to suit the specific requirements of a content analysis. In the evaluative assertion analysis, any concern about cognitive dissonance the writer may himself express, for example, when lamenting that his best friend does something horrible, cannot be handled. According to the construct, his friend would have to acquire a negative evaluation even though the writer may have a lot of different ways resolving the cognitive dilemma. There are also doubts as to whether it makes snese to decompose a whole text into pairs of concepts and whether the various explicit and inferred evaluations can be aggregated in the manner proposed. Nevertheless, in the absence of past experiences, reliance on intersubjectively agreeable theories is the best strategy a content analyst can follow.

Representative interpreters provide a somewhat uncertain justification of the "premises" for inferences. The uncertainty arises from the conflicting requirements of using individuals either as scientifically trained observers or as uncontaminated subjects.

On the one extreme, content analysis must force categories and definitions on perfectly representative coders that render their responses to stimulus material no longer similar to those of the subjects they were thought to represent. On the other extreme the use of a representative sample of untrained individuals, serving as an "analytical" construct albeit implicitly, might yield more valid interpretations, but because their responses are unstructured, this defeats the purpose of the analysis. Between the two extremes lies the situation in which coders are allowed to use their indigenous conceptions to override counterintuitive instructions which yield large unreliabilities and enhance validity only surreptitiously.

In either case, while representative interpreters are efficient and can do no harm, the content analyst cannot rest assured because they are so representative. Of the four sources of certainties for analytical constructs, this is the weakest and least defensible one.

To summarize, the certainty past successes confer on an analytical construct is the most definite of the four. All content analyses must be successful in the sense that inferences are valid. But it requires a history of using the same construct with similar data and in similar contexts. The other three are capable of providing certainties in unique content analyses. The use of an investigator's experiences with a context can provide certainties by achieving some kind of intersubjective agreement among those who can claim experiences with the same context. It calls for an explication and publication of these experiences and a debate to achieve consensus about their generality and applicability in the given situation. When analytical constructs are derived from established theories, certainty is conferred by the empirical status of the theories involved. It presupposes that the domain of interest to the analyst, specifically involving the relations between data and context, are well-researched. The use of representative coders conveys certainties in areas involving conventional symbolic interpretations of messages provided that the circumstances of their involvement in the process of analysis do not depreciate their representativeness. It requires larger numbers of individuals and provides the weakest justification.

TYPES OF CONSTRUCTS

In uses and kinds of inferences we distinguished between systems, standards, indices and symptoms, linguistic representations, communications, and institutional processes. The knowledge of how constructs are formulated in these areas of application varies widely. This section offers a few comments on each with the bulk reserved for indices for which analytical constructs are used most commonly.

The *systems* approach to content analysis was reviewed in terms of the *extrapolation* of trends, patterns, and differences. Trends involve the observation of one or more variables at different times. The extrapolation of these variables to different time periods requires analytical constructs in the form of a recursive or autocorrelative function.

The analytical constructs for identifications, evaluations, and audits involve *standards* with which content analysis results are compared. We mentioned the evaluation of press performance, the analysis of psychopathologies, journalistic biases, and the application of codes in the mass media industry. The validity of such constructs stems from the institutions that sanction their use and intend to rely on the inferences provided. Generally, analytical constructs take the form of a two-step process, one that condenses data so that they can be compared and one that applies the standard so as to ascertain possible deviation. Both are justified by institutional practice.

Indices and symptoms were said to be variables that correlate with what they claim to indicate. The most basic form of an analytical construct for what will be called *direct* indices can be conceptualized as an input-output device. And the strongest realization of such a construct embodies a one-to-one relation or mathematical function. This is assumed, for example, in dating an anthropological artifact by measuring the activity of radiocarbon, or built into the way the speedometer of a car is coupled to the wheel. In the social sciences, indices tend to be much more uncertain and correlations may not be perfect.

Besides being correlated with some phenomena of interest, indices should be chosen so as to satisfy two additional requirements.

First, an index should be sensitive enough *to distinguish* between the phenomena of interest. Significant differences in the phenomena should also be reflected in noticeable differences in the index and vice versa. Indeed, many indices are constructed to help decide between two phenomena, states, or properties, such as whether or not a patient can be classified schizophrenic, which textbook is more readable, or whether today's television programming is more violent than yesterday's. Paisley (1964), who reviewed efforts to infer the authors of unsigned documents, stated several criteria for discrimination purposes:

- An index should exhibit low variance within a communicator's known work.
- An index should exhibit high variance between the works of all communicators being compared.
- The frequency contributing to the value of an index should be high relative to the sampling error.

Second, and this applies primarily to this *direct* form of inference, an index should not be affected by variables that are accidental or irrelevant to the phenomenon indicated. For example, Mosteller and Wallace (1963), in their attempt to infer the authorship of the *Federalist Papers,* argue against Yule's (1944) use of nouns because individuals may write on different subjects in different situations and the choice of reference words may hence contaminate what might reveal an author's identity: "The words we want to use are non-contextual ones, words whose rate of use is nearly invariant under change of topic. For this reason, the little filler words, called function words, are especially attractive" (1963: 280).

One of the peculiarities of content analysis is the use of frequencies as direct indices about underlying phenomena like the proportion of discomfort words as an index of anxiety or the proportion of space as an index of the amount of attention. Analytical constructs then represent the correlation between several such frequencies and several magnitudes indicated by it.

It is important, therefore, to point out that frequencies are here used in two distinct ways, as indices and as bases for the correlation between two variables. This is often confused in the literature. For example, Berelson's (1952) insistence on quantification is justified largely in terms of the need for testing statistical hypotheses (the strength and significance of correlations) though his examples concern primarily frequencies as indicators of other phenomena, attention and emphasis, for example.

It seems only a minor shift from counting frequencies of words, symbols, and references to counting frequencies of pairs of words, co-occurrences of symbols, and patterns of references within data, but it took 50 years of content analysis to realize this step. Although Baldwin (1942) had explored such ideas in his analysis of personality structures from autobiographies, Pool (1952) still merely observed that symbols tended to occur together or in clusters, without being able to analyze this property. Osgood (1959) made these notions available to content analysis as "contingency analysis," demonstrated its power on Goebbels diary, and conducted experiments to determine what co-occurrences indicate. All work done so far seems to suggest that above and below chance co-occurrences of references to concepts within a stream of discourse indicate cognitive associations and dissociations, respectively. Inferences to the cognitive structure of speakers, writers, and listeners have since found wide application. The development and justification of analytical constructs for these purposes follow the logic of direct frequency indicators as discussed above.

Analytical constructs for *indirect* forms of inferences can no longer be represented by simple input-output devices. They recognize special conditions under which the correlation is warranted. (For an elaboration of indirect methods, see George, 1959a, 1959b.)

Analytical constructs for *linguistic representations* and for *communications* are very complex and exceed the scope of this work. It seems though that linguistic representations always involve several components, operationalizing different knowledge about language use. One component provides a syntactical description of the linguistic material being analyzed, one component infers the possible linguistic functions and meanings of words in their linguistic context, and a third maps the semantical interpretations onto a "world model," or "territory" of the discourse, whose logic allows the analyst to draw inferences about what is referred to and implied (Hays, 1969; Krippendorff, 1969a). Such analytical constructs can neither be constructed nor validated on the basis of correlations. They rely on rather elaborate theories involving interactive procedures and feedbacks.

Analytical constructs for *institutional processes* do not follow any easily generalizable format. Such constructs tend to

- be qualitative, using verbal modes of reasoning rather than quantitative and formal ones
- involve multitudes of constraints of posssibilities which are implied by known rules, regulations, and practice rather than simple paths delineated by laws
- make use of indirect and multiple methods of drawing inferences rather than direct and unicausal ones.

Although the lack of formal rigor of such constructs suggests uncertainties regarding the validity of results obtained through them, considerable success has been reported, especially when such constructs are used

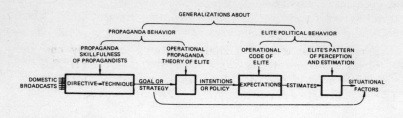

FIGURE 16:   Analytical Constructs for a Political Elite's Stable Behavior Patterns

repeatedly—allowing validation to take place in between—and conservatively—considering only the most confirmed kinds of inferences.

A good example is found in George's (1959a) account of the FCC's inferences from domestic enemy broadcasts during World War II. In the course of their work, the FCC analysts developed elaborate constructs which were intended to explain why certain broadcasts came into being and what, therefore, the antecedent perceptions and conditions were. The constructs operationalized (1) generalizations about the propaganda skillfulness of the major propagandist; (2) generalizations about the operational propaganda theory of the elite, that is, the role assigned to the mass media in pursuing a policy; (3) generalizations about the elite's operational code, that is, how estimates of the situation and capabilities are translated into policies, and (4) generalizations about the elite's pattern of perceiving and estimating itself and its environment. How these generalizations were conceived as governing the causal links between the major unstable variables of the system is shown in Figure 16 (from George, 1959a: 53). In this diagram, arrows indicate the order in which inferences are made, the direction of causality or influence goes, of course, in the opposite direction. The simplicity of Figure 16 probably belies the complexity of the task of justifying the succession of indirect references the situation called for.

10

ANALYTICAL TECHNIQUES

Computational efforts in content analysis are largely consumed by making data and applying analytical constructs. This chapter takes us one step further to the analysis, exploration, and discovery of patterns and relationships in the data.

After inferences have been made, that is, after it is known what the data mean or what they indicate, there is the need

- to summarize the data, to represent them so that they can be better comprehended, interpreted, or related to some decision the user wishes to make
- to discover patterns and relationships within data that the "naked eye" would not easily discern, to test relational hypotheses
- to relate data obtained from content analysis to data obtained from other methods or from other situations so as to either validate the methods involved or to provide missing information.

These tasks are not distinct. Usually all three are simultaneously invoked. Also these tasks are not unique to content analysis. Much scholarly work, especially statistics, is concerned with them. Since there is virtually no analytical technique that content analysis might not want to use, it is an impossible task to present a complete review here. Let me therefore focus on a few techniques that are used more in content analysis than in other empirical endeavors.

FREQUENCIES

By far the most common form of representation of data, serving primarily the summarizing function of analysis, is in terms of frequencies: *absolute frequencies*, such as the numbers of incidents found in the sample, or *relative frequencies*, such as the percentages of the sample size. Volume *measures* such as column inches, time, space, or other frequency-based indices have the same status in content analysis and need not be differentiated here. Except for their indicative qualities, such as the amount of attention or the degree to which an attitude or belief permeates a population, such frequencies do not mean much by themselves. In fact, the reader of any statistic usually has one of several standards for interpreting frequencies in mind.

The standard of *uniform distributions* is invoked when one finds that the frequency in one category is found to be larger or smaller than the average for all categories.

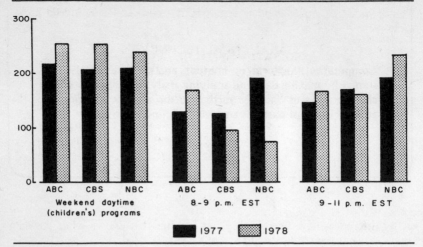

FIGURE 17:   Bar Graph Representation of Frequencies (violence index)
SOURCE: Journal of Communication, Summer 1979; reprinted by permission of
George Gerbner, and of the Journal of Communication.

The standard of *stable distribution* is invoked when one notes changes
in frequencies over time.

These standards are often implied in the way analytical results are
represented or interpreted. In Figure 17, taken from Gerbner et al.'s
(1979) work on television violence, one notes, for example, that violence
on weekend daytime television is larger than average and early evening
television is lower than average and that in 1977, programming of violence
by the three networks was about the same during weekend daytime. These
appeal to the standard of uniform distribution. One also observes changes
from 1977 to 1978 and, in considering them noteworthy, one appeals to
the standard of stable distributions.

More important is the standard of *unbiased representation* which is
invoked when one notes that the observed frequencies are larger or smaller
than what would be expected if the sample would be representative of a
population.

This standard is not absolute, however. It requires a comparison
between one sample and some other sample or population. For example,
with reference to the mass media, many content analyses using simple
frequencies have noted that the population of television characters is not
representative of the population of audience members. This has been
reported for ethnicity, occupations, socioeconomic characteristics, sex,
and age and tends to be explained in terms of prejudices, economic
interests, technological biases, and other explanatory constructs. Whether
audience characteristics should provide the standard for the mass media is
not obvious, however. Perhaps reference to literature, folklore, and other
forms of entertainment are more readily justifiable. Generalizing from the
example, any notion that the proportions of observed frequencies are

"surprising" requires that the distribution against which these observations are compared be made explicit and that the comparison is indeed justifiable.

ASSOCIATIONS, CORRELATIONS, AND CROSS-TABULATIONS

The next most common form of representing data is in terms of *relations between variables*. Such relations may be seen in a cross-tabulation of the frequencies of co-occurrences of the values of one variable and of the values of another. For example, in a content analysis, the sample of size n = 2430 acts of television violence yielded the following observed/ *expected* frequencies of co-occurrences:

character involved is	good	neutral	bad	
Associated with	369	27	23	419
law enforcement	*194*	*64*	*161*	
unrelated	751	328	454	1533
to law	*710*	*233*	*590*	
a	5	15	458	478
criminal	*221*	*73*	*184*	
	1125	370	935	2430

One might be interested not so much in frequencies, such as that most characters involved in violent acts are presented as good (1125) and of those most are unrelated to the law (751), but in the relationship that might exist between the character's legal involvement and his favorable/ unfavorable presentation. In the observed frequencies, this relation appears not so obvious and one has to apply the standard of *chance or statistical independence*. Companions of observed frequencies and those expected under conditions of statistical independence (printed below the observed frequencies) show that reports on absolute frequencies may be quite meaningless. The largest observed frequency (751) is also nearly as expected (710) and contributes nothing to a possible relationship between the two variables. The cells that make the largest contribution are the four corner cells of this table. Tests of the associations are statistically significant beyond any doubt, which supports the statement that "good guys" are more likely represented as on the side of the law, whereas "bad guys" are not. Cross-tabulations are not limited to two or three dimensions, even though these are more clearly visualized and interpreted. Multivariate techniques are available to test complex structures within multidimensional data (Reynolds, 1977).

Relations (associations and correlations) may be of two kinds:

- *within the results* of a content analysis
- *between the results* of a content analysis *and data obtained independently*.

Because the content analyst has full control over the definition and choice of his variables, there is always the danger that associations *within* content analysis results are an artifact of the recording instrument. While the frequencies in the above example were in a sense surprising because the association could have gone the other way (bad cops, good criminals), a positive correlation, for example, between the variable "feminine-masculine personality traits" and "sex of the character" is not so surprising because the two variables are already *logically codependent*. Traditional tests of the statistical significance or relations within the results of a context analysis may mean nothing more than that the researcher defined his instrument that way. Under these conditions, valid tests must assume expectations other than those of statistical independence. Correlation coefficients become uninterpretable here.

Relationships *between* the results of a content analysis and other data are not affected by this problem, largely because these other data are obtained independently, through other means at different times and from different situations. Tests of such relationships are extremely important

- to validate the results of a content analysis (see section on validity) by bringing different evidence to bear on it
- to validate the results of different techniques by providing an independent source of similar evidence (multiple operationalism)
- to test theories involving variables that are assessed by different techniques.

Examples of the latter are the use of content analysis to assess the free responses to open questions on an otherwise structured questionnaire, to assess the verbal exchanges in the course of an otherwise carefully measured group experiment, and to assess the content of those mass media to which audience members are observed to have been exposed to. The ability to correlate information obtained from content analysis with data obtained from other techniques makes content analysis part of the large system of methodology in the social sciences.

IMAGES, PORTRAYALS, DISCRIMINANT ANALYSIS

Numberous content analyses focus on a special entity, person, idea, or event and attempt to find out how it is depicted or conceptualized, what its symbolic image is. Examples of such studies are "the image of the teacher," "the portrayal of women in films made by women," "how the United States is depicted in Mexican dailies," and "what the public knows about the Bell System." There are two approaches to this form of analysis

- attributes, frequency profiles, distributional properties
- associations.

When studying the image of a political candidate by the attribution approach, the content analyst may record, tabulate, and count everything that pertains to that candidate, what is said about him, the characteristics attributed to him and by whom, what he says, the people he associates with, or his socioeconomic background.

From an attributional point of view, an image of something is a systematic presentation of all that is known or said to be unique about that something. For example, documents pertaining to the candidate may be recorded in terms of the presence or absence of

O favorable personality traits
P unfavorable personality traits
Q past record as a politician/decision maker
R attitudes toward social welfare legislation
   etc.

One document shows

```
                      O   P   Q   R   S   T  . . . .
presence of references ┌──────────────────────────────┐
to candidate X         │  √       √   √       √   √    │
                       └──────────────────────────────┘
```

All documents together yield a profile consisting of frequencies of attributes

```
                       O   P   Q   R    S   T . . . .
frequency of references ┌─────────────────────────────────┐
to candidate X          │ 25  10  0  200 186  2  20 . . . │
                        └─────────────────────────────────┘
```

Although such a profile can represent all that is known or said about the candidate, it may represent no more than what is said about all candidates implying that the particular candidate is not really outstanding.

The analysis of the *uniqueness* of an image or portrayal requires comparisons, here, comparisons with other candidates. Taking the attributes of all candidates together, if the frequency of an attribute equals that expected by chance, then there cannot be anything unique about the way this attribute is used in conjunction with the candidate. If it systematically deviates from chance, one has to check whether it deviates from chance in a direction that is unique for that candidate or whether the direction of deviation is shared with some others. Continuing with the hypothetical example, the analysis of images and portrayals involves examining one candidate in the context of all other candidates so as to partition the set of recorded attributes into three groups: A, the set of attributes whose frequencies significantly deviate from chance in a direction not found in any other candidate; C, the set of attributes whose frequencies do not significantly deviate from chance; and leaving the remainder, B, the set of attributes whose frequencies do significantly deviate from chance but in a direction shared with some others.

frequencies of references	A			B		C
	Q	Γ · R	· ·	S	P · ·	O
to candidate X	0	2 · 200	· ·	186	10 · ·	25
other candidates	113	217 · 11	· ·	78	1 · ·	29
	72	305 · 2	· ·	179	0 · ·	31
	187	212 · 31	· ·	190	18 · ·	19
	93	178 · 17	· ·	207	5 · ·	22
	·	· · ·	· ·	·	· · ·	

Attributes in A are also called the candidate's discriminators and the analysis described above in its most basic form is a discriminant analysis.

From an associational point of view an image consists of all the things with which it is associated and excludes all the things with which it is dissociated. Association/dissociation is a statistical concept assessing degrees to which selected concepts occur. The image of a candidate thus becomes that associational cluster of which the candidate is a part and which contrasts with that of others.

CONTINGENCIES, CONTINGENCY ANALYSIS

Contingency analysis aims to infer the network of a source's associations from the pattern of co-occurrences of symbols in messages. It presumes that symbols, concepts, or ideas that are closely associated conceptually will be also closely related statistically. This is assumed regardless of whether the source is an individual author, a social group with its prejudices or ideological commitments, or a whole culture with its patterns of conventions. Experiments have also shown that associations are communicated through statistical contingencies in messages so that contingency analysis can also be used to make inferences about audience associations. Regardless of these possible inferences, contingency analysis is an analytical technique in its own right.

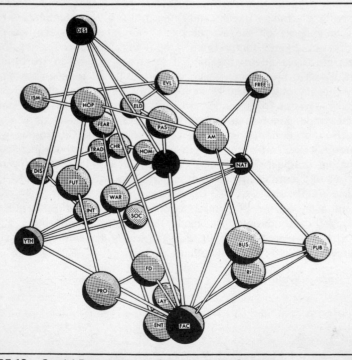

FIGURE 18:   Spatial Representation of an Association Structure

SOURCE: **Trends in Content Analysis** edited by Ithiel de Sola Pool. ©1959 University of Illinois Press.

Contingency analysis starts with a set of recording units, each of which is characterized by a set of attributes which are either present or absent. The choice of recording units is important insofar as such a unit must be informationally rich enough to contain co-occurrences. A word is too small, a sentence usually contains several concepts but large units are often preferable.

In a second step the possible co-occurrences of attributes in each unit are counted and entered as proportions.

In a third step the statistical significance of these co-occurrences must be tested. Osgood (1959), who formalized this analysis, exemplified the results by a contingency analysis of 38 talks given by W.J. Cameron on the Ford Sunday Evening Hour program. Each talk was regarded as one recording unit for which the presence or absence of 27 attributes of content were recorded. The resulting association pattern was depicted as in Figure 18.

CLUSTERING

When the table of possible co-occurrences becomes large, it may become difficult to conceptualize the results. The examination of a matrix of something like 200 × 200 associations between concepts, which is not so unusual for content analysis, is a formidable task, and, in trying to discover a pattern in this flood of information, one is likely to overlook important relationships. Happily, one often discovers that some concepts are so similar or so interrelated that they might, without much loss of detail, be regarded as one. By finding many such "clusters," the task of conceptualizing the data becomes easier.

Clustering seeks to group or to lump together objects or variables that share some observed qualities or, alternatively, to partitltion or to divide a set of objects or variables into mutually exclusive classes whose boundaries reflect differences in the observed qualities of their members.

In clustering it is important to carefully consider the criterion for the formation of clusters. Some allow the formation of long and snakelike clusters, others have a preference for compact and circular ones. Some are sensitive to how much detail is lost within a cluster, others consider only the similarities between the clusters as a whole. Under ideal circumstances, a clustering criterion reflects the way clusters are formed in reality, assessing semantic similarities rather than purely analytic ones.

Clustering procedures essentially consist of the following iteration: first, find the two clusters that are, according to criterion, most similar in the sense that their merger would have the smallest effect on the observed differences in the data as a whole. Second, lump these, taking account of the losses incurred within the newly formed cluster. Third, modify the data to reflect the latest configuration of clusters on which the next merger is computed. Fourth, record the state of the clustering process for the user. Repeat steps one through four until there is nothing left to merge. (For further reference see Krippendorff, 1980.)

Clustering results may be presented by so-called dendrograms which are treelike diagrams indicating how objects are merged into clusters and at

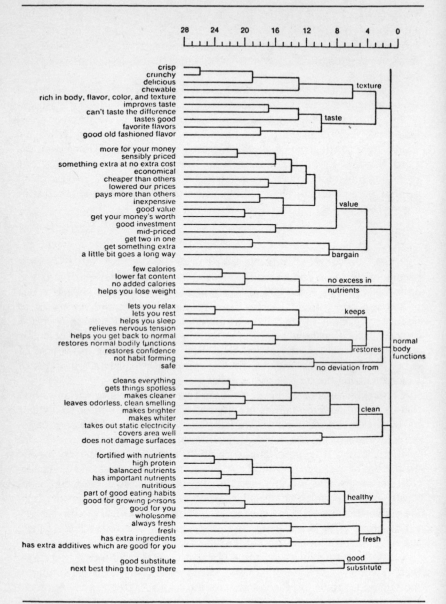

FIGURE 19: Part of a Large Dendrogram Resulting from Clustering Advertising Appeals

which level of commonality the merger took place. Figure 19 shows a fraction of an analysis of some 300 television advertising appeals (Dziurzynski, 1977). The resulting classification of appeals into those referring to texture, taste, value, or bargain has considerable face validity.

CONTEXTUAL CLASSIFICATION

Contextual classification is a multivariate technique for eliminating a certain kind of redundancy in data and thereby extracting from them what seems to be the underlying conceptualization. It assumes that objects, and most obviously, words, have more in common or are more synonymous the more the context they occur in is alike. Here, context means the linguistic environment of words or the within-date surroundings of a recording unit.

Contextual classification and clustering share the same kind of data requirements, that is, a fixed number of values for each recording unit. For example, in a study of leadership perceptions, a portion of a speech by Mao's wife (delivered on Sept. 6, 1968) was standardized in this fixed format as follows:

1	Miss Chiang	initial stage of cultural revolution	red guards	tremendous contribution	to communism
2	Miss Chiang	Initial stage of cultural revolution	red guards	tremendous contributions	to China
3	Miss Chiang	middle stage of cultural revolution	red guards	tremendous contributions	to China
4	Miss Chiang	initial stage of cultural revolution	red guards	destroy	revisionist leadership
5	Miss Chiang	middle stage of cultural revolution	red guards	destroy	revisionist leadership
6	Miss Chiang	middle stage of cultural revolution	red guards	shatter	old structure
7	Miss Chiang	final stage of cultural revolution	working class	teach	red guards
8	Miss Chiang	final stage of cultural revolution	working class	teach	red guards

In this example, one can regard the five columns as five dimensions or variables which distinguish among the authors, the situations, the actors, the actions, and the targets. Each individual author, action, and so on constitutes a value on its respective dimension and each statement occupies one of the 120 cells of this initial space. Contextual classification now examines the contexts of each value and tests whether the contexts of different values are sufficiently similar to regard these values as contextually synonymous. Procedurally, this means shrinking the size of a multivariate space, not its dimensionality, while retaining the essential relationships between the dimensions.

In the example, sentences 1 and 2 differ only in the target of the action. "China" and "Communism" have identical contexts throughout all units and may therefore be regarded as similar in meaning as far as the author is concerned. By regarding them as one class, little if anything is lost though the number of cells in the space shrinks from 120 to 96.

The next candidate for contextual classification is the distinction between the "initial . . ." and the "middle stage of cultural revolution." In sentences 2 and 3 and in 4 and 5 these two "stages" appear in identical contexts whereas in sentence 6 "shatter the old structure" occurs in the "middle stage . . ." only, and some distinction would indeed be lost here if this contextual difference would be discarded. Provided that this loss is tolerable, the space shrinks from 96 to 64 cells.

Considering the larger context of Chinese political discourse, "destroy the revisionist leadership in 5 is virtually synonymous with "shatter the old structure" in 6, but in such a small context this might not become apparent. Nevertheless, the next few steps in the analysis would bring all of the "red guard's" actions and targets together and in contrast to those of the "working class," in a space of $1 \cdot 2 \cdot 2 \cdot 2 \cdot 2 = 16$ cells.

Although Miss Chiang adheres to the convention of describing a process in three different stages, and although she mentions different actions and targets during the cultural revolution, contextual classification reveals an essential conceptual dichotomy between when and what the red guards contributed and what the working class did thereafter.

The procedure is most productive when cell frequencies within the multidimensional data space are large (see Krippendorff, 1974, 1980). Its limit is dictated by the computational efforts with the number of dimensions involved.

11

THE USE OF COMPUTERS

Done entirely by hand, content analysis is often tedious. This chapter offers an overview of the strengths and weaknesses of new efforts to use computer-based content analysis techniques with machine-readable content.

Digital computers have been widely hailed as providing content analysis with a reliable, fast, and inexpensive instrument, and, indeed, the use of computers has revolutionized certain aspects of content analysis. These deserve special attention.

The characteristics of computers that are important here are:

(1) large volumes of digital data are read into a computer sequentially
(2) logical or algebraical operations that can be defined on the internal representation of these data are executed with high speed
(3) the execution of such operations is specified by a program which determines and controls "the behavior" of the computer and is hence equivalent to a perfect theory or representation of how the computer works
(4) computational processes are deterministic and hence perfectly reliable. No ambiguities and uncertainties are tolerated within a computer.

Several analogies between the way a computer is constructed and what a content analyst does comes to mind. The sequential input of discrete symbols, (1), resembles the reading of lingistic expressions which are also stringlike and digital. The function of the program within a computer resembles that of the instructions (unitization schemes, sampling plans, recording instructions, analytical procedures) to human individuals who are expected to apply them reliably. In fact, the terms *data processing* and *symbol manipulation,* which serve as a synonym for "computation," have also been used to describe aspects of human intelligence. Let us see what these analogies are worth. In the section on Conceptual Foundations, we characterized content analysis in terms of

(a) its unobtrusive nature
(b) its ability to consider unstructured material
(c) its context sensitivity
(d) its ability to analyze large volumes of data.

The most obvious way in which computers can aid the content analyst is by processing large amounts of data (d) with high speed (2). A good example, and perhaps the ideal, is an on-line analysis of newsprint. De Weese (1977) developed a device which converts the typesetting instructions (from which the templet for printing the newspaper is produced)

into an analyzable form which enabled her to analyze a newspaper virtually while it is in print. Another example is the creation of a con-
cordance of an author's literary production. In the past this work could
easily occupy the life of a literary scholar. Now it can be a question of
hours (provided the text is in computer readable form). Even with optical
reading, progress has also been reported so that the possibility is virtually
in sight that large volumes of written material may be entered into a
computer without human interface.

The computer's ability to process textual material reliably (4) has also
been convincing to many content analysts. It virtually eliminates human
error and the effort of developing reliable coding instructions. But with
this virtue in the foreground, it is easily forgotten that a computer in
content analysis must in some sense understand or at least retain the
symbolic qualities of a text (c). Whereas traditional content analyses can
rely on human coders' common sense and their ability to interpret and to
identify subtle symbolic differences, suitable computer programs (3) need
to be developed in their place. These have to be explicit and detailed and
represent the symbolic processes involved. Nothing can be left to intuition.
The question is not whether the reliability of a content analysis can be
improved computationally but whether the researcher knows enough
about the context of his data and whether he is able to explicate this
knowledge in the form of a computer program.

Only on the surface does the need to be explicit run counter to the
claimed virtue of content analysis to accept unstructured material (b).
Computers and scientific analysts are alike in imposing their own structure
on the input text. The difference is that human coders might revolt or
become confused when they find that the analytical categories they are
asked to employ are totally alien to the symbolic nature of the text. A
computer simply does its job, leaving the analyst to wonder what the
output means.

Current computer uses in content analysis might be discussed in terms
of three major kinds:

- statistical analyses
- computational aids for survey and discovery
- computational content analyses.

STATISTICAL ANALYSES

In the social sciences, statistical techniques are standard procedures.
Practically all of them are available in the form of computer programs. In
fact, hardly anyone does and perhaps can still do a factor analysis by hand.
In addition to individual programs, several large statistical software
packages (SPSS, BMDP, LISREL, DATA-TEXT, and so on) are available
which are easy to use, even by those unfamiliar with computer programming.

To apply them, data are coded to conform to the input requirements of
the technique and computational options are specified by the user. In the
course of the computation, data are sorted, reorganized, transformed, and
accounted for by numerical indices which the user must then interpret in

view of what the technique does. Some understanding of how these indices come about is therefore essential.

Where statistical procedures are used *as a means of drawing inferences* or where they are incorporated as a part of a larger process of drawing inferences (see Analytical Techniques), their internal structure must be shown to be context sensitive (see Constructs for Inferences), that is, represent the symbolic processes in which the data are involved. In such applications the user may have to acquaint himself with the theoretical literature on the procedures and decide whether the assumptions built into the procedure are indeed justifiable in the particular context.

In content analysis it is more usual to apply statistical tests *after inferences* have been obtained, for example, to summarize classes of symbols or references made in a text, to test the statistical independence among attributes, or to relate content analysis findings to results obtained by other research methods. There is, then, no need to justify these uses in terms other than their formal properties.

COMPUTATIONAL AIDS FOR SURVEY AND DISCOVERY

Before conceptualizing his data and before deciding on data reduction techniques, dictionary constructions, and analytical procedures that might be appropriate, the researcher might want to achieve an overview of the variety, kind, and distribution of data. Computational aids for achieving such an overview are primarily motivated by the large volumes of textual material an anlyst may have to consider. Unaided, the analyst is likely to form biased, incomplete, and highly selective impressions.

One simple aid is an alphabetical tally of the units of analysis, for example, the words occurring in a text. This has also been shown to facilitate the correction of typographical errors in the data input stream.

Another, perhaps more instructive, way of listing units is by their frequency of occurrence. Such a list can be considerably shortened by a concern for word stems, roots, or kinds rather than their particular varieties. Ignoring grammatical endings of the words reduces "talks," "talked," "talking," and "talkative" to "talk," for example. Experiences with either account show the frequency of words or word stems to be exponentially declining. There usually are a few high-frequency words, articles, function words which may not distinguish one document from another and a large number of unique words which do not engage in significant associations and correlations. Thus a mere frequency account of the units in his data may enable the researcher to form an idea of the quantities he has to cope with. It may also enable him to make certain simplifying decisions such as eliminating the most frequent and least frequent words from the analysis.

Another aid is found in information retrieval programs. Such programs essentially carry out a series of "search and locate" instructions which can be formulated either on the basis of an a priori theory according to which some units, words, or word stems are more important than others, or after examining the frequency tally. The output of an information retrieval program consists of the unit's location(s) or a printout of all sentences, paragraphs, or documents which contain such a unit. It allows the analyst to systematically examime the whole data base from a particular perspective. One of the earliest research applications of information retrieval systems is attributed to Sebeok and Zeps (1958), who searched for patterns in Cheremis folktales. Janda (1969) devised another such system that stores documents on microfilm and allows the analyst to add content indicators (categories) as he examines the material. Here the whole document is the unit of retrieval. Ekman et al. (1969) describes a similar system for visual information display, used to analyze facial expressions.

Whereas all counts and alphabetical listings take words out of their original linguistic environment and make their context-dependent meanings no longer recognizable by the analyst, the Key-Word-In-Context (KWIC) approach does just the opposite. It list the occurrences of selected words together with the linguistic environment in which they occur and gives the researcher an idea of how each key-word is used. Figure 20 (Stone et al., 1966: 159) reproduces Dunphy's example of à KWIC list for the word *play*. When references to the original documents are maintained, as in this list, the analyst can moreover examine whether different senses of a word coincide with different authors, documents, or situations. KWIC lists also are important aids to develop categories of meaning such as required for dictionary construction and manual coding.

Another computational aid, approaching the nature of a statistical decision technique, is to identify a printout for inspection and select for

```
        A VIOLINIST OF THE HIGHEST CALIBRE  PLAY A CONCERTO. JIMMY HAS BEEN TAKING    5C1 WILLIAMSON UNDERGRAD
        IN HIS ROOM, HE WOULD HALF-HEARTEDLY PLAY A FEW SCALES, AND THEN WOULD PUT     5C1 WILLIAMSON UNDERGRAD
         LEADERSHIP, THAT SCOTT WILL PROBABLY PLAY A LARGER ROLE IN THIS AREA, AND      2H4 SHAPIRO SMALL GROUP
       BEST BUDDY. ..HOW ABOUT COMING OVER TO PLAY A LITTLE BALL... HIS FRIEND          5C1 WILLIAMSON UNDERGRAD
            WHILE HE IS YOUNG HE SHOULD LEARN TO PLAY A MUSICAL INSTRUMENT. THE VIOLIN. 5C1 WILLIAMSON UNDERGRAD
          A GREAT DEAL TO US) COULD CONCEIVABLY PLAY A SIGNIFICANT PART. IT SURPRISES ME 2H5 SHAPIRO SMALL GROUP
         AN AIR OF DISDAIN. HOW CAN HE POSSIBLY PLAY A SOLO IN THE CONCERT TOMORROW     5C1 WILLIAMSON UNDERGRAD
            COME TO PLAY A TUNE I HAVE COME TO PLAY A SONG. WILL YOU GIVE ME YOUR       0A3 ZINACANTAN DREAMS
      MIGUELITO HOW ARE YOU. I HAVE COME TO PLAY A TUNE I HAVE COME TO PLAY A SONG.     0A3 ZINACANTAN DREAMS
           A VIOLIN, HE WANTED TO LEARN HOW TO PLAY A VIOLIN. GO TO THE NEXT ONES HE    5A1 HARTMAN DETROIT GANGS
           SEEP, YOU KNOW, ENCOURAGED ENOUGH TO PLAY AN INSTRUMENT AND I DO NOT THINK HE 5A1 HARTMAN DETROIT GANGS
           PARENTS HAVE DECIDED THAT HE SHOULD PLAY AN INSTRUMENT, AND HAVE BOUGHT HIM  5C1 WILLIAMSON UNDERGRAD
        WELL GROWN THEY USED TO GO OUTSIDE TO PLAY AND HAVE FRESH AIR. THEY WENT ON IN  8J1 KIKUYU
          THINGS, THE CHILDREN WOULD ASK HER TO PLAY AND THAT IF SHE SEES THAT IT IS    1A1 FAM INTERACTION FRISBIE
          BOY. WHEN I WAS DOWN SOUTH, I USED TO PLAY AND THEN I WOULD GET MAD AND GO IN 5A2 HARTMAN DETROIT GANGS
          WE WANTED SOMETHING, AND SO WE WOULD PLAY AND THROW BOXES ALL OVER THE ROOM, 5A2 HARTMAN DETROIT GANGS
           I-VE DECIDED TO TAKE YOUR OFFER AND PLAY AT THE ..POPS.. TONIGHT. HOW MUCH  5D1 WILLIAMSON UNDERGRAD
         YOU SEE I WILL BE BACK I AM GOING TO PLAY AT THE HOUSE OF OUR FRIEND MANVEL    0A3 ZINACANTAN DREAMS
          AND SCOLD HIM AND TELL HIM HE CANNOT PLAY BALL AT ALL TODAY SINCE HE DID NOT  5C1 WILLIAMSON UNDERGRAD
         IS A NICE SPRING DAY AND HE WANTED TO PLAY BALL INSTEAD. HE IS NOW TRYING TO   5D1 WILLIAMSON UNDERGRAD
             COAXLE HIMSELF BY GOING OUT TO PLAY BALL, AND RESIGNEDLY RETURN TO         5F1 N ACH TAT
       HE IS IN THE ATTIC, WATCHING SOME BOYS PLAY BASEBALL ON THE OPPOSITE HILL. HE    5D1 WILLIAMSON UNDERGRAD
          I GO AROUND THERE WITH MY FRIENDS AND PLAY BASKETBALL ALL THE TIME. THAT IS   5A2 HARTMAN DETROIT GANGS
            AFRICANS IN BASKETBALL, AND I OFTEN PLAY BASKETBALL WITH THE LEBANESE.      2C2 PEACE CORPS
       WORK AND SO THEN I GOES DOWN THERE AND PLAY BASKETBALL, BECAUSE THAT HELP FIND   5A2 HARTMAN DETROIT GANGS
            BIT COCKY + LOYAL TO MY FRIENDS + A PLAY BOY + LENIENT TOWARD SOCIAL 20191  9C2 WHO AM I
         HE GREW A LITTLE BIGGER HE LEARNED TO PLAY BY HIMSELF AND WHEN HE GOT BIGGER   5G2 NAVAHO TATS
           HAD TO SIT THERE AND LET THE PIANO PLAY BY ITSELF. HE WAS IN SCHOOL AND THE  0B2 CHILDREN S DREAMS
              IN THE EVENINGS WE TALK, WRITE, PLAY CARDS OR SCRABBLE. WE HAVE A NEW     2K1 RAMALLO
         (THAT HE/SC HAS ROBBED/S HIS FATHER). PLAY EENY MEENY MINEY MOS WE/1 HAVE/3    1G1 MILLS
         BE THAT IN SIX OR SEVEN YEARS HE WILL PLAY FAIRLY WELL AND BE EXTREMELY        5C1 WILLIAMSON UNDERGRAD
         OURS THOU WHO ARE IN PAPANTAL. DO NOT PLAY FALSE BUT TURN THOU SOON ASIDE.     8E1 IFUGAO
       JUNIOR YEAR + ON THE HOUSE COMMITTEE I PLAY FOOTBALL + PLAY TENNIS + ENJOY       9C4 WHO AM I
       I SELDOM PLAY I DONT KNOW AND I PLAY I PLAY FOR MY OWN NO I CANT NOW I LEARNED   1F1 JAFFE CASE
            I WAS ON THE PITCHING MOUND. I PLAY FOR THE DETROIT TIGERS. WELL, I         5A1 HARTMAN DETROIT GANGS
          TWO TO TWELVE. WE COMB THEIR HAIR, PLAY GAMES WITH THEM, SEW CLOTHES FOR      2C5 PEACE CORPS
             TO TALK WITH THEM, SHOW AND PLAY GAMES, SING AND WATCH THEIR FACES         2K2 RAMALLO
       OBSERVE THE RITUAL PROHIBITIONS. THEY PLAY GONGS AND DANCE. ON THE EIGHTH DAY    8E1 IFUGAO
          WE WILL GET SUGAR CANE TODAY. THEY PLAY GONGS FOR THE SUGAR CANE. THEY CUT    8E1 IFUGAO
        WENT STRAIGHT TO MWENENEGAS HOUSE TO PLAY HAVOC. A LONG BLAST FROM A HORN WAS   8J1 KIKUYU
           MIGUEL HE SAID. NOW BASTARD LET US PLAY HE SAID. TAKE OFF YOUR CLOTHES WE    0A1 ZINACANTAN DREAMS
         TO HIS WOMANS HOUSE HE WOULD COME TO PLAY HIS GUITAR. WELL NO THE OLD MAN      0A2 ZINACANTAN FOLK
        EVEN LEARN THE PIANO AND I I I SELDOM PLAY I DONT KNOW AND I PLAY I PLAY FOR    1F1 JAFFE CASE
          I I I SELDOM PLAY I DONT KNOW AND I PLAY I PLAY FOR MY OWN NO. I CANT NOW I   1F1 JAFFE CASE
            AND SADDLES. THAT WAS OUR GREATEST PLAY IN OUR VILLAGE IN BASUTOLAND. THE   5B1 SUZMAN SOUTH AFRICAN
```

FIGURE 20:   Sample of Key-Word-in-Context: Play

SOURCE: Philip J. Stone et al., **The General Inquirer: A Computer Approach to Content Analysis**, MIT Press, p. 159. Reprinted by permission of MIT Press.

further analysis those units or words that exhibit some association with other words and are in this sense information bearing. The whole text is scanned by some kind of window of, say, 200 characters or 20 words in length. The observed number of occurrences are compared with their statistical expectations and those showing unusual deviations from chance are retained (see Iker, undated).

Obviously, such computational aids range over a rather wide spectrum of techniques including the qualitative KWIC listings on the one extreme and the quantitative selection of the most information bearing words on the other. These aids share their applicability to large volumes of data and involve only minimal assumptions regarding the underlying constructs. The interpretation of their outputs is left entirely to the analyst. Although they do retain some references to the symbolic qualities in the data, they do not make inferences.

Unfortunately, the development of computational aids for recognizing complex pattern and for displaying differences in meanings that are distributed over large bodies of text or other vehicles is not given sufficient attention in content analysis. Especially with an increase of interactive data processing, such devices will gain in importance.

COMPUTATIONAL CONTENT ANALYSIS

The above use of computers may not involve inferences of the kind sought by content analysis and are, in fact, not unique to content analysis. We will limit the term *computational content analysis* to situations in which a computer is programmed to mimic, model, replicate, or represent some aspect of the social context of the data it processes, that is, where the process of drawing inferences from original text (or data generally) is entirely or largely computerized.

Although the aim of computational content analysis is to accept raw text as input, the computer is often unable to recognize theoretically relevant distinctions which may have to be introduced by *manual pre-editing*. For example, it is easy to record and analyze voice patterns mechanically but it is extremely difficult to design a device for recognizing words in them. Human transcription of the human voice is simply more efficient. In the practice of content analysis, preediting of text may mean (1) repeating the period to indicate the end of a sentence; (2) marking the beginning of a paragraph or the speaker at the point of turn taking with a specialized symbol; (3) spelling out abbreviations; (4) adding special definitions; (5) replacing pronouns by proper names; (6) identifying the actors, actions, targets, and justifications; (7) distinguishing between Buffalo the city and buffalo the animal; and so on. It may also mean kernellizing complex expression or rewriting the whole text into a standard format, an effort which may turn arguments in favor of the efficiency of a computer approach into the opposite. It is simply not so easy to program a computer to understand indigenous symbolic communications. Most working systems are limited to a very reduced form of understanding, specialized for a particular discourse or limited to a form of input.

Within computational content analysis one can distinguish two principal approaches

* dictionary and thesaurus approaches
* artificial intelligence approaches.

To this we should add that the field is still in flux and perhaps not as highly developed as one may wish. A recent review of computer applications in the social sciences (*American Behavioral Scientist, 20*, 3, 1979) hardly mentions content analysis although great efforts are indeed under way.

Dictionary and Thesaurus Approaches

Dictionary and thesaurus approaches share the emphasis on single words, or short strings of characters, which are identified in a text, removed from their linguistic environment, individually classified or "tagged," and then counted. The classification or tagging of words (recording units) is intended to replicate shared judgments on the semantical similarities between pairs of words or on synonyms and is thus presumed to represent an important part of the semantical interpretation of a text. This simple form of understanding is shared by several rather different approaches. We sketch three prototypical systems here.

A purely *thesaurus approach,* as evident in a set of computer programs called VIA (Sedelow, 1967), capitalizes on the existence of thesauri of the English language, for example, *Roget's University Thesaurus* or *Webster's New Dictionary of Synonyms.* A thesaurus groups words according to the meanings they share, and in Roget's approach the shared meaning is moreover designated by a heading which is conceived of as simpler, more general, and more abstract. Thus *Roget's International Thesaurus* (1974) groups synonyms in eight classes: Abstract Relations, Space, Physics, Matter, Sensation, Intellect, Volition, and Affection. In a second-level classification, Intellect is broken down into Intellectual Faculties and Processes, States of Mind, and Communication of Ideas. In the lattermost category, 13 divisions are recognized, of which the "Nature of the Ideas Communicated" has 9 divisions, of which "Meaning" has 15 divisions, and of which the second group of nouns finally lists the words *intent, intention, purpose, aim, object, design, plan,* and *hang.*

Sedelow (1967) provides a convincing demonstration for the need to tabulate words by their thesaurus headings. She analyzed two separate English translations of *Sokolovsky's Military Strategy* and found that they differed in nearly 3000 words: 1599 appeared only in the Rand translation and 1331 appeared only in the version published by Praeger. Since both were respectable translations, it would be misleading to conclude that they differed in content. Replacing words by their categories of meaning suppresses mere stylistic variation and idiosyncratic word choices which account for these surface differences. The aim of the thesaurus approach is to yield a simpler representation of the meaning of the text, to identify certain basic concepts, to ascertain how often particular ideas occur, and by comparing different documents, to determine what is new or different.

Besides the limitations inherent in all single-word-out-of-context analyses, one common problem of the thesaurus approach is that words are listed in more than one similarity group which makes it difficult to interpret statistical accounts of the thesaurus headings. For example, *Roget's International Thesaurus* lists the word *intent* in nine different groups which in turn occur in four out of the eight primary classes. The analyst has to decide to which level of classification the meaning of a word is to be simplified. A second problem, which is considered to be the strength of this approach, is the absence of theoretical conceptions in the categories of a thesaurus. This absence is a weakness when a content analysis aims at something other than a general, complete, and commonly shared semantical interpretation of the words within a text. To this one must remark that even so, a thesaurus claims to make distinctions according to the language in use, it is not altogether clear how these categories have been obtained. They may not be free of Mr. Roget's 19th century conceptual bias and omit distinctions that are important today.

The *dictionary approach* to content analysis is best exemplified by Stone et al.'s (1966) General Inquirer. Unlike the thesaurus approach, this system incorporates a theoretically motivated classification scheme for the words or word stems occurring in a text. The development of the General Inquirer was by far the most ambitious effort to computerize content analysis and has since found numerous applications, modifications, and translations into languages other than English. We describe its principal features.

The system accepts raw or preedited text in computer readable form, usually on punch cards, which is then transferred to a tape. As a first step, word roots are identified by chopping off the suffixes "-s," "-ed," "-ing," "-ion," and so on. Thus, EDUCAT becomes the word stem for "education," "educating," and so on. These suffixes are considered unnecessary grammatical forms which merely complicate the construction of dictionaries.

In the General Inquirer, the dictionary identifies a word stem by a one-to-one match with one of its entries and assigns them to one or more categories called "tags," which are used thereafter either in conjunction with the original word or as a singular representation thereof. Several levels of tagging are possible. Dictionaries are developed independently of a text and remain fixed during an analysis although the user can add to the dictionary after inspection of a leftover list of words found in the text but not in the dictionary. A peculiarity of the General Inquirer is that tags are merely added to the tape containing the source text so that the original words can be retrieved. After tagging, several forms of analysis can be performed, including contingency analysis, evaluation assertion analysis, various frequency counts and lists according to tags, word stems, or sentences satisfying certain criteria can be obtained for inspection or further analysis.

The validity of the General Inquirer is rooted in its dictionary which represents a classification of sign-vehicles according to some semantical criterion. The original dictionary was heavily influenced by Bales's *Interac-*

tion Process Analysis and came to be known as the Harvard Psycho-Sociological Dictionary. Its 1965 version had 3500 entries and 83 tags. The fact that words can be interpreted from numerous perspectives (nitroglycerin can be an explosive, a chemical, or a drug) has led to numerous other dictionaries, for example, for analyzing survey research data, for use in alcoholism studies, for value analysis, applicable to need-achievement data, to humor, mythology, newspaper headlines, and many more. Dictionaries tend to be specific of both, a given discourse and to the domain. of the intended inferences. Some dictionaries are clearly based on theoretical conceptions, others are established after considerable experimental work on how words are grouped by subjects.

Although the original conception of the General Inquirer aimed at a tagging of *all* or nearly all content words in a text (see the need for inspecting a leftover list), several recent efforts consider only a smaller set of words of special theoretical significance. For example, Ertel (1976) developed a dogmatism scale on the frequencies of basically two classes of words, "D+" words and "D-" words. Dictionaries also do not need to follow strictly semantical conceptions. So, Holsti (in Stone et al., 1966) developed a dictionary that tags words according to Osgood's three dimensions of affective meaning: evaluation, strength, and activity. Their numerical representation feeds into an attitude theory which justifies in turn inferences about the author's attitudes.

The third of the single-word-out-of-context approaches is exemplified by a system developed by Iker (1975) called WORDS. It was developed for content analyzing psycho-therapeutic interview data and is modelled principally on early experiences with automatic abstracting. The system includes many of the General Inquirer procedures (e.g., reduction of words to roots, dictionaries, frequency lists) which need not be reviewed for these. One outstanding feature is its explicit avoidance of a priori classifications of words which are built into both the dictionary and the thesaurus classification of VIA and the General Inquirer, respectively. In many situations the researcher may not have a preconception of the theoretically significant terms or may not want to settle on categories without examination of the text to be analyzed. The WORD system commits itself to a procedure by which such a scheme emerges from the text without the theoretical bias an investigator may bring to the analysis. Clustering has been used for similar ends (Dziurzynski, 1977).

Although one may argue about the validity of the WORDS system, it demonstrates the possibility of defining computational procedures that let categories emerge from the properties of the text. Such procedures represent an important step toward generalizing content analysis procedures beyond particular theoretical conceptions and particular discourses.

Artificial Intelligence Approaches

Work on artificial intelligence aims largely at representing human intelligence in a computer. Its hope is to provide an understanding of human cognitive processes, to design mechanical devices that relieve man of undesirable or difficult decision and control processes, and to generalize intelligence beyond its human manifestations. Artificial intelligence and computational content analysis share the concern with such processes as understanding language, drawing inferences from nonlinguistic symbolic forms of communication, and making intelligent decisions on incomplete information.

When artificial intelligence attended to problems of machine translation, several researchers conceptualized content analysis as a problem of translating natural language expressions into the terms of a scientific language, and indeed, coding in content analysis involves such processes. Also the computation of abstracts from text conformed to traditional conceptions of content analysis (e.g., Iker, 1975). When artificial intelligence turned to the design of question-answering systems, many researchers (e.g., Hays, 1969) saw that this, too, was involved in content analysis. Indeed, all answers to a content analyst's question are rooted in the selective analysis of a text. Unlike in information retrieval, the search for answers is not reducible to whether some item exists in a data base. It requires some level of understanding. Also, machines that process and respond to natural language instructions can be considered analogous to a content analyst's work who is expected to interpret (perhaps without the "command" aspect implied in man-machine communication) his data and recommend appropriate actions.

Besides these obvious analogies, artificial intelligence approaches to computational content analysis have been more exploratory than the source of large-scale systems of analysis. Although it is perhaps too early to generalize, most artificial intelligence approaches to content analysis involve a syntactical analysis component, followed by a semantical analysis component, but emphasize that the outputs of these components are mapped into a *logic-of-discourse* component which represents the logical structure of the world under consideration and is capable of storing and recording knowledge about this world.

Whereas dictionary and thesaurus approaches have claimed their broad scope by reducing all complex symbolic phenomena to rather primitive forms of discourses and "worlds" (in which unordered sets of units signify or refer to a smaller unordered set of qualities or attributes), artificial intelligence approaches had to make other compromises to cope with greater complexities. For example, in a demonstration of what "understanding natural language" involves, Lindsay (1963) was satisfied by simple kernel statements in Basic English. But, stored in a memory that represented the logic of kinship systems implicitly, these statements lead to the rather complex world of existing family structures. In another system, the "world" was limited to tables of baseball scores but the system accepted a broad range of natural language questions that could be answered from these tables. The computer analyzed the syntax and semantics of these questions, such as "How many times did the Red Sox beat the Yankees in 1958," and found answers from the data (Green et al., 1963). Another simple demonstration, going beyond a dictionary and thesaurus approach, is provided by Koppelaar et al. (1978). The analyst's "world" was programmed as a simulation model. Koppelaar et al.'s data consisted of perceived causal dependencies between working conditions in social organizations and were extracted from interview transcripts. The simulation explored all functional implications of these data. Hays (1969) suggested that the "world" relative to which a discourse is content analyzed be organized as an encyclopedia, containing the presuppositions of the assertions analyzed, prior knowledge about the subject, and the logical structure of the situation.

An exciting and potentially important development in artificial intelligence approaches to content analysis is a series of computer programs able to represent discourses such as accident descriptions, social encounters, and restaurant behavior computationally and to simulate how individuals may make sense of such verbal accounts (which usually leaves many details to the imagination of the reader). The work has evolved out of early interest in models of attitude change (Abelson, 1963) and is reported by Schank and Abelson (1977). It responds particularly to the criticism of computational linguistics, which has limited its attention largely to the understanding of single sentences, by aiming to represent a whole discourse in terms of scripts, plans, themes, and goals. Although the aim of the authors is primarily psychological, that is, to understand how individuals store and process knowledge which may ultimately control their behavior, the inferences they are able to draw from a text are those several content analysts have hoped to obtain by noncomputational techniques.

Judging from the current state of knowledge, computational content analysis is likely to be most successful when

(a) attention is restricted to data from a particular discourse which is limited in vocabulary, syntax, and semantics. The relative success of specialized dictionaries attests to the wisdom of this restriction.

(b) The logic of the context of this discourse (causality, scripts, social structures) is either explicitly statable or implicit in the form in which data are represented computationally. It seems difficult to compute meanings and implications and to draw inferences for all possible situations or worlds. Only those which are reasonably formalizable can lead to valid results.

(c) A priori knowledge and presuppositions relevant to the discourse can enter the analysis either in the form of additional data, or in the form of the logic of the context. Either must contribute to the desired inferences.

12

RELIABILITY

This chapter gives an extended review of the ways in which reliability can be and should be assessed in content analysis. Designs are offered for examining stability, reproducibility, and accuracy. Computational techniques, comparative standards, and diagnostic devices are developed and discussed.

If research results are to be valid, the data on which they are based, the individuals involved in their analysis, and the processes that yield the results all must be reliable. Reliability is a necessary though not a sufficient condition for validity.

Reliability assessments serve as important safeguards against the contamination of scientific data by effects that are extraneous to the aims of observation, measurement, and analysis. In Kaplan and Goldsen's words:

> The importance of reliability rests on the assurance it provides that data are obtained independent of the measuring event, instrument or person. Reliable data, by definition, are data that remain constant throughout variations in the measuring process [1965: 83-84].

Reliability assesses the extent to which any research design, any part thereof, and any data resulting from them represent variations in real phenomena rather than the extraneous circumstances of measurement, the hidden idiosyncrasies of individual analysts, and surreptitious biases of a procedure.

To test *reliability,* some duplication of efforts is essential. A reliable procedure should yield the same results from the same set of phenomena regardless of the circumstances of application. To test *validity,* on the other hand, the results of a procedure must match with what is known to be "true" or assumed to be already valid. It follows that, whereas reliability assures that the analytical results represent something real, validity assures that the analytical results represent what they claim to represent. Two propositions relate reliability to validity in content analysis.

Reliability sets limits to the potential validity of research results. Clearly, in a totally unreliable process, whose results are merely chance events, one cannot expect conclusions to be valid to a degree better than chance. Totally unreliable processes rarely occur in practice, nevertheless, the probability of a valid result cannot exceed the probability with which that result is obtainable in the process of repeated analysis.

Reliability does not guarantee the validity of research results. Two judges with the same prejudices may agree on what they see but be wrong by all other standards. An analytical procedure may be deterministic, like a computer program, but has nothing in common with the context from which the data stem and repeat its mistakes over and over again. Thus, high reliability cannot provide any assurance that results are indeed valid.

One could add a third proposition to the above which does not, however, have the definite force of the other two: *Reliability often gets in the way of validity*. This empirical fact stems in part from the real difficulties of analyzing complex symbolic forms systematically, and in part from a researcher's natural tendency to improve that quality of the data which is most easily measurable. An example, discussed by Holsti (1969), is Merrit's (1966) study of national consciousness among 13 American colonies on the basis of newspaper accounts. Because themes with manifestations of such sentiments are difficult to unitize, to record, to compare, and are hence likely to be unreliable, the analysis enumerated place names instead. Indeed, counting words rarely poses reliability problems but the validity of such counts remains obscure.

In the following we will distinguish between several conditions for generating suitable data for reliability tests, define a general measure of agreement for reliability studies, discuss standards for accepting data as sufficiently reliable to warrant further analysis, and offer several diagnostic devices that will aid various forms of quality control particularly during the pretesting phase of a content analysis.

RELIABILITY DESIGNS

Actually, the term *reliability* covers at least three distinct types and it would be better to designate which of these applies in a given situation. For example, a coder may duplicate what he has done before and, finding no major deviations between the two, conclude that his data are reliable. Now, compare this with a situation in which that coder's assignment of units to categories is compared with those made by another coder. Here too, the absence of deviation is an indication of the reliability of the data but it is a much stronger test because it is sensitive to more than the internal noise or inconsistencies of one coder. The difference between the two situations is one of design, that is, of the way reliability data are obtained and not related to how the two sets of data are evaluated.

We distinguish three types:

- stability
- reproducibility
- accuracy.

Stability is the degree to which a process is invariant or unchanging over time. Stability becomes manifest under test-retest conditions, such as when the same coder is asked to code a set of data twice, at different points in time. Disagreements between the two ways units are described, coded, measured, or assigned to numerical values or categories reflect intraobserver inconsistencies or noise, the cognitive changes that took place *within* that observer, or that coder's difficulty in interpreting the recording instructions. Stability is the weakest form of reliability and should not be trusted as the sole indicator of the acceptability of content analysis data for inference and analysis. Stability is also known as "intra-observer reliability" or simply "consistency."

Reproducibility is the degree to which a process can be recreated under varying circumstances, at different locations, using different coders. To establish reproducibility, data must be acquired under test-test conditions. An example is when two or more individuals apply the same recording instructions independently on the same set of data. Disagreements between the ways these individuals record the data reflect both intra-observer inconsistencies and interobserver differences in the way a recording instruction is interpreted. Reproducibility is also termed "inter-coder reliability," "intersubjective agreement," or the "consensus" achieved among observers.

Accuracy is the degree to which a process functionally conforms to a known standard, or yields what it is designed to yield. To establish accuracy data are obtained under test-standard conditions, which are met, for example, when the performance of one coder or measuring instrument is compared with what is known to be the correct performance or measure. Differences between the two ways of recording then reflect intraobserver inconsistencies, interobserver disagreements, as well as the systematic deviations from the standard. Accuracy is the strongest reliability test available. It is surpassed in strength only by a measure of validity, which conforms to this design except that the standard must also be known to be true, which is nowhere assumed in reliability assessments.

The differences between the three types of reliability designs are best illustrated in Table 2.

Accuracy measurements have proved useful for testing the performance of coders in the course of training where a standard may have been established previously or by a panel of experts. When the handling of data

Table 2
Types of Reliability

Types of Reliability	Reliability Designs	Errors Assessed	Relative Strengths
Stability	test-retest	intra-observer inconsistencies	weakest
Reproducibility	test-test	intra-observer inconsistencies and inter-observer disagreements	
Accuracy	test-standard	intra-observer inconsistencies, inter-observer disagreements and systematic deviations from a norm	strongest

is merely clerical or computational, the meaning of accuracy is also clear. But in most situations in which observations, message contents, and texts are coded into the categories of a data language, the standards against which the accuracy would be established are rarely available. In content analysis it is therefore largely unrealistic to insist on this strongest reliability criterion. *Data should at least be reproducible,* by independent researchers, at different locations, and at different times, using the same instructions for coding the same set of data.

Note that reproducibility requires that coders are *independent.* Unfortunately, the content analysis literature describes many violations of this requirement. For example, several coders may be asked to discuss each unit of observation and to reach an agreement regarding which descriptive category would be best. However, the practice neither assures reproducibility nor does it reveal its extent. While group processes may suppress individual idiosyncrasies, communication among coders introduces other errors. And, since the process is designed to yield only one score per unit (all individuals function as one observer), the data provide no indication as to reliability. In another example, individual coders work independently and are allowed to communicate with each other only when problems arise. Communication invariably influences coding toward higher agreement and this *lack of independence is likely to make data appear more reliable than they are.*

Another practice, assertedly aimed at bypassing problems of unreliability, is to take averages or majority judgments as true values whenever disagreements among independent observers are encountered. Such data do contain evidence about reproducibility *before* the "undesirable" variance is eliminated. But, since disagreement implies nothing about who is right and who is wrong, neither the mean nor the mode has the wisdom required to improve data reliability by computational means.

An even more deceptive practice is to admit only those data to an investigation on which independent coders achieve perfect agreement. The bias here is two-fold. The procedure does not prevent chance agreements from entering the data (which can be as much as 50% of all units) and it biases the data toward what is easily codable. In any scientific inquiry, data must be chosen to be representative of a phenomenon of interest and not to suit the needs of a particular method.

One design that is mistakenly used to assess reliability in content analysis is the split-half technique. Here a sample of recording units is split into two equal parts. If differences between these two parts are statistically insignificant, data are taken to be reliable; otherwise, they are taken to be unreliable. However, this technique only tests the statistical homogeneity within a sample. It may establish the degree to which that sample is large enough to represent the characteristics of the population from which it is drawn (see sampling). But it does not test whether the units as recorded are individually information bearing, described in a consistent manner, and can therefore be taken to be descriptive of some real phenomenon.

AGREEMENT

Reliability data require that at least two coders independently describe a possibly large set of recording units in terms of a common data language. These terms may be descriptive categories, numerical values of a variable, or complex classification schemes.

Reliability is expressed as a function of the agreement achieved among coders regarding the assignment of units to categories. If agreement among coders is perfect for all units, then reliability is assured. If the agreement among coders is not better than chance, which might be observed when coders do not care to examine the units or instead throw a die to decide on category assignments, reliability is absent. Whether reliability takes the form of stability, reproducibility, or accuracy, it always boils down to measuring the agreement achieved among observers, coders, or judges regarding how they independently process scientific information.

An Example

Let us take a simple example. Suppose someone wishes to study U.S. foreign policy perceptions in the Chinese press and instructs two native speakers to identify the presence or absence of references to such perceptions by marking the document "1" and "0," respectively. Let the data from this test-test situation be as follows:

document	1	2	3	4	5	6	7	8	9	10
Jin	0	1	0	0	0	0	0	0	1	0
Han	0	1	1	0	0	1	0	1	0	0

The data in this table show that Jin and Han agree in 6 out of 10, or 60%, of all assignments of news items to categories. But such a percentage does not mean much. It says nothing about whether this is much or little, or how it compares with chance. To consider such questions, we tabulate the data in the 2 X 10 matrix into a 2 X 2 contingency table of frequencies:

		Han		
		0	1	
Jin	0	5	3	8
	1	1	1	2
		6	4	10

Obtaining a similar table in which agreement is a matter of chance presupposes some knowledge of how references to U.S. foreign policy are distributed in the Chinese press. Although we do not know this distribution, we may estimate it from both coders' experience. With Jin claiming to have identified 2 out of 10 and Han claiming 4 our of 10, they jointly claim that 6 out of the 20, or 30%, of all news items contain U.S. foreign policy references. This is exactly the proportion of "1"s in the 2 × 10 matrix of reliability data. Suppose now, the 14 "0"s and the 6 "1"s are put into an urn from which two individuals draw at random. In drawing 2 "1"s, the first individual will draw a "1" in 6 out of 20 cases. And, after drawing a "1" and thereby removing that "1" from the urn, the second coder would draw a matching "1" in 5 out of 19 cases. The probability of agreeing on the presence of a reference by mere chance is then the product of these two probabilities (6/20)(5/19) = .08. When multiplied by the number of recording units, here 10, the expected frequency is .8 or less than one. The other expected frequencies are obtained by similar logic.

A table in which agreement is perfect has only diagonal entries, here in the 0-0 cell and in the 1-1 cell, with all off-diagonal entries empty. In such a table entries correspond to the estimated population proportions. Thus, the three tables to which a suitable measure of agreement must make reference to are:

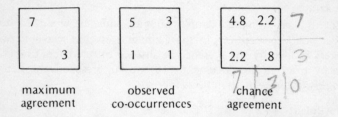

| maximum | observed | chance |
| agreement | co-occurrences | agreement |

The most convincing measure that expresses the amount of agreement in reliability data is the extent to which the table of observed co-occurrences resembles the table with the maximum agreement rather than that in which agreement is merely chance. The following expresses this idea with α being the agreement coefficient wanted:

$$\begin{matrix}\text{observed}\\\text{co-occurrences}\end{matrix} = \alpha \begin{pmatrix}\text{maximum}\\\text{agreement}\end{pmatrix} + (1-\alpha)\begin{pmatrix}\text{chance}\\\text{agreement}\end{pmatrix}.$$

If the table of observed co-occurrences equals the table with the maximum agreement, then α = 1, and if it equals the table in which agreement is chance, then α = 0. With a little bit of algebraic manipulation, this coefficient can be expressed by:

$$\alpha = 1 - \frac{\text{observed disagreement}}{\text{expected disagreement.}}$$

In the 2 × 2 table, disagreements are contained in the 0-1 and 1-0 cells, the observed disagreement is 3 + 1 = 4, and the expected disagreement is 2.2 + 2.2 = 4.4, so that the agreement within the reliability data is:

$$\alpha = 1 - \frac{(3+1)}{(2.2+2.2)} = 0.095.$$

Thus, agreement turns out to be barely 10% above chance. One could say that the two coders' performance is equivalent to having read and correctly identified the reference in only about 10% of all news items and thrown dice to determine the categories for the remaining ones. Perhaps one or both coders did not know Chinese well enough or failed to understand the English instructions. Perhaps the instructions were ambiguous or inappropriate to the data at hand. Whatever the case may be, one would have to reject these data as not reproducible. Under these circumstances, conclusions to which such data would lead are largely misleading or true only by chance. The fact that 60% of all category assignments matched, turned out to have no meaning. This should be considered a warning against using percent agreement as a reliability yardstick. Although it is often reported in the content analysis literature, it is wholly deceptive.

According to the above, the agreement coefficient indicates how the original table (or one that is equivalent in the distribution of agreements) can be reconstructed from the two tables containing maximum and chance agreement, respectively:

from maximum
agreement: .095 $\begin{array}{|cc|}\hline 7 & \\ & 3 \\\hline\end{array}$ = $\begin{array}{|cc|}\hline .7 & \\ & .3 \\\hline\end{array}$

from chance
agreement: (1 - .095) $\begin{array}{|cc|}\hline 4.8 & 2.2 \\ 2.2 & .8 \\\hline\end{array}$ = $\begin{array}{|cc|}\hline 4.3 & 2 \\ 2 & .7 \\\hline\end{array}$

the symmetrical
equivalant of the
    observed table: $\begin{array}{|cc|}\hline 5 & 2 \\ 2 & 1 \\\hline\end{array}$

where it is worth noting that the following tables are all equivalent in the amount of agreement/disagreement they contain:

$\begin{array}{|cc|}\hline 5 & 4 \\ 0 & 1 \\\hline\end{array}$ $\begin{array}{|cc|}\hline 5 & 3 \\ 1 & 1 \\\hline\end{array}$ $\begin{array}{|cc|}\hline 5 & 2 \\ 2 & 1 \\\hline\end{array}$ $\begin{array}{|cc|}\hline 5 & 1 \\ 3 & 1 \\\hline\end{array}$ $\begin{array}{|cc|}\hline 5 & 0 \\ 4 & 1 \\\hline\end{array}$

This example is too simple and the agreement coefficient so defined is too limited. First, the data involve only two coders. One often needs to assess agreements among many observers. And, second, the data concern only dichotomous choices. Content analysis data may contain very many distinctions and complex metrics or scales. With this simple example in mind, we shall now state the agreement coefficient in more general terms.

Canonical Form of Reliability Data

Instead of two, we now consider m coders; and instead of the dichotomous distinction, we now consider a system of categories or values of which k_{ij} is assigned to the ith recording unit by the jth judge, observer, or coder. Reliability data then assume the form of an m X r matrix which will be called their *canonical form*:

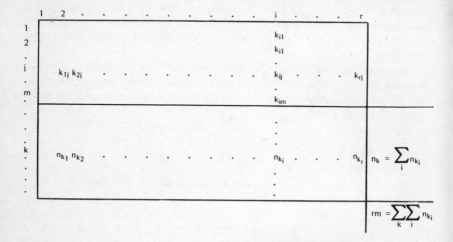

Below this matrix is an account of the frequencies n_{ki} with which the category k occurs in column i and the frequencies n_k of category k in the table as a whole.

Differences and Disagreements

To evaluate any disagreement within this table, it is important to know how different two categories or values are. This depends on the nature of the metric involved. The idea is fairly simple. When the categories of a variable are unordered, like names, places of birth, or occupations, then it does not matter which two categories are confused. Any mismatch is as good or as bad as any other mismatch. On the other hand, if the categories are ordered as would by the case with time, lengths, or attitude strength, it may make a great deal of difference how far apart mismatching values are. The difference between 1 and 20 is surely greater than the difference between 1 and 2 whether one considers miles, dollars, or age. As has been discussed under data languages, there are many kinds of metrics. Age, for example, is a ratio scale. Thus, guessing accurately within one year the age of an 80-year-old person is a good performance but being within a year of guessing the age of a baby is not. In ratio scales, distances depend on how far away from the zero point they occur. The following definitions take account of nominal scales, ordinal scales, interval scales, and ratio scales.

With b and c as two categories or values of a variable, differences between them are as follows:

for *nominal scales* or unordered variables:

$$d_{bc} = \begin{cases} 0 & \text{iff } b=c \\ \\ 1 & \text{iff } b \neq c \end{cases}$$

for *ordinal scales*:

$$d_{bc} = (\sum_{k>b} \frac{n_k}{rm} - \sum_{k<b} \frac{n_k}{rm} + \sum_{k<c} \frac{n_k}{rm} - \sum_{k>c} \frac{n_k}{rm})^2$$

for *interval scales*:

$$d_{bc} = (b-c)^2$$

for *ratio scales*:

$$d_{bc} = (\frac{b-c}{b+c})^2$$

Other differences are possible but will not be presented here.

Now, each column of the m $\times$ r matrix of reliability data in canonical form contains m entries, which are the categories or values associated with one unit. Within each column it is possible to form $m(m-1)$ pairs with no attention paid to order. With nb_i as the number of categories b in column i and n_{c_i} as the number of categories c in column i, the *number of b-c pairs in column i* is $nb_i \, n_{c_i}$ when $b \neq c$ and $nb_i(n_{c_i}-1)$ when b = c. It sums, of course, to:

$$m(m-1) = \sum_b \sum_c n_{b_i}(n_{c_i} - \Delta_{bc}) \quad \text{where} \quad \Delta_{bc} = \begin{cases} 0 & \text{iff } b \neq c \\ \\ 1 & \text{iff } b=c \end{cases}$$

where the Kronecker Δ assures that entries are not compared with themselves. Since there are r columns, the *observed disagreement* may now be expressed as the average within column (unit) difference:

$$D_o = \frac{1}{r} \sum_i \sum_b \sum_c \frac{n_{b_i} \, n_{c_i}}{m(m-1)} d_{bc}.$$

By dropping reference to columns, the *number of possible b-c pairs in the whole matrix* is $n_b n_c$ which sums to:

$$rm(rm-1) = \sum_b \sum_c (\sum_i n_{b_i} (\sum_i n_{c_i} - \Delta_{bc}) = \sum_b \sum_c n_b (n_c - \Delta_{bc}).$$

And the *expected disagreement* is again expressed as an average difference but now within all possible pairs in the whole matrix:

$$D_e = \sum_b \sum_c \frac{n_b \, n_c}{rm(rm-1)} d_{bc}.$$

Agreement Coefficient for Canonical Data

In terms of the reliability data in canonical form, the *agreement coefficient* is defined by:

$$\alpha = 1 - \frac{D_o}{D_c}$$

$$= 1 - \frac{\dfrac{1}{r}\sum\limits_i \sum\limits_b \sum\limits_c \dfrac{n_{b_i} n_{c_i}}{m(m-1)} d_{bc}}{\sum\limits_b \sum\limits_c \dfrac{n_b n_c}{rm(rm-1)} d_{bc}}$$

$$= 1 - \frac{rm-1}{m-1} \cdot \frac{\sum\limits_i \sum\limits_b \sum\limits_{c>b} n_{b_i} n_{c_i} d_{bc}}{\sum\limits_b \sum\limits_{c>b} n_b n_c d_{bc}}$$

The first expression presents the general idea. It makes transparent that whenever no disagreement is encountered in the data, the numerator is zero and the agreement coefficient is one, indicating that reliability is perfect. When the observed disagreement equals what would be expected by chance, the agreement coefficient is zero, indicating that reliability is absent.

In the second expression the observed and expected disagreements are inserted as average differences. The third expression gives a more convenient computational formula.

It is important to note that when the number of coders is exactly two, the categories of the variables are unordered (nominal scale), and the sample size is very large, then our agreement coefficient equals Scott's (1955) pi:

$$pi = \frac{\% \text{ of observed matches} - \% \text{ of expected matches}}{100 - \% \text{ of expected matches}}$$

$$= 1 - \frac{100 - \% \text{ of observed matches}}{100 - \% \text{ of expected matches}}.$$

Whereby, unlike in Cohen's (1960) kappa, the percentage of expected matches is computed from the proportion with which a category is used, both coders taken together. The expression (100 - % of matches) is one of disagreement and shows pi's conformity to our form. Our coefficient corrects for small sample sizes. For two coders and interval scale judgments, our coefficient also equals the intraclass correlation coefficient. For more than two coders it formalizes a method suggested by Spiegelman et al. (1953a), who involved subjective rank orderings of patterns of disagreement among individuals making nominal scale category assignments. Our coefficient is thus a generalization to many coders, many kinds of orders (metric) in data, and for any sample size. It provides a uniform measure that is comparable across numerous situations.

A hypothetical example of reliability data obtained by three coders will illustrate the computation:

unit i:	1	2	3	4	5	6	7	8	9		
coder: A	1	1	2	4	1	2	1	3	2		
B	1	2	2	4	4	2	2	3	2		
C	1	2	2	4	4	2	3	3	2		
$n_{1i} =$	3	1			1		1			$n_1 = 6$	
$n_{2i} =$		2	3			3	1		3	$n_2 = 12$	
$n_{3i} =$							1	3		$n_3 = 4$	
$n_{4i} =$				3	2					$n_4 = 5$	

For units with perfect agreement, all differences within columns are zero. Hence, units 1, 3, 4, 6, 8, and 9 do not contribute to the observed disagreement. Assuming the values in this variable to be unordered (nominal scale), the difference between nonmatching pairs is 1 and is 0 otherwise. The value of the numerator of the coefficient in the computational form is:

$$\sum_i \sum_b \sum_{c>b} n_{bi} n_{ci} d_{bc} = n_{12} n_{22} + n_{15} n_{45} + n_{17} n_{27} + n_{17} n_{37} + n_{27} n_{37}$$
$$= 1\cdot2 + 1\cdot2 + 1\cdot1 + 1\cdot1 + 1\cdot1$$
$$= 7$$

and the value of the denominator in the computational form is:

$$\sum_b \sum_{c>b} n_b n_c d_{bc} = n_1 n_2 + n_1 n_3 + n_1 n_4 + n_2 n_3 + n_2 n_4 + n_3 n_4$$
$$= 6\cdot12 + 6\cdot4 + 6\cdot5 + 12\cdot4 + 12\cdot5 + 4\cdot5$$
$$= 254$$

with r = 9 units and m = 3 coders, the coefficient measures:

$$\alpha = 1 - \frac{9\cdot3-1}{3-1}\ \frac{7}{254} = .642.$$

This agreement would indicate that in about 65% of the cases, the observed co-occurrences are explainable by the pattern of perfect agreement rather than by what would be expected by chance, or, for short, observed co-occurrences are 65% above chance.

In case this example is still bewildering, consider the example from the beginning of this section, involving dichotomous choices, 0 or 1, by m = 2 coders on r = 10 units. The difference between mismatching categories is again $d_{01} = d_{10} = 1$ and $d_{00} = d_{11} = 0$. In each column there either is or is not a mismatch, so that the observed disagreement simply expresses the number of mismatches as the proportion of the total number of pairs within columns:

$$D_o = \frac{1}{r} \sum_i \sum_b \sum_c \frac{n_{b_i} n_{c_i}}{m(m-1)} d_{bc} = \frac{\text{number of mismatching units}}{r}$$

and the expected disagreement is similarly simplifiable, in this case:

$$D_e = \sum_b \sum_c \frac{n_b n_c}{rm(rm-1)} d_{bc} = \frac{n_0 n_1}{r(2r-1)}$$

so that the agreement coefficient for bivariate agreement ($m = 2$ coders only) on dichotomous choices (0 or 1) reduces to:

$$\alpha = 1 - \frac{D_o}{D_e} = 1 - \frac{(2r-1) \text{ number of mismatching units}}{n_0 n_1}$$

With 4 mismatching units in the example, the value of the coefficient becomes:

$$\alpha = 1 - \frac{(2 \cdot 10 - 1)4}{14 \cdot 6} = .095$$

which corresponds to what had been obtained before.

Reliability Data in Coincidence Matrix Form

It is often conceptually more convenient to examine reliability data not in their canonical form, but rather in the form of a symmetrical table of co-occurrences, called the *coincidence matrix*. Such a matrix should not be confused with a contingency matrix, which is not symmetrical and is applicable to only two coders. Entered in a coincidence matrix are the *number of pairs*, x_{bc}, of values b and c within all units. It can be constructed from the canonical form by

$$x_{bc} = \sum_i n_{b_i} (n_{c_i} - \Delta_{bc}) \text{ where again } \Delta_{bc} = \begin{cases} 0 \text{ iff } b \neq c \\ 1 \text{ iff } b = c \end{cases}$$

The table has the following form, with marginals obtained by summing as indicated:

$$x_{.c} = \sum_b x_{bc} = n_c (m-1)$$

$$x_{..} = \sum_b \sum_c x_{bc} = rm (m-1)$$

In such a matrix the matching pairs occupy the diagonal entries and the nonmatching pairs are distributed around this diagonal. Since the differences between matching values are always zero, the observed disagreement is the average difference in pairs in the off-diagonal entries. The expected disagreement computes such an average under the assumption of statistical independence ($p_{bc} = p_b p_c$).

Agreement Coefficient for Matrix Forms

In terms of this coincidence matrix representation of reliability data, the *agreement coefficient* then becomes somewhat easier:

$$\alpha = 1 - \frac{D_o}{D_c}$$

$$= 1 - \frac{\sum_b \sum_c \frac{x_{bc}}{x_{..}} d_{bc}}{\sum_b \sum_c \frac{x_b \cdot x_{.c}}{x_{..}(x_{..} - m + 1)} d_{bc}}$$

$$= 1 - \frac{rm-1}{rm} \frac{\sum_b \sum_c \frac{x_{bc}}{x_{..}} d_{bc}}{\sum_b \sum_c \frac{x_b \cdot x_{.c}}{x_{..} \cdot x_{..}} d_{bc}}$$

$$= 1 - (x_{..} - m + 1) \frac{\sum_b \sum_{c>b} x_{bc} d_{bc}}{\sum_b \sum_{c>b} x_b \cdot x_{.c} d_{bc}}$$

The first expression is again the general form into which the observed and expected disagreement is entered to obtain the second expression. The third expression reveals how the agreement coefficient is corrected for small sample sizes. If either the number of coders, m, or the number of units, r, becomes very large, the factor $(rm - 1)/rm$ approaches 1 and may be ignored. Small sample sizes would have the effect of deflating the coefficient which is hereby corrected. With this correction factor separated, the remainder can be seen as expressing the observed differences as they are found in the matrix and the expected differences as they would appear under the assumption of statistical independence. The fourth expression gives a convenient computational formula.

In the three coder, nine unit example, the coincidence matrix of observed co-occurrences would be this:

	1	2	3	4	
1	6	3	1	2	12
2	3	20	1		24
3	1	1	6		8
4	2			8	10
	12	24	8	10	54

categories:

Note that this table is symmetrical. It does not recognize the individual contributions of the coders and its margins are inflated by a factor of $(m-1)$, the number of degrees of freedom in each column (unit).

The observed number of mismatching pairs in one off-diagonal triangle is

$$\sum_b \sum_{c>b} x_{bc} = 3 + 1 + 2 + 1 = 7$$

and the observed disagreements expressed as an average over all possible pairs $x_{..}$ is

$$D_o = \sum_b \sum_c \frac{x_{bc}}{x_{..}} d_{bc} = \frac{3+1+2+3+1+1+1+2}{54} = \frac{14}{54} = .259.$$

The products of the marginal entries in one off-diagonal triangle which amounts to $x_{..}$ times the number of expected mismatching pairs is:

$$\sum_b \sum_{c>b} x_{b.} x_{.c} = 12 \cdot 24 + 12 \cdot 8 + 12 \cdot 10 + 24 \cdot 8 + 24 \cdot 10 + 8 \cdot 10 = 1016$$

which is the sum over the entries in the lower off-diagonal triangle of the following matrix of $(x_{..} - m + 1) = 52$ times the expected frequencies:

12·10	24·12	8·12	10·12	12·52
12·24	24·22	8·24	10·24	24·52
12·8	24·8	8·6	10·8	8·52
12·10	24·10	8·10	10·8	12·52
12·52	24·52	8·52	10·52	54·52

and the expected disagreement is:

$$D_c = \sum_b \sum_c \frac{x_{b.} x_{.c}}{x_{..}(x_{..} - m+1)} d_{bc} = \frac{12\ 24+12\ 8+12\ 10+24\ 12+\ldots}{54\ (54-3+1)} = \frac{2032}{54 \cdot 52} = .724$$

so that the agreement coefficient, computed both ways, becomes:

$$\alpha = 1 - \frac{D_o}{D_c} = 1 - \frac{.259}{.724} = .642$$

$$\alpha = 1 - (x_{..} - m+1) \frac{\displaystyle\sum_b \sum_{c>b} x_{bc}\, x_{bc}}{\displaystyle\sum_b \sum_{c>b} x_{b.}\, x_{.c}\, d_{bc}} = 1 - (54-3+1) \frac{7}{1016} = .642$$

Coincidence matrices not only summarize reliability data for an easier identification of coding errors but they also reveal the meaning of the differences between categories and values more clearly. Let us consider the differences as a weight assigned to each cell of a coincidence matrix, say, with categories 0 through 7 (see page 144).

In the nominal case all off-diagonal entries are equally different and the two disagreement measures, therefore, simply enumerate the observed and expected occurrences in these cells. This has been illustrated in the examples above. Interval differences depend on how far apart the categories are and, inasmuch as interval scales do not recognize any one reference point, it does not matter between which values a difference is observed or expected. The lines of equal difference are thus parallel to the diagonal. Ratio distances, on the other hand, weigh value-pairs heavier, the closer they are to the absolute zero point. One could say that it is here the angular deviation from the diagonal that indicates the magnitude of the difference between two values. Accordingly, the difference between nothing and something is as great as between nothing and a lot, but being cheated out of a dollar means a lot more for someone who only has two than for a millionaire. This is what the ratio difference explicates. The difference between the ranks in ordinal scales is more difficult to depict because it does not depend on the numerical value of their categories, but rather on how many ranks are used between them. Suppose 10 units are assigned the following ranks: 1, 2, 3, 3, 4, 4, 4, 4, 5, 10. Intuitively the difference between 1 and 3 should be much smaller than that between 3 and 5 because the latter case recognizes many more ranks in between. For the same reason, the difference between 1 and 2 should be the same as between 5 and 10. Even though their numerical difference is greater, the number of intermediate ranks is the same. Applying the definition for ordinal differences to the frequencies just given yields distances which are twice the number of ranks between the center of each class.

	1	2	3	4	5	10	
1	0	2	5	11	15	18	$n_1 = 1$
2	2	0	3	9	14	16	$n_2 = 1$
3	5	3	0	6	11	13	$n_3 = 2$
4	11	9	6	0	5	7	$n_4 = 4$
5	16	14	11	5	0	2	$n_5 = 1$
10	18	16	13	7	2	0	$n_{10} = 1$

ordinal d_{bc} (exemplified)

Only if the frequencies of ranks are uniformly distributed does the ordinal difference equal the interval difference in effect.

Suppose the values in the example in fact constituted an interval scale, and differences (b–c) were consequently meaningful. Then the coefficient would have to weigh a 1–3 confusion 4 times and a 1–4 confusion 9 times

nominal d_{bc}

	0	1	2	3	4	5	6	7
0	0	1	1	1	1	1	1	1
1	1	0	1	1	1	1	1	1
2	1	1	0	1	1	1	1	1
3	1	1	1	0	1	1	1	1
4	1	1	1	1	0	1	1	1
5	1	1	1	1	1	0	1	1
6	1	1	1	1	1	1	0	1
7	1	1	1	1	1	1	1	0

interval d_{bc}

	0	1	2	3	4	5	6	7
0	0	1	4	9	16	25	36	49
1	1	0	1	4	9	16	25	36
2	4	1	0	1	4	9	16	25
3	9	4	1	0	1	4	9	16
4	16	9	4	1	0	1	4	9
5	25	16	9	4	1	0	1	4
6	36	25	16	9	4	1	0	1
7	49	36	25	16	9	4	1	0

ratio d_{bc}

	0	1	2	3	4	5	6	7
0	0	1	1	1	1	1	1	1
1	1	0	$\frac{1}{3}$	$\frac{2}{4}$	$\frac{3}{5}$	$\frac{4}{6}$	$\frac{5}{7}$	$\frac{6}{8}$
2	1	$\frac{1}{3}$	0	$\frac{1}{5}$	$\frac{2}{6}$	$\frac{3}{7}$	$\frac{4}{8}$	$\frac{5}{9}$
3	1	$\frac{2}{4}$	$\frac{1}{5}$	0	$\frac{1}{7}$	$\frac{2}{8}$	$\frac{3}{9}$	$\frac{4}{10}$
4	1	$\frac{3}{5}$	$\frac{2}{6}$	$\frac{1}{7}$	0	$\frac{1}{9}$	$\frac{2}{10}$	$\frac{3}{11}$
5	1	$\frac{4}{6}$	$\frac{3}{7}$	$\frac{2}{8}$	$\frac{1}{9}$	0	$\frac{1}{11}$	$\frac{2}{12}$
6	1	$\frac{5}{7}$	$\frac{4}{8}$	$\frac{3}{9}$	$\frac{2}{10}$	$\frac{1}{11}$	0	$\frac{1}{13}$
7	1	$\frac{6}{8}$	$\frac{5}{9}$	$\frac{4}{10}$	$\frac{3}{11}$	$\frac{2}{12}$	$\frac{1}{13}$	0

that of a 1-2 confusion. Assuming interval differences rather than the nominal ones assumed earlier,

$$\alpha = 1 - \frac{\displaystyle\sum_{b}\sum_{c>b} \frac{x_{bc}}{x_{..}} d_{bc}}{\displaystyle\sum_{b}\sum_{c>b} \frac{x_{b.}\,.\,x_{.c}}{x_{..}(x_{..}-m+1)} d_{bc}} = 1 - \frac{\dfrac{3\cdot1^2+1\cdot2^2+2\cdot3^2+1\cdot1^2+\cdots}{54}}{\dfrac{12\cdot24\cdot1^2+12\cdot8\cdot2^2+12\cdot10\cdot3^2+\cdots}{54(54-3+1)}} = .547.$$

If the mismatches appeared closer to the diagonal, as would be expected in a "true" interval scale, then the interval coefficient would exceed the coefficient with nominal scale assumptions in value. In this case the 1-4 mismatch reduces the interval coefficient below the previously obtained value. An inspection of the matrix suggests that ratio scale assumptions would be worse and indeed the ratio coefficient amounts to .483.

Coincidence matrices between just two observers are again much more easily interpretable. Such matrices may be obtained by simply adding the contingency matrix between two observers to their transpose, for example, from the dichotomous example:

	Han			Jin				
Jin	5	3	+ Han	5	1	=	10	4
	1	1		3	1		4	2

in which the marginal sums equal the total number of occurrences of a category $x_{b.} = n_b$. This simplifies the conceptualization and computation of the coefficient. When the number of categories is two in addition (one dichotomous distinction between 0 and 1), then the coefficient takes its simplest computational form:

$$\alpha = 1 - (x_{..} - 1)\frac{x_{01}}{x_{0.}\,x_{.1}}.$$

A common mistake against which one must give warning here is to confuse agreement with association. The following contingency table shows high association and no agreement.

	1	2	3
1			10
2	10		
3		10	

The practice of using correlation coefficients for reliability assessments is particularly misleading. When all data fall along a line $X = aY + b$, correlation is perfect but agreement requires $X = Y$ which is not what correlation coefficients measure. Association measures and correlation coefficients fail to register systematic coding errors and are therefore inadequate as measures of reliability.

DATA RELIABILITY AND STANDARDS

The ultimate aim of testing reliability is to establish whether data obtained in the course of research can provide a trustworthy basis for drawing inferences, making recommendations, supporting decisions, or accepting something as fact. In this ultimate aim, reliability is an attribute of all relevant distinctions within the data and is called data reliability. Data reliability is thus contrasted with several other characteristics of a process whose reliability may be assessed mainly for diagnostic purposes.

It is important to recognize that data reliability is an attribute of the data, not of the reality of interest. The distinction is important for sampling considerations. Because reliability designs call for a duplication of coding and data processing efforts, generating suitable reliability data at least doubles the costs of generating the data on which research findings are to be based. Usually, therefore, not all, but rather a sample of, data are subjected to a reliability test. This subsample need not be representative of the population characteristics (which serve as a basis for sampling data for analysis), but rather *must be representative of all distinctions made* within the sample of data at hand. Sampling from a population for the purpose of analysis and the subsampling from a sample of data for the purpose of testing reliability is different. The latter is served best by a stratified sampling design that assumes that all categories of analysis, all decisions specified by various forms of instructions, are indeed represented in the reliability data regardless of how frequently they may occur in the actual data.

Thus, in testing the reliability of data, one question that needs to be answered is whether reliability data are sufficiently representative of the distinctions within the data to be analyzed. The other is how high the level of agreement must be in order for the data to be judged sufficiently reliable to warrant analysis. This is now addressed.

To begin with, in a content analysis involving many variables, data reliability cannot be a single figure. There are good reasons why the foregoing defined agreement only for a single variable. Although one could compute an average agreement over all variables of a study, this would be a deceptive figure because it would assume that any reliable variable could compensate for any unreliable one. This is not possible, particularly when the variables are logically distinct and free of conceptual redundancy which is what many data languages in content analysis aim at. If a summary account is needed at all, *the lowest agreement measure in the set is the best indicator of the reliability of the data.* Any variable could become the bottleneck for the trustworthiness of the data as a whole.

Having argued the need to take the smallest agreement as a measure of the reliability of multivariate data, the question still remains how high the level of agreement must be. Should one require data reliability to be at least .95, .90, or .80? Although every content analyst is faced with such a question, there is no set answer.

To shed light on how different levels of reliability could be interpreted, a Dutch colleague of mine, Marten Brouwer, once set up a set of categories, gave them complicated Dutch names without resemblance to English words, and asked coders to describe television characters in their terms. Although such words connoted at best some vague morphophonemical-personality associations, the agreement measured was already .44. From the categories thus recorded, nobody in his right mind can justify making statements about what these coders had in fact observed. In several content analyses I found that correlations among variables with agreements of less than .7 tend to be statistically insignificant. This is of course quite obvious for they are then excessively polluted by noise. In a study by Brouwer et al. (1969) we adopted the policy of reporting on variables only if their reliability was above .8 and admitted variables with reliability between .67 and .8 only for drawing highly tentative and cautious conclusions. These standards have been continued in work on cultural indicators (Gerbner et al., 1979) and might serve as a guideline elsewhere.

Where possible, *standards for data reliability* should not be adopted *ad hoc*. They *must be related to the validity requirements imposed upon research results, specifically to the costs of drawing wrong conclusions.* If it were a matter of life and death, even a content analyst should not accept a standard for data reliability that would lead to an error in the result with a probability of, say, less than that of being killed in a car accident (which is what people seem to be willing to live with). If it is an exploratory study without serious consequences, that level may be relaxed considerably, but it should not be so low that the findings can no longer be taken seriously.

To establish a meaningful level of reliability, the content analyst will have to determine how the unreliabilities encountered in the data will affect his findings. Some content analyses are very robust in the sense that unreliabilities become hardly noticeable in the result. In other situations small numbers of errors may make a great deal of difference and can turn an affirmative answer into its opposite. To test the sensitivity of a content analysis to unreliabilities in data, one has to analyze and process not just one set of data but as many sets as can be obtained by permutation of the categories between which disagreement was encountered. *Unreliabilities in the data define a distribution of possible results* among which the "true" finding is likely to occur. If this distribution is wider than can be tolerated, data reliability is too low.

To demonstrate what is meant, suppose it is important to establish whether two variables are associated. Suppose further that both are recorded by two independent coders:

units:		1	2	3	4	5	6	7	8	9
variable X	coder A	1	2	3	1	2	3	1	2	3
	coder B	1	2	3	2	3	1	1	2	3
variable Y	coder A	b	c	a	a	b	c	a	b	c
	coder B	a	b	c	a	b	c	a	b	c

For both variables the reliability is .628. Since it is impossible to know whether and when coder 1 or coder 2 is to be trusted, by merely choosing for each unit either from the first or from the second column, a whole range of patterns of possible co-occurrences can be constructed from these data:

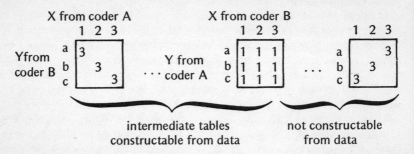

intermediate tables
constructable from data

not constructable
from data

By not checking the effects of the error variance unreliability introduces, any one of these patterns could have been taken as the result. Since, by this reasoning, about half of the possible co-occurrences cannot be constructed from the data, this suggests that associations are not likely to be negative. But actually, nothing can be said about whether a positive association exists or about its extent. Only a higher level of agreement between coders will narrow the wide distribution of possible patterns. With the aim of establishing associations, .628 would not be an acceptable level of agreement.

A mistake commonly found in the content analysis literature is to test the null hypothesis on reliability data and accept data as reliable if this hypothesis turns out not to be tenable. This is a serious error. In testing data reliability, one wants to be sure that errors are within tolerable limits or, equivalently, that the achieved level of agreement deviates only minimally from perfect correspondence. An agreement that merely deviates from chance, however significant this deviation may be, offers no assurances that data can be trusted. Since it does not seem possible to test the statistical significance of the deviation from perfect agreement, what is required is, first, that all agreements be higher than required for a particular analysis. Second, if they are higher, then one needs to test the hypothesis that they could have been obtained from a population of reliability data with agreement less than that required. If this hypothesis fails, data are indeed reliable above what is expected.

DIAGNOSTIC DEVICES

While developing a content analysis instrument and much before final data reliability is tested, many preliminary and detailed reliability tests may be conducted to identify sources of unreliability in the research design. The diagnosis of problems in the research design may lead to modifications of the categories of the analysis, changes in instructions to coders, and even decisions on whom to involve in the process until all bottlenecks are removed. It is quite usual that two or three diagnostic reliability tests are conducted before the researcher feels confident to proceed with testing data reliability and generating the remainder of the data for analysis.

In the following we distinguish and illustrate four diagnostic devices:

- unit reliability
- individual reliability
- single-category reliability
- conditional reliability.

The first locates problems of unreliability in the source material, the second in the coders employed, and the last two in the recording instructions.

Unit Reliability

Unit reliability locates the source of unreliability in the units that are recorded. Some units are more difficult to describe than others and those that cause difficulties in coding need to be examined more carefully to find ways of adjusting the recording instructions to the properties that are found in the data. In the example given earlier:

	units:	1	2	3	4	5	6	7	8	9
	A	1	1	2	4	1	2	1	3	2
coder:	B	1	2	2	4	4	2	2	3	2
	C	1	2	2	4	4	2	3	3	2

No mismatches are found in units 1, 3, 4, 6, 8, and 9. For these units observed disagreement is 0 and their reliability becomes 1. In units 2 and 5, 2 out of 6 possible pairs mismatch, the observed disagreement is .333 in each of these units which yields a reliability of .539 for these units. In unit 7 all pairs mismatch, observed disagreement is 1, and its reliability becomes −.382 which is less than chance.

As a diagnostic device, unit reliability must not be used as a criterion for inclusion or exclusion of particular units in an analysis. This has been argued above. It is permissible, however, to use it as a criterion for restricting the use of a recording instruction to a *class* of recording units that is defined by criteria other than reliability. For example, in a study of television programming, we found that cartoons were the most unreliable units, which was substantiated after computing the reliability for cartoons and for other programs separately. It turned out that our recording instrument was simply unsuited for the categorization of cartoon characters. Faced with the option of either generalizing the instruction to include these characters or limiting the study, we decided on the latter. It limited the generalizations we could make but did not bias the findings toward easily codable units.

Individual Reliability

Individual reliability measures the extent to which an individual is the source of unreliable data. Quite often, some coders are more careful than others, work more consistently, or understand the instructions and the source language better than others do. Where reliability matters, only the most capable individuals can be employed. Individual reliability provides a means of determining how reliable each observer, coder, or judge is.

Individual reliability data can be obtained in two situations. Under test-standard conditions, individual reliability becomes an accuracy measure, which is what one would like individual reliability to be. Only in rare cases, such as the aforementioned training situation, do such conditions exist. Under test-test conditions, the performance of one individual must be compared with the remaining individuals taken as a group. It thus requires more than two, preferably many, coders. The performance of the group against which the performance of one individual is compared then becomes the standard, with individual reliability assessing how close that individual is to the center of the group.

In the reliability data of the example, coder A, with his apparent preference for category 1, is clearly deviant. To construct the coincidence matrix of co-occurrences involving only A, we substract from the coincidence matrix of all pairs of co-occurrences those between B and C which do not contribute to the comparison:

$$
\begin{array}{ccc}
\text{A:B:C} & \text{B:C} & \text{A:B+C} \\[6pt]
\begin{array}{cccc}
6 & 3 & 1 & 2 \\
3 & 20 & 1 & \\
1 & 1 & 6 & \\
2 & & & 8
\end{array}
&
-\quad
\begin{array}{cccc}
2 & & & \\
& 8 & 1 & \\
& 1 & 4 & \\
& & & 4
\end{array}
\quad =
&
\begin{array}{cccc}
4 & 3 & 1 & 2 \\
3 & 12 & & \\
1 & & 4 & \\
2 & & & 4
\end{array}
\end{array}
$$

$$D_o = \frac{14}{54} = .259 \qquad D_o = \frac{2}{18} = .111 \qquad D_o = \frac{12}{38} = .316$$

$$D_e = \frac{2032}{2808} = .724 \qquad D_e = .724 \qquad D_e = .724$$

$$\alpha = .642 \qquad\qquad \alpha = .846 \qquad\qquad \alpha = .564$$

For all three coders there are 14 mismatching out of 54 possible pairs, for coders B and C it is 2/18, whereas for A and B+C it is 12/38. The expected disagreement for all three coders was previously computed to be .724 and must be taken here as the safest estimate for the chance situation in all three cases. The three coefficients are listed above. The conclusion this analysis supports is that coder A is indeed unreliable. If the data he contributes to a study could be removed, checked, or recoded by the other two coders, data reliability would improve from .642 to .846.

Single-Category Reliability

Single-category reliability assesses the extent to which one category is confused with the remainder of a set of categories. Confusions of this kind are usually the result of an ambiguous definition or caused by the coder's inability to understand the meaning of that value or category. Of all the distinctions within a variable, single-category reliability concerns only those involving the one variable in question. In the coincidence matrix for our example, one can see that most disagreements involve category 1. To eliminate distinctions between the remaining categories, a 2 X 2 coincidence matrix is constructed by summing the entries in this matrix so that only the distinction between one category and all others is preserved. The following depicts this for categories 1 and 2 separately:

	1	2	3	4
1	6	3	1	2
2	3	20	1	
3	1	1	6	
4	2			8

$\alpha = .642$

	1 other	
1	6	6
other	6	36

$$D_o = \frac{12}{54} = .222$$

$$D_e = \frac{1008}{2808} = .358$$

$\alpha = .381$

	2 other	
2	20	4
other	4	20

$$D_o = \frac{8}{54} = .148$$

$$D_e = \frac{1152}{2808} = .256$$

$\alpha = .711$

The coefficients given above quantify what is intuitively obvious: Category 1 is ill-defined and unreliable whereas category 2 has more definition.

Single-category reliability presupposes unordered variables. When the reliability of a single category is low, the researcher has two options. He may either redefine the unreliable category, making the distinction between it and the others clearer and then perform another reliability test to see whether the modification was indeed effective. Or, he may decide not to use the distinction in the subsequent analysis and focus instead on the remaining categories. He will then have to test reliability conditionally.

Conditional Reliability

Conditional reliability assesses the reliability of a subset of categories within a variable. It is needed when some categories are so unreliable that no conclusions can be based on them while the remaining categories may still be salvageable. Such situations are quite common in content analysis. For example, it tends to be much harder to obtain agreement on whether or not a particular characteristic is present in some unit than on how it is classified after that characteristic is judged present. This is true particularly when identifying personality traits, themes, moods, emotional expressions, and so on. Suppose the categories in our example could be construed as the result of two decisions, the outcome of the first being a condition for the second to apply. Conditional reliability then removes or discounts the effect of the first decision.

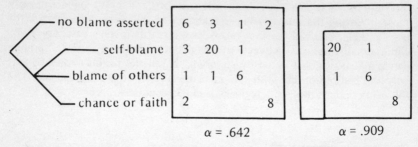

$\alpha = .642$ $\alpha = .909$

To obtain conditional reliabilities, observed and expected disagreements are averaged only within the submatrix that contains the relevant distinctions, whereby the probabilities for the expected disagreement take account of all distinctions made. In the example, there are 36 agreements on categories other than the 1 of which two are observed to mismatch within 2, 3, and 4, so that the observed disagreement is 2/36. How the expected disagreement comes about may be seen in the following matrices: (a) the expected frequencies for the whole matrix, which were used above to compute data reliability and so on; (b) the expected frequencies for the first decision in which the expected agreement on categories other than 1 amounts to 32.31 entries; (c) the expected probabilities in the submatrix conditional on the agreement on categories other than 1. To obtain these probabilities, expected frequencies in the cells of the submatrix are divided by the total frequency in this submatrix. The contributions of the cells in this submatrix to the expected disagreement are contained in its off-diagonal entries and sum to 64/105. The conditional reliability is .909.

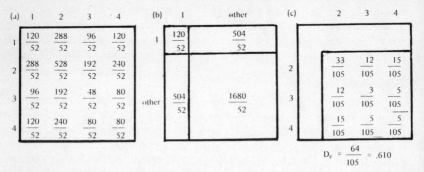

Single-category reliability and conditional reliability may be seen as two complementary parts of what we have elsewhere (Krippendorff, 1971) termed decision reliability. It allows the analyst to examine the reliability of each decision in a complex decision tree by removing the effects of antecedent decisions in the manner described as conditional reliability and by ignoring the disagreements of subsequent decisions as exemplified in single-category reliability. An example of such a decision tree is depicted as Figure 21. To evaluate the reliability of the decision on value types, one

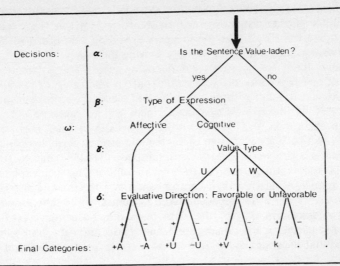

FIGURE 21: Decisions in a Branching Process Which Are Separately Evaluable for Reliability

eliminates, by summing, the distinctions introduced by all subsequent decisions and considers the outcome of the preceding decision as the condition for making value type judgments.

Improvement of Reliability

Conditional reliability is one device to determine which parts of a variable, whose reliability as a whole is unacceptably low, might be worth keeping in the final analysis. There are a few others, all of which boil down to testing whether some transformation of the data will improve reliability.

Testing the effects of *lumping categories* is one such practice. For example, in the following coincidence matrix, categories 2 and 4 appear confused. The two coders cannot reliably distinguish between them. If the researcher can afford loosing the distinction and lump the two categories into one, this modified variable may well become reliable enough to be admitted into the analysis.

	1	2	3	4	5
1	10				
2		6	1	6	
3		1	8		
4		6		6	
5					12

$\alpha = .692$

	1	2&4	3	5
1	10			
2&4		24	1	
3		1	8	
5				12

$\alpha = .950$

Needless to say, lumping presupposes nominal scale assumptions. But deciding on rougher distinctions within an ordered variable (e.g., changing from coding the age of a person in years to coding it in broad social age categories) has the same effect while preserving the order.

Finally, there are occasions when coding errors are systematic. For example, one coder may place a certain concept into category X while the other consistently and without bad intention places the same concept into category Y. If this error is systematic there will be more X-Y or Y-X co-occurrences than X-X or Y-Y co-occurrences. Agreement may become negative (which is always a sign of systematic errors). Such errors may be identified in a *contingency matrix* and subsequently eliminated by finding an explanation for the error. (When erros are random, no such explanation can be found.) Similarly, when coding concepts into semantic differential scales from +3 to -3, some coders avoid extremes, while others avoid the center. A transformation of the data from one coder may rectify the systematic nature of the disagreement and render the data more reliable, provided that the systematic nature of these errors is well-understood.

13

VALIDITY

All scientific findings are intended to be valid in the sense of representing real phenomena. This chapter develops a typology of the kinds of validity that are important to content analysis and shows what is needed to assess the kinds of validity quantitatively.

"Validity" designates that quality of research results which leads one to accept them as indisputable facts. Closest relatives of the term are "empirical truth," "predictive accuracy," and "consistency with established knowledge." We speak of a measuring instrument as being valid if it measures what it is designed to measure, and we consider a content analysis valid to the extent its inferences are upheld in the face of independently obtained evidence.

The importance of validation lies in the assurance it provides that research findings have to be taken seriously in constructing scientific theories or in making decisions on practical issues. Such assurances are particularly desirable when content analysis results or theories arising from them are intended to have policy implications, when they are meant to aid government and industry, when they are proposed as evidence in court, or when they affect individual human beings. In such situations wrong conclusions may have costly consequences. Validation may be said to reduce the risk involved in acting on misleading research findings as if they were true.

In the past, content analysts have been rather casual about validating their results. This may explain the fact that other research techniques, notably controlled experiments and survey research, are often preferred to content analyses whenever such options present themselves. There are at least two obstacles to validation in content analysis. One is conceptual and the other methodological. Our conceptual framework aims to overcome both.

The conceptual obstacle to validation stems primarily from uncertainties regarding a target for inferences from data and, what is the other side of the same coin, from ambiguities regarding where one may find independent evidence that could corroborate the results. Suppose a content analyst claims to have found a shift in the United States from material values to spiritual ones whereby this shift is observed exclusively in terms of symbol uses. Unless this analyst is willing to specify in advance the class of independently observable phenomena in which such a shift should be manifest if true, such a finding cannot be validated and stand entirely on its own. Uncertainties of this kind are built into conceptions of content analysis as "merely descriptive of a medium of communication." One must suspect that some content analysts thrive on such conceptual uncertainties for it helps them to avoid the threats of disconfirming evidence, even at the risk of being empirically irrelevant.

The methodological obstacle to validation stems primarily from a narrow interpretation of validity. Consider the following trilemma: if the content analyst has no direct knowledge about what he is inferring, then he actually cannot say anything about the validity of his findings. If he possesses some knowledge about the context of the data and uses it in the development of his analytical constructs, then this knowledge is no longer independent from his procedure and cannot be used to validate the findings. And if he manages to keep the knowledge about the target of his inferences separate from his procedure, then the effort at inferring it from data is in fact superfluous and adds at best one incident to the generalization of the procedure. The trilemma is resolvable, however, by relying on various forms of *partial and indirect evidence* about the phenomena of interest or on evidence in a form *similar* but not identical to the findings, leaving *direct-evidence* for postfact and hence retroactive validation efforts.

The kind of indirect evidence that might be brought to bear on content analysis results and the way this evidence might contribute to the validity of findings is the principal focus of this section. Our classification deviates somewhat from that proposed in the literature on psychological testing mainly because the situation in which the content analyst finds himself differs from that of an experimental psychologist.

A TYPOLOGY FOR VALIDATION EFFORTS

Following Campbell (1957), we distinguish between internal validity and external validity. *Internal validity* is merely another term for reliability. It employs criteria that are internal to an analysis and evaluates whether research findings have anything to do with the data at hand without saying what. Here we are concerned only with external validity or validity proper. *External validity* assesses the degree to which variations inside the process of analysis correspond to variations outside that process and whether findings represent the real phenomena in the context of data as claimed. The requirement that content analysis procedures be context sensitive is a demand for their external validity. Ideally, all stages of a content analysis should be justified using external validity criteria. In practice this is possible only at certain critical points.

Although several content analysts have followed the *Technical Recommendations for Psychological Tests and Diagnostic Techniques* (American Psychological Association, 1954) for their concepts of validity, we respond here to the special problems of content analysis. According to our typology we start by distinguishing between whether the validating evidence concerns the nature of the *data,* the analytical *results,* or the nature of the *process* connecting the two.

Data-related validity assesses how well a method of analysis represents the information inherent in or associated with available data. Whereas reliability assures that the representation of raw data in an analysis is consistent within a method, across different methods, or relative to a standard, data-related validity assesses moreover the degree to which the representation of the raw data in an analysis correspond to an outside criterion. Although data-related validity tends to be used to justify the initial steps of a content analysis, it is not limited to these. We further distinguish between the two kinds of data-related validity, semantical validity and sampling validity.

Semantical validity assesses the degree to which a method is sensitive to the symbolic meanings that are relevant within a given context. In content analysis high semantical validity is achieved when the semantics of the data language corresponds to that of the source, the receiver, or any other context relative to which data are examined. The concern for emic or indigenous rather than etic or imposed categories of analysis is a reflection of the concern for semantical validity as well. Semantical validity is rarely a problem in research techniques in which the data gathering process is structured (see distinctions in Conceptual Foundations).

Sampling validity assesses the degree to which available data are either an unbiased sample from a universe of interest or sufficiently similar to another sample from the same universe so that the data can be taken as statistically representative of that universe. Ideally, data are actively sampled from a universe by the analyst. But in content analysis, data are more often than not made available by a source using own and usually biased selection criteria that the analyst cannot control. In either case a sample is valid to the extent its composition, whether in proportion, scale, or distribution, corresponds to the composition of the universe for which it is intended to stand.

Pragmatical or product-oriented validity assesses how well a method "works" under a variety of circumstances. There is no concern for the internal make-up of the procedure. The over-all success of a content analysis is established by showing that its results correlate or agree with what they claim to represent. We distinguish again between two kinds, correlational validity and predictive validity.

Correlational validity is the degree to which findings obtained by one method correlate with findings obtained by another and thus justify their substitutability. Here correlational validity means both, high correlations between the inferences from a content analysis and other measures of the same contextual characteristics (convergent validity) and low correlations between such inferences and measures of different characteristics (discriminant validity).

Predictive validity is the degree to which predictions obtained by one method agree with directly observed facts. In content analysis, predictive validity requires that the obtained inferences show high agreement with the states, attributes, events, or properties in the context of data to which these inferences refer (regardless of whether these are past, concurrent, or future phenomena) and high disagreement with the contextual characteristics that these inferences logically exclude.

Process-oriented validity assesses the degree to which an analytical procedure models, mimics, or functionally represents relations in the context of data. In content analysis this form of validity is concerned principally with the nature of the analytical construct which is accepted or rejected on the basis of a demonstrated structural-functional correspondence of the processes and categories of an analysis with accepted theories, models, and knowledge of the context from which data stem. We find no reason for finer distinctions and call process-oriented validity *construct validity*. The typology thus proposed is depicted as Figure 22.

It might be useful to elaborate briefly on similarities and differences between our distinctions and those proposed by others. The distinction between predictive and correlational validity corresponds to Janis's (1965) distinction between *direct* and *indirect* methods of validation. A direct method involves showing that the results of a content analysis describe what they purport to describe, but since, according to Janis, the meanings of messages mediate between individual perceptions and responses and are not directly observable in this capacity, an indirect method of validation involves "inferring validity from productivity" (1965: 70) whereby "a content analysis procedure is (said to be) productive insofar as the results it yields are found to be correlated with other variables" (1965: 65).

The *Technical Recommendations* distinguish between predictive and concurrent validity depending on whether a test leads to inferences about an individual's future or about his present status on some variables that are measured at the time of the test. In both cases, the *Technical Recommendations* require that findings and criterion variables correlate with each other. In content analysis, the time dimension appears somewhat secondary to the fact that a high correlation is sought which indicates substitutability rather than predictive accuracy. Hence both types are regarded here as correlational validity.

In the *Technical Recommendation,* "content validity" is established "by showing how well ... the test samples the class of situations or subject matter about which conclusions are to be drawn" (1954: 13). This is identical to our definition for "sampling validity." The choice of different terms is motivated merely by the possible confusion the term *content* may precipitate in our situation.

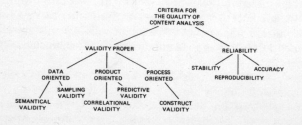

FIGURE 22:   A Typology for Validity in Content Analysis

The term *pragmatic validity* has been taken from Selltiz et al. who add to their definition that "the researcher then does not need to know *why* the test performance is an efficient indication of the characteristic in which he is interested" (Selltiz et al., 1964: 157).

The distinction between construct validity and pragmatic validity has also been implied

> by differentiating between two types of justification that Feigl (1952) termed validation and vindication. In this context, *validation* is a mode of justification according to which the acceptability of a particular analytical procedure is established by showing it to be derivable from general principles or theories that are accepted quite independently of the procedure to be justified. On the other hand, *vindication* may render an analytical method acceptable on the grounds that it leads to accurate predictions (to a degree better than chance) regardless of the details of that method. The rules of induction and deduction are essential to validation while the relation between means and particular ends provide the basis for vindication [Krippendorff, 1969a: 12].

In the *Technical Recommendations*, construct validity refers to an unarticulated manifestation of a trait or phenomenon in several different tests, whereas our definition stresses the structural correspondence of an analysis with articulated knowledge about the system of interest.

It might be noted that the typology does not include the term *face validity* because this form of justifying research results does not require any formal test and is entirely governed by intuition. While intuition cannot be ignored in any step of a content analysis, it defies systematic accounts which is the concern in this section.

The diagram in Figure 23 depicts the kind of comparisons involved in testing the five types of validity.

SEMANTICAL VALIDITY

Almost all content analyses involve some recognition of the meaning conveyed by recording units, some identification of references, or of other semantic features in the data at hand. In fact older definitions made "the classification of sign-vehicles" (Janis, 1965), the "description of the manifest content of communication" (Berelson and Lazarsfeld, 1948: 6), the "coding" (Cartwright, 1953: 424), the "putting (of) a variety of word patterns into . . . (the categories) . . . of a classification scheme" (Miller, 1951: 96) a definitional requirement of content analysis. Although many modern content analyses aim at inferences far beyond such accounts, entirely descriptive tasks in content analysis should not be underestimated in their scientific importance or in their practical significance. Whether the inferences aimed at by a content analysis go far beyond the description of conventional meanings, a correct representation of the symbolic qualities in data may be essential.

We have stated earlier that any description, however simple, must be regarded as a form of inference, posing the question why, by what standard, different units of analysis are put into the same category. The analyst may justify his descriptions in terms of scientific practice, in terms

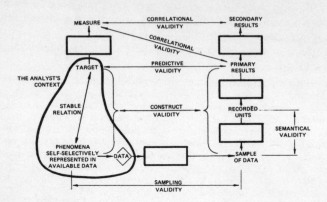

FIGURE 23:   Comparisons Involved in Different Types of Validity

of conformity to popular distinctions, or in terms of the idiosyncracies of a particular source. Whatever the case may be, his descriptions are never entirely arbitrary and may have to be validated, especially when the subsequent analysis is no longer justifiable in terms of the context of data. This is the case, for example, in most content analyses that result in frequency counts, and in which data are subjected to more sophisticated forms of data manipulation such as factor analysis. The operation of counting and of extracting factors from multivariate data rarely has functional equivalents in the social world and their construct validity is therefore often uncertain. But what may be assessed in such situations is whether the data capture those symbolic qualities that are "real" by some standard and whether the procedure is therefore valid up to the point of representing these qualities.

An analysis of values in political documents may serve as a very simple example of an effort at improving semantical validity. As a first step of an elaborate analytical scheme, we had to identify in a given text what we called "value-laden sentences." A panel of political experts could pick them out fairly reliably. But, following our explicit recording instructions, coders varied greatly in their ability and a computer program we had hoped to employ turned out to be virtually powerless in this case. Without going into the whole history of this effort, we started out by distinguishing between sentences that did or did not contain political symbols from a list, including democracy, freedom, victory, and the like, and ended up by testing each sentence for its conformity to any one of a set of structural definitions of the way values could be expressed (Krippendorff, 1970b). During the evolution of the recording instrument, "improvement" was measured by the degree to which the set of sentences identified as value-laden by the instrument approximated the set of sentences identified as value-laden by experts. One could question, of course, whether the use of expert judgments as semantical validity criteria is meaningful, why we did not use subjects, or political actors instead. But there were practical limitations and theoretical motivations for the choice of this context as reference for the analysis and we were satisfied that the instrument ultimately approximated what political experts could do.

The test for the semantical validity of a content analysis is very simple in construction. Any classification of sign-vehicles, any description of recording units, any coding of observations into a descriptive language effectively partitions the sample of units of analysis into mutually exclusive and exhaustive equivalence classes. Differences that might exist between units that find themselves assigned to the same category are ignored.

Semantical validity is indicated by a substantial agreement between two different partitions of the same set of units of analysis. One is obtained from the way the analytical procedure assigns units to its categories. The other is obtained according to an external criterion, for example, involving judges familiar with the symbolic nature of the same language who group these units according to their semantic similarity. Agreement on these partitions assures that units within one equivalence class share the properties indicated by the category to which they are assigned and units in different equivalence classes differ according to the differences between the categories.

Although semantical validations have been undertaken accordingly, they can require large efforts. Two easy validity checks may be used before proceeding to a formal test.

First, the analyst may obtain a listing of all units, grouped according to the distinctions maintained within a study. In obtaining such a breakdown, the analyst often finds himself surprised how his instrument fails to distinguish between vastly different units and why his instrument makes distinctions between units that are seemingly alike. An example is provided by Dunphy who obtained a Key-Word-In-Context printout for the word *play* (see Figure 20) to show which senses would be ignored by a computer program that merely identifies occurrences of the word (Dunphy, 1966: 159). It demonstrates that an analysis, in which a distinction between the different senses of "play" is important, cannot afford to rely on mere lexical identifications. A semantically valid procedure would have to be sensitive to the linguistic contexts of the word. It also shows that even though a tagging dictionary may be valid with respect to single-word assignments to tags, the procedure in which it is embedded may not be adequate to represent the symbolic qualities conveyed in larger units of a text.

Second, the analyst may create a set of hypothetical units with well-known properties and examine how the procedure would distinguish between them. The method is well-established in linguistics where, as soon as some linguist proposes a grammar that claims to distinguish between grammatical and nongrammatical sentences, another linguist comes up with counter examples of sentences that the proposed grammar will misidentify. In the critique of contingency analysis, Osgood (1959: 73-77) employs this mode of reasoning. In effect, he observes that when a psychoanalytic patient states:

(1)"I love my mother."

contingency analysis would add this incident, as it should, to the *association* between LOVE and MOTHER. But consider the following statements:

(2) I have always loved my mother more than anyone else.
(3) Mother loved me dearly.
(4) I have loved my mother.
(5) "I have always loved my Mother? What a joke."
(6) My (be)loved father hated mother.

Since the two critical words co-occur in all six statements, contingency analysis would cast them into the same equivalence class of LOVE-MOTHER co-occurrences. However, relative to (1), (2) shows contingency analysis to be insensitive to the strength of an expressed association, (3) shows contingency analysis to be unable to distinguish active and passive constructions, (4) shows contingency analysis to be insensitive to negation, (5) shows contingency analysis to be insensitive to irony, and (6) shows contingency analysis to be insensitive to grammatical considerations.

A critical examination of the semantical distinctions that an analysis makes or discards may thus give valuable insights into the nature of the procedure and provides perhaps sufficient reasons to reject its results.

Sampling Validity

Sampling validity is in question whenever the sample under scrutiny differs from the universe of interest and when this difference is due to probabilistic processes of selecting units for analysis. Such processes of selection are omnipresent in virtually all content analysis data. Two kinds of such processes must be distinguished: sampling by the content analyst and self-sampling within the data source.

The theory of *sampling by an analyst* is well-developed. Following a suitable sampling plan, which assures, as it should, that each unit in the universe has an even chance to be included in the sample, the sampling validity of large samples is virtually guaranteed. As samples become smaller, the sampling error reduces the sampling validity up to the point at which the resemblance of the sample and the universe is no longer certain.

Regarding the second process, communication research knows too well that all social processes that are mediated by communications and represented in symbols or indices are selective, statistically biased, and, in effect, the product of *processes of self-sampling.* Consider the overrepresentation of marrying age and well-to-do WASPs among television characters; consider the selective way witnesses in court recall events from memory; consider how few individuals are known to us through histories and mythologies; or consider how little public assertions on civil rights issues correspond to the frequency of social prejudice and injustice. Processes of *self-sampling almost always assign unequal probabilities to events* that individuals, institutions, or cultures deem worthwhile to retain and make available for analysis. Such processes tend to be rather systematic, describable statistically or in sociological or psychological terms, and, hence, to some extent accountable.

Processes of self-sampling precede the availability of data. *Sampling must undo the statistical biases inherent in the way data are made available to the analyst.* And sampling validity intends to evaluate the success of this effort whereby the external validity criterion involves knowledge about the self-sampling characteristics of the data source.

For example, suppose the task is to estimate the perceptions by political decision makers in Vietnam of some political issue, say, of relations between the United States and the People's Republic of China. A foolproof but, in this situation, impractical technique would be to list the members of the decision-making elite and to interview a random sample of them, making sure that opinions are expressed freely. A content analysis could try to approximate the results of a survey without being obtrusive. A simple-minded content analyst might start by finding out which data, newsprints, reports, and journalistic accounts are available and draw a representative sample from these. Although he might stratify such a sample, considering that foreign policy issues are more likely discussed in government publications and political instructions rather than agricultural reports, such a sample may be representative of available mass communications but will be biased with respect to elite perceptions precisely because of the self-sampling characteristics involved. One probability that needs to be estimated is the probability of a decision maker to be visible. Some have easier access to public communications than others, whether because of their office, status, or personality. The other probability concerns how likely an opinion that someone may have is asserted in public. Opinions that are consistent with established policies or serve recognized functions in political processes are more likely to find their way into a publication than opinions that deviate from overall purposes.

Given an estimate of the probability with which a phenomenon of interest is represented in the stream of the available data, an unbiased sample from these data must assure that the frequency of that phenomena in the sample is proportional to the inverse of the likelihood that the phenomena is available for sampling. With n_i as the frequency of phenomena i in the sample, and p_i as the estimated probability that the phenomenon i will be made available to the analyst, the criterion against which sampling validity is to be measured is

$$n_i \text{ is proportional to } p_i^{-1}$$

when p_i is uniformly distributed and self-sampling is, hence, unbiased, sampling validity reduces to showing that sampling from available data was random. In the example, a valid sample of opinions would give decision makers who rarely express opinions publicly larger attention than those highly visible communicators who dominate the public media. Kops's (1977: 230-240) discussion of "disproportional stratified random sampling" designs in content analysis should be mentioned as the closest relative of a sampling plan that satisfies our criterion for sampling validity.

The example is not to suggest that content analysis should replicate the result that other techniques would normally yield. On the contrary, content analysis could consider, for example, that some decision makers are more influential than others and use this knowledge to draw a sample that is representative of a universe of possible consequences. Or, the nature of the expressed opinions could be discarded altogether in favor of inferring the dynamics of political intentions behind the front of a staged appearance. In each of these cases, samples may have to be drawn differently. In content analysis *a demonstration of sampling validity is important, especially when processes of self-sampling are involved.* Defining the universe of interest so that it coincides with the data at hand avoids sampling problems but curtails the power of content analysis so severely that it renders the technique virtually useless.

CORRECTIONAL VALIDITY

A fact well-recognized in the psychological literature is that both *test results and test criteria are measures,* neither of which should be confused with the phenomena either might represent. Moreover, statistical correlations assess the *strength of an association* between two or more variables and thereby indicate the degree to which a (linear) relationship between them may be stated with certainty. Hence, correlations do not predict events or phenomena, but they indicate, what is very important in the development of measuring instruments, whether one measure is *substitutable* for another. Correlational validity is important in that it may transfer validity from one or more established measures to a new measure that has certain practical advantages. Thus, content analysis results may become more acceptable if they correlate with the results of established psychological tests, interviews, experiments, direct observation, and the like.

Campbell and Fiske (1959) were the first to develop the idea of validation by correlational techniques into a full-fledged methodology. They recognize that any justification for a novel measure requires not only a high correlation with established measures of the trait it intends to measure but also low or zero correlations with established measures of traits it intends to discriminate against. The former requirement is called *convergent* validity, the latter *discriminant* validity. Thus, a research result may be invalidated by either or both, too low correlation with independent measures of the same phenomenon and too high correlation with measures of phenomena it intends to discriminate against.

To show that a measure possesses both convergent and discriminant validity calls for a multitrait-multimethod matrix of all correlations between measures of a variety of traits, each obtained by several independent methods. (See Campbell and Fiske, 1959; Alwin, 1974; Krippendorff, 1980a.)

In the domain of content analysis, correlational validity is of particular importance when the phenomena of interest mediate between the reception and production of messages. This refers most obviously to all mediational concepts of meaning which underly a large number of research designs and are explicit in, among others, Osgood's affective meaning system. The first one to recognize this is Janis (1965), who, in 1943, suggested that the content analyst's job is to "estimate the significations attributed to signs by an audience" (1965: 61). He thought of significations as internally represented meanings that come immediately to mind whenever someone is confronted with some sign, verbal assertation, or symbol and that will effect the verbal or nonverbal behavior of audience members. Janis points out that significations cannot be observed directly. Because of the presumed effects of these significations on the behavior of message receivers, in order for a content analysis to be valid, its results must at least correlate with some aspect of audience behavior.

PREDICTIVE VALIDITY

Prediction is a process by which available knowledge is extended to an unknown domain. The predicted phenomena may have existed somewhere in the past—as for historical events or the antecedent conditions of available messages—may be concurrent with the data being analyzed—as for attitudes, psychopathologies, or personalities of interviewees—or are anticipated to be observable sometime in the future—as expected in aptitude tests or trend extrapolations. Although the *Technical Recommendations* distinguish between types of validity along this time dimension, in content analysis this distinction is subordinate to the fact that specific inferences are made to phenomena in the context of available data.

Substitutability must not be confused with predictability. One measure is substitutable by another if it can be shown that both occupy the same position within the network of possible correlations. Correlational validity assesses just that. In contrast, one measure is predictive of some phenomenon if it can be shown that the measure *agrees* with what it claims to predict. Ideally, predictions and facts stand in a one-to-one semantical correspondence, that is, a prediction unambiguously designates phenomena that are observable in principle, whether directly or indirectly, whether in the past, in the present, or in the future, and regardless how evidence about these phenomena reaches the analyst.

One aspect of the distinction lies in the difference between agreement and correlation: A slow watch correlates highly with time but disagrees systematically. Unless one knows the bias of this watch, one could not tell the (conventional) time. The famous body-count during the Vietnam war may have correlated highly with military activity but its numerical value turned out to have no agreement with the number of victims. High correlations may be a necessary, but not a sufficient, requirement for predictability.

A second aspect of the distinction lies in the evidential status attributed to the variable against which a measure is validated. In testing for correlational validity, all measures are considered *indices of some underlying phenomenon* and, when substitutability is shown, of each other as well. In testing for predictive validity, the variable against which a measure is validated is taken to be *the final criterion*, as "fact," so to speak. Although also "facts" are accessible only through the medium of describable observations and are thus not fundamentally different from measurements, it is this variable as observed which provides the content of predictions, not what it might indicate. For example, employers may not be impressed by how well the scores of their job-applicants correlate between different aptitude tests, but they may want to know how well the individuals will *actually* perform on the job. And measures of the dramatic violence on television, whatever their correlation with other indices may be, they obtain predictive validity only when agreement with observable phenomena (audience behavior, crime rate, public fear, or expectation of violence, etc.) can be demonstrated. To test correlational validity any index may serve as a criterion variable. To test predictive validity, the factuality of the criterion is essential. Qualitatively, predictive validity is assured by entering each of a set of possible events in the following four-fold table and measuring the agreement between prediction and observation.

	events predicted	events excluded by prediction
events that did occur	A	B
events that did not occur	C	D

Events Counting for and Against Predictive Validity

Obviously, the A and D cells count in favor of predictive validity and the B and C cells count against. Neither column must be empty else discrimination is not evident and neither row must be empty else convergence cannot be demonstrated.

A classical, though not entirely conclusive, example of this form of validation is George's (1959a) attempt to evaluate the FCC predictions made from enemy domestic propaganda during World War II. All inferences were available in form of reports by the propaganda analysts and could be matched, one by one with documents that became available after the war. Those inferences for which validating evidence was available were judged either correct, nearly so, or wrong. The result showed the analysis efforts to have had considerable predictive success. The validation effort was not quite adequate because, by putting predictions in these three (or similar) categories, cells B and C are not differentiated and cell D probably remains empty.

In a more quantitative mode, predictive validation can follow Campbell and Fiske's criteria with one important difference, that the entries in the multitrait-multimethod matrix are *agreement coefficients*, not correlations. (For the nature of these coefficients see the section on Reliability.) In these terms, a content analysis may be said to have predictive validity if its inferences can be shown to exhibit both high agreement with (past, present, or future) phenomena that it claims to predict in the context of its data and low agreement with phenomena it intends to discriminate against.

CONSTRUCT VALIDITY

When a content analysis procedure is designed *de novo*, pragmatic validation is likely to be impossible for it requires either past experiences with analyzing the kind of data at hand and/or the availability of concurrent indicators about the phenomena to be inferred. And, because semantical and sampling validity typically govern only the initial phases of a content analysis, during which the identity of units is maintained, data-oriented validity does not go as far as one might wish. For content analyses that are unique to a particular set of data, or unprecedented in a given situation, the validation of their procedures as constructs of the data-context relation might be the only recourse.

The work of historians is most typically of this nature. Whether the statement "history never repeats itself" reflects a philosophical position or a historical fact, it is a position that many content analysts assume as well. When this is assumed to be the case, statistical validation procedures are practically ruled out. Dibble (1963), who analyzed the arguments made by historians in favor or against inferences drawn from documents, came to the conclusion that they all involved *assumptions* about psychological characteristics of the observers, about rules of the social system keeping the records, and about physical-social conditions surrounding the writing of the documents. While historical documents and the inferences drawn from them are thought to be unique and outstanding, the assumptions linking a text with some event have the logical status of *generalizations regarding documentary evidence*.

Leites et al.'s (1951) inferences from Stalin's birthday speeches, discussed earlier, is another, particularly transparent example of construct validation in an essentially unique situation. The inferences simply followed from the construct. The validity of the construct was established by careful arguments for the generality of the relationship and by showing that the operationalization indeed captured his relationship.

In a previous section we identified four sources of knowledge that a content analyst might utilize in the development and justification of analytical constructs.

- past successes with similar constructs and/or similar situations
- experiences with the context of available data
- established theories and models of the contextual dependencies of data
- representative interpretes and experts.

These are also the sources that may have to be used in validating given analytical procedure. Construct validation involves basically two steps.

(1) There is an effort to *generalize available knowledge* to the particular context within which data are content analyzed, taking account of (a) the relative strength of the dependencies between data and their context,

such as whether the relations are deterministic or merely probabilistic, (b) the confidence in the validity of this knowledge in terms of number of independent confirmations, conformity to established theory, or absence of counter examples, and (c) the appropriateness of the knowledge in the particular context, whether the contextual relations are likely to have been invariant, in which way the system under investigation differs from the one known. These points have been discussed under "uncertainties" in Constructs for Inference and need no further elaboration here.

(2) There is an effort to *logically derive* from valid generalizations the particular *propositions underlying the analytical procedure* used. In developing new analytical constructs, this would mean operationalizing, or deriving, defendable rules for data transformation from given theory. In validating existing constructs, this means testing whether the construct is in fact logically derivable from the generalizations. We need to examine in particular (a) errors of omission, such as dependencies postulated by the generalizations that the construct does not operationalize, and (b) errors of commission, or dependencies built into the construct that have no basis in the generalizations.

It is also possible to design experiments or create other situations in which data are obtained pertaining directly to the construct. One example, already mentioned, is Osgood's (1959) effort to obtain validating evidence for contingency analysis. He exposed subjects to various pairs of names and found that the associations subjects acquired between the names were influenced significantly by their co-occurrence in the stimulus material, thus suggesting that a statistical account of co-occurrences in the mass media might indeed predict audience associations.

It should be re-emphasized that our term *construct validity* differs somewhat from that in the *Technical Recommendations*. However, this difference does not pertain to the spirit of these arguments. In applications these recommendations consider, "construct validity is evaluated . . . by demonstrating that certain explanatory constructs account to some degree for (the individuals') performance on the test." The *Technical Recommendations* conceptualize this form of validation as a two-way process: "First the investigator inquires: From (the) theory (underlying the test), what predictions would he make regarding the variation of scores from person to person or occasion to occasion? Second, he gathers data to confirm these predictions" (1954: 14). When a content analysis is unique, only the first part of the process envisioned in the recommendations can be completed: the justification of the procedure and categories of analysis from valid theory. Most situations in content analysis make it difficult to proceed to the second step of gathering data to confirm the predictions, which we have discussed under correlational and predictive validity.

14

A PRACTICAL GUIDE

This chapter outlines the steps content analysts typically follow, starting with conceptualizing the research problem and ending with the report. A clear outline of the procedures used facilitates the interpretation of the findings and the replication of the process leading up to them.

Whereas the preceding sections introduced analytical concepts and elaborated on some of the methodological problems, we now attempt to summarize these with the practice in mind.

To begin with, we find that any content analysis involves three logically separate activities:

- design
- execution
- report.

The logical order of these activities, however, does not imply their temporal sequence. Very often, the researcher decides on an analytical scheme, following a viable idea, only to find out that it cannot be executed the way it was planned. Whether he had a wrong conception of his data, whether he could not find enough literature to justify his contentions, or whether he underestimated the resources required, he may have to go back to the drawing board until he has found a design that is workable *and* leads to results that are meaningful to him. Or, when writing up the results, it is also not uncommon that certain patterns may become apparent that call for further computation and quality checks to be substantiated. It means going back from reporting to execution until a clear and complete picture is ascertained. Despite this going back and forth, making adjustments to constraints, and finding compromises between conflicting requirements, the logical priorities are maintained. The design that is finally arrived at spells out what is to be executed, and the execution yields results that are finally reported.

As is true for most research, content analyses are also rarely ever finished. Although a good content analysis will answer some question, it is also expected to pose new ones, leading to revisions of the procedures for future applications, stimulating new research into the bases for drawing inferences, not to mention suggesting new hypotheses about the phenomena of interest. The beginning and end of a content analysis mark but an arbitrary segment in time.

DESIGN

Designing means realizing an idea and operationalizing a way of observing reality vicariously. Developing a research design is intellectually the most exciting activity of content analysis where the researcher clarifies his own interests and what he knows, where he explores available literature for insights about the surrounding conditions of his data, where he plays with and pretests ideas until plans emerge that bring all together into a research procedure that can be executed. (see the Logic of Content Analysis Designs). This is where methodology is used creatively and for practical ends. The following discusses nine aspects of designing a content analysis:

- applying the framework for content analysis
- searching for suitable data
- searching for contextual knowledge
- developing plans for unitizing and sampling
- developing coding instructions
- searching for contextually justifiable procedures
- deciding on qualitative standards
- budgeting and resource allocation.

Applying the Framework for Content Analysis

Whereas all scientific research is motivated by the desire to know or to better understand a portion of the real world, a content analysis must show interest in *two kinds of reality,* the reality of the data and the reality of what the researcher wants to know about. In content analysis these two realities do not overlap so that the researcher will have to find ways of regarding the data he can analyze as symbolic manifestations or as indicative of the phenomena of interest.

Ideally, a content analyst starts out by clarifying for himself what he really wants to know about and yet cannot observe directly. Then he looks for data that might allow him to draw inferences about the portion of the world of interest. It means first of all delineating *the target for inferences.*

Questions concerning audience perceptions, psychopathologies, military intelligence, and the nature of historical events exemplify such targets (see Conceptual Foundations). In practice, many content analysts start from the other end, with available data, whose symbolic nature they then explore to see what could possibly be inferred that might be of interest. This latter approach is also called a "fishing expedition." Although Berelson (1952) and many others after him speak against this approach, the methodological problems it poses can largely be bypassed if the content analyst, after an initial exploration, clearly distinguishes the data from what he wishes to infer and then reexamines the data to see whether they would still be meaningful, representative, and appropriate in the context of concern. In content analysis the choice of data must be justified by what the analyst wants to know, hence the logical priority of the target.

Research results must be validatable in principle. In delineating a target for his inferences, the analyst must be willing to specify in unambiguous

terms the kind of *evidence that would demonstrate the validity* or inva-
lidity of the inferences he wishes to make. This may be obvious when one
is concerned with inferring psychological states or identifying unknown
authors. It may be difficult when the content analyst attempts to infer the
attitudes of historical figures or "predict" the nature of certain symbolic
events that took place in an extinct civilization. But even by defining a
measure, for example, of "symbolic salience," on the frequency of certain
words within text, the analyst should commit himself to say what this
measure is meant to indicate.

Searching for Suitable Data

Data for content analysis must be known to have something to do with
what the researcher wants to infer. The connection between data and the
target of the analyst's inferences may be very tenuous and in fact is rarely
strong and obvious to begin with. But, there is no sense to collect data that
may be symbolic or have meanings in a different context when these
meanings have nothing to do with the content analyst's interest. Presumably, the reason for content analyzing mass communications is rooted in
the conviction that the mass media, beyond being merely entertaining,
reflect (social-economical-) institutional arrangements in society, are
powerful molders of public opinion, or are perhaps causally connected
with several social pathologies.

The search for suitable data may follow any known or anticipated
connection between what is to be inferred and what could conceivably be
observed, sampled, and analyzed. Traditional content analyses have
emphasized *semantical reference* and *expressions* of attitudinal evaluations. But modern uses of content analysis may see data as *correlates* of
the phenomena of interest, such as wear and tear of library books to assess
the popularity of certain topics; as *by-products* of these phenomena when
mass media content is used to infer the economic make-up and ideological
biases in the communications industry; as *causes*, in an attempt to infer
audience perceptions or political agendas; or as *instrumental* when data are
taken to be a manifestation of particular values or interests of their
producer. Webb et al. (1966) review such connections in terms of *physical
traces* that the phenomena of interest leave behind and *actuarial records*
that are maintained for reasons other than the analyst's interest in them.
Thus, to search for suitable data, the analyst needs to explore how the
phenomena of interest might affect or be affected by what could be
observed, how these phenomena come into being, and where traces from
them or linguistic representations of them may be found. *Anything connected with the phenomena of interest qualifies as data for content
analysis.*

Searching for Contextual Knowledge

Evidence about the empirical connection between data and what is to
be inferred from them is obviously important in any content analysis. We
already argued that a high frequency of symbols for love and sex may not
be indicative of a promiscuous society. With a symbolic substitution

hypothesis in mind, one might well infer the opposite, repression. Also the interpretation of such frequencies as indices of attention may not hold water either. To justify any inferences from data, some hard knowledge, some empirical evidence about the connections between data and what is to be inferred from them, is essential. It is this knowledge that enables the researcher to place his data in a suitable context, to render them indicative of phenomena outside of themselves, and thus provides him with *a logical bridge* for making inferences. In this search, the content analyst becomes a consumer of knowledge.

Typical sources of contextual knowledge are: *theories and models* about the system under investigation, *experiences with the context* of data that the analyst may want to operationalize, *past successes* with content analyses of similar data in similar situations, and *representative interpreters* such as experts or informants of the symbolic qualities of the data (see Constructs for Inference). The designer of a content analysis should not be surprised that the search for this kind of knowledge typically absorbs much of his time and effort. Inferences do not justify themselves. Depending on how well-researched the area is, there are likely to exist many studies investigating hypotheses which could justify the constructs to obtain the desired inferences. There may exist reports on completed content analyses making similar assumptions. The success of such content analysis may favor the repetition of such assumptions. There may exist experts who know or have internalized the dependencies between data and the phenomena of interest. Some of the difficulties of applying knowledge of this kind have been mentioned (see Constructs for Inference).

Very often the search for contextual knowledge may mean conducting preparatory experiments, using subjects, for example, to test whether the theory "works out" in contexts that resemble the one of the analysis. Osgood's (1959) validation experiments on contingency analysis and Stone and Hunt's (1963) experiments on suicide notes are examples. Correlations between frequencies of key symbols and attention/importance assigned to their referents by authors or by readers have been surprisingly low. In view of how little one knows about the relationships between the use of language and media expressions on the one hand and antecedent conditions, behavioral correlates, and consequences on the other, there is a need for exploring such relationships more systematically.

Developing Plans for Unitizing and Sampling

Given the universe of possible data, at least in outline, the researcher has to find ways of securing all or obtaining a sample of them. When the analyst has complete control over the choice of including or excluding a particular datum in his analysis, he can follow one of the standard sampling procedures.

In most content analyses, control over the process of collecting data is limited. There are usually good reasons why some data are made more readily available to the analyst than others. The survival of historical documents is selective, what patients tell their psychiatrist is selective, and what is printed as news is selective from a large range of possibilities.

Selectivity of this kind indicates sampling processes that are indigenous to the source. Whether such processes are unconscious, as perhaps in psychiatric interviews, or governed by rational decisions, as perhaps in advertising and television programming, the analyst can choose only among what survives the self-sampling processes. And with this choice he may have to rectify the self-sampling bias inherent in available data.

The knowledge that goes into the design of plans for unitizing and sampling concerns:

- the nature of the sampling units which must be individually information bearing (see Unitizing)
- the spacial or temporal location of units of different kinds (see Sampling)
- the nature of the distribution of information in the universe
- the self-sampling characteristics for different kinds of units and/or information (see Sampling and Validity).

Random processes should be used to make the final choice of including data in the sample but only after all available knowledge about the universe of possible data has been exhausted.

In practice, a sampling plan has to cope with a large number of irregularities. Some of the back issues of newspapers requested from publishers turn out to be no longer available. Some sections of taped interviews selected for analysis turn out to contain too much noise. Some television shows sampled for a study on personality characteristics turn out to have no actors at all. In all such cases the researcher will have to decide whether (1) the deficiency is entirely accidental, in which case he may continue with the random choice process until the sample has the appropriate size. (2) The deficiency is the result of self-sampling biases, in which case he has to make a special effort to obtain the missing unit and, failing this, investigate why this unit has dropped out and by which other unit it might be replaced to retain the sample's representativeness. Or, (3) the deficiency is the result of an inadequate conceptualization either of the universe of possible data or of the stratification, grouping, or organization within it. This requires a revision of the sampling plan if not a revision of what constitutes the universe of possible data for the study.

The sampling plan has to be detailed and explicit so as to result in a procedure that is replicable and yields similar samples from the same universe.

Developing Coding Instructions

Many researchers seem to value their own categories of analyses, formulate and pretest new instructions to coders until they are sufficiently reliable, and then apply them to data that have never been analyzed before. Thus, large numbers of content analyses are undertaken whose results are neither comparable with each other nor cumulatively contributory to theory. Although ingenuity is always welcome, the researcher who relies on existing conceptualizations has more of a chance to contribute to knowledge.

One obvious starting point is an examination of available *literature of how data are related to their context*. Not all describable message characteristics are related to the phenomena of interest and it does, therefore, make little sense to extend a content analysis beyond its purpose. There usually are well-formulated theories or at least hypotheses that can supply concepts and categories in terms of which new data can be described. This allows the researcher to thereafter rely on well-developed constructs. Also categories used in other endeavors should be relied upon where possible. A content analysis that requires occupational categories, for example, may be based on official Federal Trade Commission listings or sociological studies of occupational status and prestige. This opens access to comparable data. The common difficulty is one of operationalizing theoretical concepts and categories from a different field so that they conform to a suitable data language with its variables and mutually exclusive categories (see Data Languages) on the one side, and indigenous conceptions of the data source on the other side and remain understandable to human coders or to computer applications.

Published *content analyses with similar aims* are a second source of ideas for coding instructions. Various systems of categories have been illustrated thoughout the preceding sections (especially in Recording and Data Languages). Other examples are found in Berelson (1952) and particularly in Holsti (1969). Some studies rely on a few variables others define very many. Some studies require only a page of instructions, others a whole book (see Dollard and Auld, 1959). But there is no need to invent a new scheme if existing ones have not been shown to be defective. Even if the validity of these instruments is not quite established, the use of existing recording instructions or only slight adaptations thereof offers two distinct advantages over new ones: first, it provides the possibility of comparing results across different situations out of which standards or expectation may emerge (see Uses and Kinds of Inferences) and, second, it shortcuts the efforts of making such instructions reliable.

Good coding or recording instructions should contain:

- a prescription of the characteristics of the observers (coders, judges) employed in the recording process
- an account of the training these observers undergo to prepare themselves for the task
- a definition of the recording units including procedures for their identification
- a delineation of the syntax and the semantic of the data language (variables, categories) including, when necessary, an outline of the cognitive procedures to be employed in placing data into categories
- a description of how data sheets are to be used and administered.

Inasmuch as the final coding instructions provide the basis for reproducing the analysis elsewhere, or for applying it on similar data, instructions must be explicit and detailed and if not part of the final research report at least available upon request.

Searching for Contextually
Justifiable Procedures

The Conceptual Foundations elaborated on the contention that the target of a content analysis lies outside the syntax and form of the data whose symbolic nature mediate, point to, or indicate something in the context of these data. The analytical procedures should therefore be sensitive to and represent or be justifiable in terms of the context from which the data stem. Contingency analysis (see Analytical Techniques) exemplifies a computational device that operationalizes certain propositions in psychology and is thus sensitive to a context in which these propositions are true. Evaluative Assertion Analysis, too, is an outgrow of certain theories of cognition. Other sections (notably Constructs for Inference and Validity) elaborated on the difficulties of operationalization and on the criteria that analytical constructs should satisfy.

It should be stressed that *any analytical procedure by its very nature can be said to imply certain assumptions about the context of data which must be defendable from what is known about this context.* When one examines the assumptions implied by the procedures that content analysts have employed (usually without explicit justification), one is often surprised to see how much the analyst's stated conception about the symbolic environment deviates from the conception built into the analytical techniques chosen.

Deciding on Quality Standards

Much of content analysis can be characterized as a game in which the analyst tries to guess what his opponent hides, and in order to perform better than chance, he is advised to rely on any information his opponent happens to reveal about himself. There are likely to be errors and these can be costly. In practical situations, where the well-being of people may be affected (see Validation), the certainty with which inferences are made may have to be higher than in scholarly work where only the reputation of the researcher is at stake. Generally, the higher the cost of errors, the more expensive a content analysis, either because of a larger volume of data required during analysis or because of the need for more sophisticated techniques including preparatory studies of the analytical constructs involved. Thus, high qualitative standards, while always desirable, are also costly and a content analyst may not wish to accept a project whose standards are beyond what he can afford, both in terms of the resources at his disposal and in terms of the costs of errors in analytical results.

It is important, however, to decide on such standards *before* an analysis is evaluated. In content analysis, qualitative standards are concerned principally with reliability and validity. The researcher derives these standards by working backward, from the required validity (accuracy, certainty, or specificity) of the results to the requirements each component of the analysis must satisfy so that valid results are assured. To do this, he must know the net effect of the individual standards on the result.

Since high reliability is a requirement for high validity but does not assure it, standards for validity are clearly more powerful and hence preferable to standards for reliability. However, the measurement of reliability is important for two reasons. First, when validating evidence is absent, the researcher really has no option but to use everything he can to assure the results are valid. This is what reliability does. Second, since low reliability means that data cannot be trusted, there is really no point in proceeding to a generally more expensive validity test if reliability is low. Thus, reliability indicates whether validation efforts could provide additional assurances.

Budgeting and Resource Allocation

A content analysis is made up of many different kinds of activities. Some activities can be performed by a single person, others require the collaboration of several people, such as in testing the reliability of recording instructions. Some activities take a long time, others fractions of seconds, such as data processing by computer. Some activities must be executed in sequence while others can be arranged in parallel. Some activities occupy scarce facilities which then delay the execution of others. Some activities can only be done by the researcher himself while others can be delegated to trained assistants. Unless the content analysis is small, and exploratory, the researcher must develop a clear idea about the work organization needed to perform the analysis: when and where resources are needed and how long it takes at what cost.

One approach is to develop a flowchart. Thus, starting with a general picture, we develop the activities that are involved in handling the data from sampling to writing of the report. This forces the researcher to anticipate the inputs each step needs.

Other useful aids from operation research are PERT (Program Evaluation and Review Technique) and CPM (Critical Path Method; Elmaghraby, 1970). The methods transform a whole research process into a network of arrows. Each represents an activity, like cardpunching or sorting, and each links two nodes, the states of the research, like data sheets completed and data punched, and analysis completed. To each arrow is assigned the time or the resource it takes to execute the process. The methods enable the researcher to schedule the various activities, to find the most efficient ways of concluding the research, and thus to come up with a work organization and an assessment of the manpower requirements for a viable plan.

There are, of course, many planning techniques that may be consulted. Whichever is used, it should give the content analyst and perhaps funding agencies and clients the assurance that

- there is at least one practical way to proceed (deviations from this way may later appear more fruitful, but the design should designate at least one). The researcher needs to know at each point exactly where he stands and where he will go next.
- the research can be managed organizationally in terms of available personnel, skills, facilities, and so on. The researcher needs to know where, when, which people are engaged in which activities, who is responsible or where the services come from.
- the research can be executed within a reasonable time frame. Whenever the question arises, the researcher needs to know how long it will take and whether he is on schedule or exceeded his time.
- there are sufficient resources available to complete the content analysis, broken down into the costs for wages, facilities, and services, by hours, months, or by years and in terms of individual budgets. Whatever seems

convenient, the researcher should be able to assess at any point in the process how well he is doing, how much money he spent, and what he still has.

EXECUTION

Ideally, the execution of a well-designed content analysis is routine. With all intellectual problems solved during the design phase, the execution could be delegated to a research organization. In reality, unanticipated problems are bound to emerge, even in the most well-thought through research plan. Many problems of this kind arise from inadequacies in available data and unexpected costs for labor and facilities. However, the most severe problems stem from the inability to meet given standards of reliability and validity. When the solution to such problems cannot be specified in advance, short of discontinuing the content analysis altogether, one has to go back and modify the design, keeping the over-all research objective in mind.

The order in which a typical content analysis is executed is outlined in The Logic of Content Analysis. Whether the content analysis is done by hand or by computer, whether its emphasis is on description or on elaborated inferences, it contains at least one or more of the following:

- sampling by sampling units until the sample can be judged sufficiently representative of the universe
- identification and description of recording units which must be reproducible and satisfy criteria of semantical validity where applicable
- data reduction and transformation of data into a form required for analysis, retaining all relevant information
- application of context-sensitive analytical procedures (analytical constructs) to yield inferences
- analysis, identification of pattern within inferences, testing hypotheses regarding relations between inferences, and results obtained by the methods and pragmatic validation of findings.

When it appears that a representative sample cannot be obtained, whether because of the high costs of large sample sizes or, more typically, because certain items are simply unavailable for analysis, little can be done other than limiting the inferences that were intended to be drawn from the data to those that can be drawn with some degree of validity. Individuals and societies are alike in their ability to suppress information that might be valuable for a content analysis and what is not available cannot be examined. Thus, redefining the universe is one remedy. The other is reducing the status of the content analysis to that of a preliminary examination until relevant data can be included.

When the recording of data cannot be done reliably, the first task is to locate the sources of unreliability (see Reliability). Possibly the unreliability is due to some inadequately trained coders. Possibly, the unreliability occurs only between a few ill-defined categories the others being unambiguous and clear. Possibly, the unreliability is restricted to only a few variables with the remainder being acceptable as is.

When unreliability is located, there are essentially two options. First, *unreliable features are omitted* from analysis. For example, data recorded

by unreliable   ,e sample. Categories that are
consistently c_   and thereafter are no longer
distinguished. Unreliable variables are dropped from further analysis. The
data that survive such a screening process then carry less information than
before and the researcher must decide whether the retained information is
unbiased by the process of omission and sufficient to warrant subsequent
analysis.

More usually, second, *data are recoded using modified instruments* that
exclude the causes for the initial unreliability. This means that recording
instructions to coders are modified, coders are retrained, and new reliability tests are administered until all criteria are met. In fact, it is not
unusual that reliable recording instructions emerge only after two or three
preceding efforts failed. A good research design should provide for the
need to improve recording instructions iteratively. In training coders, care
must be taken that the content of the training process appears codified in
the recording instructions. And in testing reliability, the researcher must
assure that the coders remain independent both of each other and of prior
coding assignments (see Recording and Reliability).

When text is processed directly by computer, in which case units
(words, phrases, sentences) are identified and categorized algorithmically,
without human judgment, reliability is no longer a problem but the
semantical validity of the process may be in question. To achieve suitable
levels of semantical validity, it is also common to go through several cycles
until the processes (dictionaries and dictionary routines in the case of
coding by computer and the categories of the recording instruction for
manual coding) conform to desired standards.

Data reduction by selecting according to some criteria and data transformation such as copying from one medium to another, tabulating and
key punching are clerical tasks that are often ignored. They, too, are
subject to human errors whose magnitudes often exceed those of recording. All such activities have to be checked to assure that data are accurate
and nothing is omitted that is relevant for the analysis. Cleaning up what is
often called "dirty" data is a time-consuming task. Typical errors that
need to be checked are:

(1) *missing records.* Sometimes whole card images are omitted from the set which
    can lead to a wrong reading of nearly all data.
(2) *Out-of-sequence records.*
(3) *Illegitimate values* are labels for categories that have no meaning in the data
    language as defined in the coding instructions. A "5" is illegal when the scale
    ranges between "+ 3" and "−3," a letter is illegal when numerical values are
    expected, and the absence of a value is illegal when all boxes should have one.
(4) *Inconsistencies* occur when a unit of analysis is described in mutually exclusive
    terms; for example, a pregnant bachelor, a 999-year old child.
(5) *Improbabilities* occur when values are legitimate within the context of a
    measuring instrument but outside the range of expectations, for example a
    television show that is violent but employs no characters (when violent is
    defined in terms of intentional acts of destruction), a juvenile professor.

The detection of 1 and 2 is aided by sequence numbers for cases and
identification numbers for cards. Researchers are advised to consider a
data organization that can be checked easily. Missing records can lead to

out-of sequence reading of the data and may yield totally uninterpretable results. Errors 3 and 4 can easily be identified by special programs that print out all out-of-range values and illegal co-occurrences. Although the researcher can easily correct these errors, this check does not safeguard against errors within the range of possible values or within what is logically possible. A high frequency of errors 3 and 4 suggests that the data may be dirtier than can be checked without going back to where the data came from. Improbabilities (5) are not errors as such for it may indeed be possible to produce a violent television show without recorded actors. Improbabilities merely signal the need for further examination of the source material.

REPORT

The report of a research effort is an authoritative account of what was done, why it was undertaken, its accomplishment, and its contribution to existing knowledge. In highly institutionalized settings where the motivation is understood and the procedures are codified, a research report may be limited to what deviated from standard procedure. A decision maker may well be interested only in the results, relying on the researcher's reputation to have done the job well. However, in scientific pursuits, findings are not accepted independently of the procedure through which they are obtained and this procedure must be replicable elsewhere. A research report needs to be specific about some or all of the following:

(1) a statement of *the general problem* to which the research pertains. It should convince the reader of the theoretical or practical importance of solving such a problem relative to what is currently known and/or the benefits that might accrue from solving it.

(2) an account of *the background of the problem* containing a review of the literature, where available, on how the problem has been approached in the past, what similar research efforts have shown, and arguments for why a content analysis promises to yield interesting findings. (See Distinctions in the section on Conceptual Foundations.)

(3) a statement of *the specific objectives of the content analysis* which governs the choice of data, methods, and design and how the objective relates to the general problem above. Specifically, an outline of the system under consideration, the data being analyzed, their context, and the target of inferences all as seen by the content analyst (see Framework in the section on Conceptual Foundations) including, perhaps, the empirical constraints under which the research was undertaken. This should also contain a statement or at least an outline of the kind of evidence that would be accepted to invalidate the inferences made (see Validity).

(4) a justification of *the choice of data, methods and design.* This requires matching the assumptions built into the analytical constructs and techniques with what is known about the context of the data (whether in the form of theories, past successes, or practical experiences). (See Constructs for Inference and Validity.)

(5) a description of *the procedures actually followed* (see the Logic of Content Analysis Designs) so that the research can be replicated by others. This includes a description of the *unitization schemes* (see Unitizing), the *sampling plan* (see Sampling), the *recording instructions*, training schedules, a sample of the data sheets (see Recording and Data Languages), the procedures employed for data handling and *analysis* (see Analytical Techniques), and most particu-

larly the *results of the reliability tests* (see Reliability) and all efforts at validating parts or the whole procedure (see Validity).

(6) a presentation of *the findings,* their statistical significance—goodness of fit where appropriate, the reliability scores associated with each, and an assessment of their probable validity. For the sake of advancing knowledge, it is important to report also approaches to analysis that failed to yield interesting findings. The apparent lack of structure may be as important as its presence, one should not be suppressed in favor of the other.

(7) *A self-critical appraisal* of the procedures followed and the results obtained in relation to the stated objectives (has the goal been accomplished?), regarding the costs and benefits of its results (was it worth the effort?), or in contrast with what is known through other methods (was content analysis appropriate?). After completing a project, the analyst usually has accumulated many experiences, insights, and warnings he may want to share with others. Most research, while providing some answers to initial questions, also poses new problems for further inquiries which the researcher should not keep to himself.

This list of possible contents is not meant to be exhaustive. Content analysts are known to invent ingenious devices to obtain apparently valid inferences. The analyst may want to report on activities not mentioned above. Neither is this list meant to prescribe a standard form for content analysis reports. Some accounts can be delegated to an appendix (lists of data, pretest findings, complex category schemes), some can be substituted by reference to other publications (description of analytical techniques, standard tests, and justifications given by others), and some may be made available upon request by those who indicate a special interest in them (data, written coding instructions which can become quite voluminous, computer printouts). A content analyst is obligated to make everything transparent, if not in the context of a publication, so at least for those interested in using the findings, replicating the analysis, or further developing the techniques.

Content analysis results should be firm enough to withstand the threat of empirical evidence and informed criticism of its procedures, to show that is an important aim of its methodology. All of the above tried to advance the logic of demonstrating the validity of content analysis findings.

REFERENCES

ABELSON, R. P. (1963) "Computer simulation of hot cognition," pp. 277-298 in S. S. Tomkins and S. Messick (eds.) Computer Simulation of Personality. New York: John Wiley.

—— (1968) "Simulation of social behavior," pp. 274-356 in G. Lindzey and E. Aronson (eds.) The Handbook of Social Psychology. Reading, MA: Addison-Wesley.

ADORNO, T. W. (1960) "Television and the patterns of mass culture," pp. 474-488 in B. Rosenberg and D. M. White (eds.) Mass Culture. New York: Free Press.

ALBIG, W. (1938) "The content of radio programs—1925-1935." Social Forces 16: 338-349.

ALBRECHT, M. C. (1956) "Does literature reflect common values?" American Sociological Review 21: 722-729.

ALLEN, L. E. (1963) "Automation: substitute and supplement in legal practice." American Behavioral Scientist 7: 39-44.

ALLPORT, G. W. (1942) The Use of Personal Documents in Psychological Science. New York: Social Science Research Council.

—— [ed.] (1965) Letters from Jenny. New York: Harcourt Brace Jovanovich.

—— and J. M. FADEN (1940) "The psychology of newspapers: five tentative laws." Public Opinion Quarterly 4: 687-703.

ALWIN, D. F. (1974) "Approaches to the interpretation of relationships in the multitrait-multimethod matrix," pp. 79-105 in H. L. Costner (ed.) Sociological Methodology 1973-1974. San Francisco: Jossey-Bass.

American Psychological Association (1954) "Technical recommendations for psychological tests and diagnostic techniques." Psychological Bulletin Supplement 51, 2: 200-254.

ARMSTRONG, R. P. (1959) "Content analysis in folkloristics," pp. 151-170 in I. de Sola Pool (ed.) Trends in Content Analysis. Urbana: University of Illinois Press.

ARNHEIM, R. and M. C. BAYNE (1941) "Foreign language broadcasts over local American stations," pp. 3-64 in P. F. Lazarsfeld and F. N. Stanton (eds.) Radio Research 1941. New York: Duell, Sloan & Pearce.

ASH, P. (1948) "The periodical press and the Taft-Hartley Act." Public Opinion Quarterly 12: 266-271.

ASHEIM, L. (1950) "From book to film," pp. 299-306 in B. Berelson and M. Janowitz (eds.) Reader in Public Opinion and Communication. New York: Free Press.

BALDWIN, A. L. (1942) "Personality structure analysis: a statistical method for investigating the single personality." Journal of Abnormal and Social Psychology 37: 163-183.

BALES, R. F. (1950) Interaction Process Analysis. Reading, MA: Addison-Wesley.

BARCUS, F. E. (1959) "Communications content: analysis of the research 1900-1958: a content analysis of content analysis." Ph.D. dissertation, University of Illinois.

BARTON, A. H. (1968) "Bringing society back in: survey research and macro-methodology." American Behavioral Scientist 12, 2: 1-9.

BATESON, G. (1972) Steps to an Ecology of Mind. New York: Ballantine.

BECKER, H. P. (1930) "Distribution of space in the American Journal of Sociology, 1895-1927." American Journal of Sociology 36: 461-466.

—— (1932) "Space apportioned forty-eight topics in the American Journal of Sociology, 1895-1930." American Journal of Sociology 38: 71-78.

BELL, D. (1964) "Twelve modes of prediction—a preliminary sorting of approaches to the social sciences." Daedalus 93, 3: 845-880.

BERELSON, B. (1952) Content Analysis in Communications Research. New York: Free Press.

—— and P. F. LAZARSFELD (1948) The Analysis of Communication Content. Chicago and New York: University of Chicago and Columbia University.

BERELSON, B. and P. J. SALTER (1946) "Majority and minority Americans: an analysis of magazine fiction." Public Opinion Quarterly 10: 168-190.

BERELSON, B. and G. A. STEINER (1964) Human Behavior: An Inventory of Scientific Findings. New York: Harcourt Brace Jovanovich.

BERKMAN, D. (1963) "Advertising in *Ebony* and *Life:* Negro aspirations vs. reality." Journalism Quarterly 40: 53-64.

BRODER, D. P. (1940) "The adjective-verb quotient: a contribution to the psychology of language." Psychological Record 3: 310-343.

BROOM, L. and S. REECE (1955) "Political and racial interest: a study in content analysis." Public Opinion Quarterly 19: 5-19.

BROUWER, M., C. C. CLARK, G. GERBNER, and K. KRIPPENDORFF (1969) "The television world of violence," pp. 311-339 and 519-591 in R. K. Baker and S. J. Ball (eds.) Mass Media and Violence: A Report to the National Commission on the Causes and Prevention of Violence. Washington, DC: Government Printing Office.

BUDD, R. W. (1964) "Attention score: a device for measuring news 'play.'" Journalism Quarterly 41: 259-262.

CAHNMAN, W. J. (1948) "A note on marriage announcements in the *New York Times.*" American Sociological Review 13: 96-97.

CAMPBELL, D. T. (1957) "Factors relevant to the validity of experiments in social settings." Psychological Bulletin 54, 4: 297-311.

―――― and D. W. FISKE (1959) "Convergent and discriminant validation by the multitrait-multimethod matrix." Psychological Bulletin 56, 2: 81-105.

CANTRIL, H. (1948) "Opinion trends in World War II: some guides to interpretation." Public Opinion Quarterly 12: 30-44.

CARTWRIGHT, D. P. (1953) "Analysis of qualitative material," pp. 421-470 in L. Festinger and D. Katz (eds.) Research Methods in the Behavioral Sciences. New York: Holt, Rinehart & Winston.

CHOMSKY, N. (1959) "Review of B. F. Skinner, *Verbal Behavior.*" Language 35: 26-58.

COHEN, B. C. (1957) The Political Process and Foreign Policy: The Making of the Japanese Peace Settlement. Princeton, NJ: Princeton University Press.

COHEN, J. (1960) "A coefficient of agreement for nominal scales." Educational and Psychological Measurement 20, 1: 37-46.

"Content analysis: a new evidentiary technique." (1948) University of Chicago Law Review 15: 910-925.

Council on Inter-Racial Books for Children (1977) Stereotypes, Distortions and Omissions in U.S. History Textbooks. New York: Racism and Sexism Resource Center for Educators.

DALE, E. (1937) "The need for the study of newsreels." Public Opinion Quarterly 1: 122-125.

DEICHSEL, A. (1975) Elektronische Inhaltsanalyse. Berlin: Volker Spiess.

De WEESE, L. C., III (1977) "Computer content analysis of 'day-old' newspapers: a feasibility study." Public Opinion Quarterly 41: 91-94.

DIBBLE, V. K. (1963) "Four types of inferences from documents to events." History and Theory 3, 2: 203-221.

DOLLARD, J. and F. AULD, Jr. (1959) Scoring Human Motives: A Manual. New Haven, CT: Uale University Press.

DOLLARD, J. and O. H. MOWRER (1947) "A method of measuring tension in written documents." Journal of Abnormal and Social Psychology 42: 3-32.

DOVRING, K. (1954-1955) "Quantitative semantics in 18th century Sweden." Public Opinion Quarterly 18, 4: 389-394.

DUNPHY, D. C. (1966) "The construction of categories for content analysis dictionaries," pp. 134-168 in P. J. Stone et al. (eds.) The General Inquirer. Cambridge: MIT Press.

DZIURZYNSKI, P. S. (1977) "Development of a content analytic instrument for advertising appeals used in prime time television commercials." M.A. thesis, University of Pennsylvania.

EKMAN, P. and W. V. FRIESEN (1968) "Nonverbal behavior in psychotherapy research," in J. Shlien (ed.) Research in Psychotherapy. Washington, DC: American Psychological Association.

—— and T. G. TAUSSIG (1969) "VID-R and SCAN: tools and methods for the automated analysis of visual records," pp. 297-312 in G. Gerbner et al. (eds.) The Analysis of Communication Content. New York: John Wiley.

ELLISON, J. W. (1965) "Computers and the testaments," pp. 64-74 in Proceedings, Conference on Computers for the Humanities. New Haven, CT: Yale University Press.

ELMAGHRABY, S. E. (1970) "Theory of networks and management science." Management Science 17: 1-34, 1354-1371.

ERTEL, S. (1976) "Dogmatism: an approach to personality," pp. 34-44 in A. Deichsel and K. Holzenscheck (eds.) Maschinelle Inhaltsanalyse, Materialien I. Hamburg: University of Hamburg.

FENTON, F. (1910) "The influence of newspaper presentations on the growth of crime and other anti-social activity." American Journal of Sociology 16: 342-371, 538-564.

FLESH, R. (1948) "A new readability yardstick." Journal of Applied Psychology 32: 221-233.

—— (1951) How To Test Readability. New York: Harper & Row.

FOSTER, C. R. (1938) Editorial Treatment of Education in the American Press. Cambridge, MA: Harvard University Press.

FOSTER, H. S. (1935) "How America became belligerent: a quantitative study of war news 1914-17." American Journal of Sociology 40: 464-475.

GARFIELD, E. (1979) Citation Index: Its Theory and Application to Science, Technology and Humanities. New York: John Wiley.

GELLER, A., D. KAPLAN, and H. D. LASSWELL (1942) "An experimental comparison of four ways of coding editorial content." Journalism Quarterly 19: 362-370.

GEORGE, A. L. (1959a) Propaganda Analysis: A Study of Inferences Made from Nazi Propaganda in World War II. Evanston, IL: Row, Peterson.

—— (1959b) "Quantitative and qualitative approaches to content analysis," pp. 7-32 in I. de Sola Pool (ed.) Trends in Content Analysis. Urbana: University of Illinois Press.

GERBNER, G. (1959) "The social role of the confession magazine." Social Problems 6: 29-40.

—— (1964) "Ideological perspectives and political tendencies in news reporting." Journalism Quarterly 41: 495-508.

—— (1966) "An institutional approach to mass communications research," pp. 429-445 in L. Thayer (ed.) Communication: Theory and Research. Springfield, IL: Charles C Thomas.

—— (1969) "Toward 'cultural indicators': the analysis of mass mediated public message systems," pp. 123-132 in G. Gerbner et al. (eds.) The Analysis of Communication Content. New York: John Wiley.

—— and G. MARVANYI (1977) "The many worlds of the world's press." Journal of Communication 27, 1: 52-75.

GERBNER, G., L. GROSS, N. SIGNORIELLI, M. MORGAN, and M. JACKSON-BEECK (1979) "Violence profile no. 10: trends in network television drama and view conceptions of social reality, 1967-1978." Annenberg School of Communications, University of Pennsylvania. (mimeo)

GERBNER, G., O. R. HOLSTI, K. KRIPPENDORFF, W. J. PAISLEY, and P. J. STONE [eds.] (1969) The Analysis of Communication Content: Developments in Scientific Theories and Computer Techniques. New York: John Wiley.

GIEBER, W. (1964) "News is what newspapermen make it," pp. 173-182 in L. A. Dexter and D. M. White (eds.) People, Society, and Mass Communications. New York: Free Press.

GREEN, B. F., A. K. WOLF, C. CHOMSKY, and K. LAUGHERY (1963) "Baseball: an automatic question answerer," pp. 207-216 in E. A. Feigenbaum and J. Feldman (eds.) Computers and Thought. New York: McGraw-Hill.

GROTH, O. (1948) Die Geschichte der Deutschen Zeitungswissenschaft, Probleme und Methoden. Munich: Konrad Weinmayer.

HATCH, D. L. and M. HATCH (1947) "Criteria of social status as derived from marriage announcements in the *New York Times*." American Sociological Review 12: 396-403.

HAYS, D. C. (1960) Automatic Content Analysis. Santa Monica, CA: Rand Corporation.

––– (1969) "Linguistic foundations for a theory of content analysis," pp. 57-67 in G. Gerbner et al. (eds.) The Analysis of Communication Content. New York: John Wiley.

HERDAN, G. (1960) Type-Token Mathematics: A Textbook of Mathematical Linguistics. The Hague: Mouton.

HERMA, H., E. KRISS, and J. SHOR (1943) "Freud's theory of the dream in American textbooks." Journal of Abnormal and Social Psychology 38: 319-334.

HOLSTI, O. R. (1962) "The belief system and national images: John Foster Dulles and the Soviet Union." Ph.D. dissertation, Stanford University.

––– (1969) Content Analysis for the Social Sciences and Humanities. Reading, MA: Addison-Wesley.

––– R. A. BRODY, and R. C. NORTH (1965) "Measuring affect and action in international reaction models: empirical materials from the 1962 Cuban crisis." Peace Research Society Papers 2: 170-190.

IKER, H. P. (1975) WORDS System Manual. Rochester, NY: Computer Printout.

––– (n.d.) "SELECT: a computer program to identify associationally rich worlds for content analysis." New York. (mimeo)

INNIS, H. A. (1951) The Bias of Communication. Toronto: University of Toronto Press.

Institute for Propaganda Analysis, Inc. (1937) "How to detect propaganda." Propaganda Analysis 1: 5-8.

JANDA, K. (1969) "A microfilm and computer system for analysing comparative politics literature," pp. 407-435 in G. Gerbner et al. (eds.) The Analysis of Communication Content. New York: John Wiley.

JANIS, I. L. (1965) "The problem of validating content analysis," pp. 55-82 in H. D. Lasswell at al. (eds.) Language of Politics. Cambridge: MIT Press.

––– and R. H. FADNER (1965) "The coefficient of imbalance," pp. 153-169 in H. D. Lasswell et al. (eds.) Language of Politics. Cambridge: MIT Press.

KAPLAN, A. and J. M. GOLDSEN (1965) "The reliability of content analysis categories," pp. 83-112 in H. D. Lasswell et al. (ed.) Language of Politics. Cambridge: MIT Press.

KATZ, E., M. GUREVITCH, B. DANET, and T. PELED (1967) "Petitions and prayers: a content analysis of persuasive appeals." University of Chicago. (mimeo)

KLAUSNER, S. Z. (1968) "Two centuries of child-rearing manuals." Technical Report to the Joint Commission on Mental Health of Children, Department of Sociology, University of Pennsylvania. (mimeo)

KLEIN, M. W. and N. MACCOBY (1954) "Newspaper objectivity in the 1952 campaign." Journalism Quarterly 31: 285-296.

KLEIST, K. (1934) Gehirn Pathologie. Leipzig: Johan Ambrosius Barth.

KLIR, G. and M. VALACH (1965) "Language as a means of communication between man and machine," pp. 315-373 in Cybernetic Modelling. Princeton, NJ: D. Van Nostrand.

KOPPELAAR, H., B. VAN KONIGSVELD, and H. WEIJENBURG (1978) "Verbale modelvorming." Sociologische Gids 25, 3: 201-211.

KOPS, M. (1977) Answahlverfahren in der Inhaltsanalyse. Meisenheim/Glan: Anton Hain.

KRACAUER, S. (1947) From Caligari to Hitler: A Psychological History of German Film. London: Dennis Dobson.

––– (1952-1953) "The challenge of quantitative content analysis." Public Opinion Quarterly 16: 631-642.

KRENDEL, E. S. (1970) "A case study of citizen complaints as social indicators." IEEE Transactions on Systems Science and Cybernetics SSC-6, 4: 267-272.

KRIPPENDORFF, K. (1969a) "Theories and analytical constructs: introduction," pp. 3-16 in G. Gerbner et al. (eds.) The Analysis of Communication Content. New York: John Wiley.
––– (1969b) "Models of messages: three prototypes," pp. 69-106 in G. Gerbner et al. (eds.) The Analysis of Communication Content. New York: John Wiley.
––– (1970a) "On generating data in communication research." Journal of Communication 20, 3: 241-269.
––– (1970b) "The expression of value in political documents." Journalism Quarterly 47: 510-518.
––– (1971) "Reliability of recording instructions: multivariate agreement for nominal data." Behavioral Science 16, 3: 222-235.
––– (1974) "An algorithm for simplifying the representation of complex systems," pp. 1693-1702 in J. Rose (ed.) Advances in Cybernetics and Systems. New York: Gordon & Breach.
––– (1980a) "Validity in content analysis," pp. 69-112 in E. Mochmann (ed.) Computerstrategien fuer die Kommunikations analyse. Frankfurt: Campus.
––– (1980b) "Clustering," in P. R. Monge and J. N. Capella (eds.) Multivariate Techniques in Communication Research. New York: Academic Press.
LABOV, W. (1972) Sociolinguistic Patterns. Philadelphia: University of Pennsylvania Press.
LANDIS, H. H. and H. E. BURTT (1924) "A study of conversations." Journal of Comparative Psychology 4: 81-89.
LASSWELL, H. D. (1927) Propaganda Technique in the World War. New York: Knopf.
––– (1938) "A provisional classification of symbol data." Psychiatry 1: 197-204.
––– (1941) "The world attention survey: an exploration of the possibilities of studying attention being given to the United States by newspapers abroad." Public Opinion Quarterly 5, 3: 456-462.
––– (1960) "The structure and function of communication in society," pp. 117-130 in W. Schramm (ed.) Mass Communications. Urbana: University of Illinois Press.
––– (1963) Politics: Who Gets What, When, How. New York: Meridian.
––– (1965a) "Why be quantitative?" pp. 40-52 in H. D. Lasswell et al. (eds.) Language of Politics. Cambridge: MIT Press.
––– (1965b) "Detection: propaganda detection and the courts," pp. 173-232 in H. D. Lasswell et al. (eds.) Language of Politics. Cambridge: MIT Press.
––– and A. KAPLAN (1950) Power and Society: A Framework for Political Inquiry. New Haven, CT: Yale University Press.
LASSWELL, H. D., D. LERNER, and I. DE SOLA POOL (1952) The Comparative Study of Symbols. Stanford, CA: Stanford University Press.
LASSWELL, H. D., et al. (1965) Language of Politics: Studies in Quantitative Semantics. Cambridge: MIT Press.
LAZARSFELD, P. F., B. BERELSON, and H. GAUDET (1948) The People's Choice: How the Voter Makes Up His Mind in a Presidential Campaign. New York: Columbia University Press.
LEITES, N., E. BERNAUT, and R. L. GARTHOFF (1951) "Politburo images of Stalin." World Politics 3: 317-339.
LINDSAY, R. K. (1963) "Inferential memory as the basis of machines which understand natural language," pp. 217-233 in E. A. Feigenbaum and J. Feldman (eds.) Computers and Thought. New York: McGraw-Hill.
LIPPMANN, W. (1922) Public Opinion. New York: Macmillan.
LOEBL, E. (1903) Kultur und Presse. Leipzig: Duncker & Humblot.
LOEVENTHAL, L. (1944) "Biographies in popular magazines," pp. 507-548 in P. F. Lazarsfeld and F. N. Stanton (eds.) Radio Research 1942-1943. New York: Duell, Sloan & Pearce.
LORR, M. and D. M. McNAIR (1966) "Methods relating to evaluation of therapeutic outcome," pp. 573-594 in L. A. Gottschalk and A. H. Auerbach (eds.) Methods of Research in Psychotherapy. Englewood Cliffs, NJ: Prentice-Hall.
LYNCH, K. (1965) The Image of the City. Cambridge: MIT Press.
MACCOBY, N., F. O. SABGHIR, and B. CUSHING (1950) "A method for the analysis of news coverage of industry." Public Opinion Quarterly 14: 753-758.

MAHL, G. F. (1959) "Exploring emotional states by content analysis," pp. 89-130 in I. de Sola Pool (ed.) Trends in Content Analysis. Urbana: University of Illinois Press.

MANN, M. B. (1944) "Studies in language behavior: III. The quantitative differentiation of samples of written language." Psychological Monographs 56, 2: 41-47.

MARANDA, P. and E. K. MARANDA [eds.] (1971) Structural Analysis of Oral Tradition. Philadelphia: University of Pennsylvania Press.

MARKOV, A. A. (1913) "Essai d'une recherche statistique sur le texte du roman 'Eugene Onegin' illustrant la liaison des epreuves en chaine (Russian)." Bulletin de L'Académie Impériale des Sciences de St. Pétersbourg 6, 7: 153-162.

MARTIN, H. (1936) "Nationalism and children's literature." Library Quarterly 6: 405-418.

MATHEWS, B. C. (1910) "A study of a New York daily." Independent 68: 82-86.

McCLELLAND, D. C. (1958) "The use of measures of human motivation in the study of society," pp. 518-552 in J. W. Atkinson (ed.) Motives in Fantasy, Action and Society. Princeton, NJ: D. Van Nostrand.

McDIARMID, J. (1937) "Presidential inaugural addresses: a study in verbal symbols." Public Opinion Quarterly 1: 79-82.

MERRILL, J. C. (1962) "The image of the United States in ten Mexican dailies." Journalism Quarterly 39: 203-209.

MERRITT, R. L. (1966) Symbols of American Community, 1735-1775. New Haven, CT: Yale University Press.

MIDDLETON, R. (1960) "Fertility values in American magazine fiction: 1916-1956." Public Opinion Quarterly 24: 139-143.

MILES, J. (1951) "The continuity of English poetic language," pp. 517-535 in University of California Publications in English. Berkeley: University of California Press.

MILLER, G. A. (1951) Language and Communication. New York: McGraw-Hill.

MINSKY, M. [ed.] (1968) Semantic Information Processing. Cambridge: MIT Press.

MORTON, A. Q. (1963) "A computer challenges the church." Observer (November 3).

——— and M. LEVINSON (1966) "Some indications of authorship in Green prose," pp. 141-179 in J. Leed (ed.) The Computer and Literary Style. Kent, OH: Kent State University Press.

MOSTELLER, F. and D. L. WALLACE (1963) "Inference in an authorship problem." Journal of American Statistical Association 58: 275-309.

——— (1964) Inference and Disputed Authorship: The Federalist. Reading, MA: Addison-Wesley.

MURRAY, E. J., F. AULD, Jr., and A. M. WHITE (1954) "A psychotherapy case showing progress but no decrease in the discomfort-relief quotient." Journal of Consulting Psychology 18: 349-353.

NAMENWIRTH, J. Z. (1973) "Wheels of time and the interdependence of value change in America." Journal of Interdisciplinary History 3: 649-683.

NEWELL, A. and H. A. SIMON (1956) "The logic theory machine." IRE-Transactions on Information Theory IT-2 3: 61-79.

——— (1963) "General Problem Solver: a program that simulates human thought," pp. 279-293 in E. A. Feigenbaum and J. Feldman (eds.) Computers and Thought. New York: McGraw-Hill.

NIXON, R. B. and R. L. JONES (1956) "The content of non-competitive newspapers." Journalism Quarterly 33: 299-314.

NORTH, R. C., O. R. HOLSTI, M. G. ZANINOVICH, and D. A. ZINNES (1963) Content Analysis: A Handbook with Applications for the Study of International Crisis. Evanston, IL: Northwestern University.

OSGOOD, C. E. (1959) "The representation model and relevant research methods," p. 33-88 in I. de Sola Pool (ed.) Trends in Content Analysis. Urbana: University of Illinois Press.

——— S. SPORTA, and J. C. NUNNALLY (1956) "Evaluative assertion analysis." Litera 3: 47-102.

—— G. J. SUCI, and P. H. TANNENBAUM (1957) The Measurement of Meaning. Urbana: University of Illinois Press.

O'SULLIVAN, T. C., Jr. (1961) "Factor analysis concepts identified in theoretical writings—an experiment design." Itek Laboratories, Lexington, MA., September.

PAISLEY, W. J. (1964) "Identifying the unknown communicator in painting, literature and music: the significance of minor encoding habits." Journal of Communication 14: 219-237.

PHILLIPS, D. P. (1978) "Airplane accident fatalities increase just after newspaper stories about murder and suicide." Science 201: 748-749.

PIAULT, C. (1965) "A methodological investigation of content analysis using electronic computers for data processing," pp. 273-293 in D. Hymes (ed.) The Use of Computers in Anthropology. The Hague: Mouton.

PIERCE, B. (1930) Civic Attitudes in American School Textbooks. Chicago: University of Chicago Press.

POOL, I. DE SOLA (1951) Symbols of Internationalism. Stanford, CA: Stanford University Press.

—— (1952a) The "Prestige Papers": A Survey of Their Editorials. Stanford, CA: Stanford University Press.

—— (1952b) Symbols of Democracy. Stanford, CA: Stanford University Press.

—— [ed.] (1959) Trends in Content Analysis. Urbana: University of Illinois Press.

—— R. P. ABELSON, and S. L. POPKIN (1964) Candidates, Issues and Strategies: A Computer Simulation of the 1960 Presidential Election. Cambridge: MIT Press.

RAINOFF, T. J. (1929) "Wave-like fluctuations of creative productivity in the development of West-European physics in the eighteenth and nineteenth centuries." ISIS 12: 287-307.

RAPOPORT, A. (1969) "A system-theoretic view of content analysis," pp. 17-38 in G. Gerbner et al. (eds.) The Analysis of Communication Content. New York: John Wiley.

REYNOLDS, H. T. (1977) Analysis of Nominal Data. Beverly Hills, CA: Sage.

Roget's International Thesaurus (1974) London: Collins.

SCHANK, R. C. and R. P. ABELSON (1977) Scripts, Plans, Goals and Understanding: An Inquiry into Human Knowledge Structures. Hillsdale, NJ: Erlbaum.

SCHUTZ, W. C. (1958) "On categorizing qualitative data in content analysis." Public Opinion Quarterly 22, 4: 503-515.

SCOTT, W. A. (1955) "Reliability of content analysis: the case of nominal scale coding." Public Opinion Quarterly 19: 321-325.

SEBEOK, T. A. and L. H. ORZACK (1953) "The structure and content of cheremis charms." Anthropos 48: 369-388.

SEBEOK, T. A. and V. J. ZEPS (1958) "An analysis of structured content with application of electronic computer research in psycholinguistics." Language and Speech 1: 181-193.

SEDELOW, S. Y. (1967) Stylistic Analysis. Santa Monica, CA: SDC.

—— and W. A. SEDELOW, Jr. (1966) "A preface to computational stylistics," in J. Leed (ed.) The Computer and Literary Style. Kent, OH: Kent State University Press.

SELLTIZ, C., M. JAHODA, M. DEUTSCH, and S. W. COOK (1964) Research Methods in Social Relations. New York: Holt, Rinehart & Winston.

SHANAS, E. (1945) "The *American Journal of Sociology* through fifty years." American Journal of Sociology 50: 522-533.

SHANNON, C. E. and W. WEAVER (1949) The Mathematical Theory of Communication. Urbana: University of Illinois Press.

SHNEIDMAN, E. S. (1963) "The logic of politics," pp. 178-199 in L. Arons and M. A. May (eds.) Television and Human Behavior. Englewood Cliffs, NJ: Prentice-Hall.

—— (1966) The Logics of Communication: A Manual for Analysis. China Lake, CA: U.S. Naval Ordnance Test Station.

—— (1969) "Logical content analysis: an exploration of styles of concludifying," pp. 261-279 in G. Gerbner et al. (eds.) The Analysis of Communication Content. New York: John Wiley.

SIMPSON, G. E. (1934) "The Negro in the Philadelphia press." Ph.D. dissertation, University of Pennsylvania.

SINGER, J. D. (1964) "Media analysis in inspection for disarmament." Journal of Arms Control 1: 248-260.

SMYTHE, D. W. (1954) "Some observations on communications theory." Audio-Visual Communication Review 2, 1: 248-260.

SPEED, G. J. (1893) "Do newspapers now give the news?" Forum 15: 705-711.

SPIEGELMAN, M., C. TERWILLIGER, and F. FEARING (1953a) "The reliability of agreement in content analysis." Journal of Social Psychology 37: 175-187.

——— (1953b) "The content of comics: goals and means to goals of comic strip charatters." Journal of Social Psychology 37: 189-203.

STEMPEL, G. H., III (1952) "Sample size for classifying subject matter in dailies: research in brief." Journalism Quarterly 29: 333-334.

STEVENS, S. S. (1946) "On the theory of scales of measurement." Science 103, 2684: 677-680.

STONE, P. J. and E. B. HUNT (1963) "A computer approach to content analysis using the general inquirer system," pp. 241-256 in E. C. Johnson (ed.) American Federation of Information Processing Societies, Conference Proceedings. Baltimore: Author.

STONE, P. J., D. C. DUNPHY, M. S. SMITH, and D. M. OGILVIE (1966) The General Inquirer: A Computer Approach to Content Analysis. Cambridge: MIT Press.

STREET, A. T. (1909) "The truth about newspapers." Chicago Tribune (July 25).

SUCI, G. and T. R. HUSEK (1957) "A content analysis of 70 messages with 55 variables and subsequent effect studies." Institute for Communication Research, University of Illinois, Urbana. (mimeo)

TANNENBAUM, P. H. and B. S. GREENBERG (1961) "J. Q. references: a study of professional change." Journalism Quarterly 38: 203-207.

TAYLOR, W. L. (1953) " 'Cloze procedure': a new tool for measuring readability." Journalism Quarterly 30: 415-433.

TENNEY, A. A. (1912) "The scientific analysis of the press." Independent 73: 895-898.

THOMPSON, S. (1932) Motif-Index of Folk Literature: A Classification of Narrative Elements in Folk-Tales, Ballads, Myths, Fables, Mediaeval Romances, Exempla, Fabliaux, Jest-Books, and Local Legends. Bloomingdale: Indiana University Studies.

TUKEY, J. W. (1980) "Methodological comments focused on opportunities," in P. R. Monge and J. N. Cappella (eds.) Multivariate Techniques in Communication Research. New York: Academic Press.

WALWORTH, A. (1938) Social Histories at War: A Study of the Treatement of Our Wars in the Secondary School History Books of the United States and in Those of Its Former Enemies. Cambridge, MA: Harvard University Press.

WATZLAWICK, P., J. H. BEAVIN, and D. D. JACKSON (1967) Pragmatics of Human Communication. New York: W. W. Norton.

WEBB, E. J., D. T. CAMPBELL, and R. D. SCHWARTZ (1966) Unobtrusive Measures: Nonreactive Research in the Social Sciences. Chicago: Rand McNally.

WEBER, M. (1911) " 'Geschaeftsbericht' in Verhandlungen des ersten deutschen Soziologietages vom 19.-22. Oktober 1910 in Frankfurt a. M.," pp. 39-62 in Schrift der Deutschen Gesellschaft fuer Soziologie.

Webster's New Dictionary of Symbols (1973) Springfield, MA: Merriam.

Webster's Seventh New Collegiate Dictionary (1967) Springfield, MA: Merriam.

WEIK, K. E. (1968) "Systematic observational methods," pp. 357-451 in G. Lindzey and E. Aronson (eds.) The Handbook of Social Psychology. Reading, MA: Addison-Wesley.

WHITE, D. M. (1964) "The 'Gatekeeper': a case study in selection of news," pp. 160-172 in L. A. Dexter and D. M. White (eds.) People, Society and Mass Communication. New York: Free Press.

WHITE, P. W. (1924) "Quarter century survey of press content shows demand for facts." Editor and Publisher 57 (May 31).

WHITE, R. K. (1947) *"Black Boy*, a value analysis." Journal of Abnormal and Social Psychology 42: 440-461.

——— (1951) Value-Analysis: The Nature and Use of the Method. Glen Gardiner, NJ: Libertarian Press.

WILCOX, D. F. (1900) "The American newspaper: a study in social psychology." Annals of American Academy of Political and Social Science 16: 56-92.

WILLEY, M. M. (1926) The Country Newspaper: A Study of Socialization and Newspaper Content. Chapel Hill: University of North Carolina Press.

WOODWARD, J. L. (1934) "Quantitative newspaper analysis as a technique of opinion research." Social Forces 12: 526-537.

WRIGHT, C. E. (1964) "Functional analysis and mass communication," pp. 91-109 in L. A. Dexter and D. M. White (eds.) People, Society and Mass Communication. New York: Free Press.

YULE, G. U. (1944) The Statistical Study of Literary Vocabulary. London: Cambridge University Press.

ZADEH, L. A. (1965) "Fuzzy sets." Information and Control 8, 3: 338-353.

ZILLMAN, D. (1964) Konzept der Semantischen Aspektanalyse. Zurich: Institut fuer Kommunikationsforschung.

ZUCKER, H. G. (1978) "The variable nature of news media influence." Communication Yearbook 2: 225-240.

ABOUT THE AUTHOR

KLAUS KRIPPENDORFF is Professor of Communication at the University of Pennsylvania's Annenberg School of Communication. Besides numerous publications in the *Journal of Communication, Journalism Quarterly, Sociological Methodology, General Systems,* among others, he coedited *The Analysis of Communication Content* and *Developments and Scientific Theories and Computer Techniques,* edited *Communication and Control in Society,* and contributed to such books as *Mass Media and Violence, Communication and Behavior, General Systems Theory and Human Communication, Communication Yearbook I,* and *Multivariate Techniques in Communication Research.*